6

First published 1979 by Ebury Press Ltd.,
National Magazine House,
72, Broadwick Street,
London W1V 2BP

© Sackett and Squire Ltd.
ISBN 0 85223 158 X

This book was designed and produced by Sackett and Squire Ltd.,
2, Great Malborough Street, London, W.1., for Ebury Press Ltd.

Printed and bound in England by Waterlow (Dunstable) Ltd.

Plants
For All Places

Plants
For All Places

Peter McHoy & David Squire

Ebury Press · London

Contents

Introduction

The joys of gardening are many, and one of the charms of this hobby is that it's so easy to make a start . . . and to experience the satisfaction of watching things grow. Even a child can sow a packet of hardy annuals and witness the miracle of germination, growth and bloom – just as the seed packet promised.

Many plants have an amazing tenacity for life, and seem determined to succeed no matter what we do to them. But not all of them are so obliging, however, and a garden of outstanding merit is the result only of skill acquired from years of experience and accumulated knowledge. Even in these days of 'instant' gardens, when so many plants are container-grown, there is no substitute for know-how and planning.

Planning is important because it is the association of plants, one with another, that makes a garden, not individual plants alone – and know-how often makes the difference between a plant that merely exists and one that thrives. By sheer chance some plants will grow well enough without careful selection and planning, but attractive gardens are not built on chance.

It is possible to learn by one's mistakes, and by a process of elimination gradually reject the plants that don't grow and replace them with new ones . . . which _may_ be right. The problem is that it takes time – many valuable years – and it costs money.

The alternative is to draw upon the experience of others – to start at the point others have reached through trial and error. That has been the object of this book.

Success in gardening can never be guaranteed – only made more likely. Every garden is different, every season a variation on those that have gone before, and every soil has a unique structure and chemical composition. There can be no blue-print for each and every garden – they all must be planted with the imagination and inspiration of the individual gardener. That is what gardening is all about . . . it is this element that gives each garden its uniqueness and the gardener a tremendous thrill and satisfaction when plants grow well.

Getting the Best From Your Garden

Gardening is a stimulating and rewarding hobby – as the fifteen or so million British gardeners can testify. There is a tremendous sense of satisfaction in growing something well . . . in creating an object of beauty in the form of a well-planned garden. There is also the special feeling of achievement when a plant selected and purchased becomes established, grows and thrives.

Sometimes, however, the plants we choose to grow do not thrive – they linger half-heartedly to grow only slowly, or even die. These are the disappointments all gardeners experience at some time. Occasionally, failure is due to circumstances beyond our control – the weather especially can claim many victims. Frequently, however, if a plant lacks vitality it is because the wrong one has been chosen for the situation. Even the tough Beech (*Fagus sylvatica*) will not grow enthusiastically on heavy clay soils, yet the Hornbeam (*Carpinus betulus*), which is so similar to Beech, will thrive on clay. Rhododendrons, no matter how beautiful and desirable their blooms, should be passed by for planting in alkaline (chalky) soil in favour of some other subjects such as hibiscus or Lilac, which enjoy soils of that nature.

There will always be gardeners who wish to battle with nature and to try and make the unlikely happen, and to them such challenges are part of the thrill of gardening. But for most of us the most direct road to success is the best one. Rhododendrons *can* be grown and flowered successfully on chalk – if you are prepared to excavate a special area, line it with polythene to prevent water seepage from the surrounding ground, fill the special planting area with a peaty soil, and perhaps water the plant with special chemicals (chelates, sold as Sequestrene). Even then it's important to remember not to use hard, limy, water. Whether it's worth all the effort is a matter of opinion – but it is certainly much easier to grow something different and yet equally as beautiful.

Although beauty is in the eye of the beholder, there are so many exquisite plants in cultivation that it is not so much a question of finding suitable plants as choosing which have to be rejected, because there is neither time nor space to grow them all.

No one can guarantee success – fortunately, nature and gardening are not that predictable, and if they were, much of the excitement would be lost – but careful planning and the selection of the correct plant for the right place will go a long way to meeting that goal. It is to that end that this book has been written. Hundreds of species are mentioned, which is only a tiny fraction of the vast

Ficus elastica
Rubber Plant
(see page 218)

Title page: Garden plants often look at their best when grouped together in a pleasing association. At the bottom right of this illustration a dwarf Balsam Fir, *Abies balsamea* 'Hudsonia', nestles against a pink, *Dianthus* 'Baby Treasure', with a Broom, *Genista lydia*, at the back.
Far left: Shrub borders can be planned to provide colour and texture the year round, but for extra colour herbaceous plants can be set among the shrubs.

Ribes sanguineum
Flowering Currant
(see page 107)

Stokesia laevis
Stokes Aster
(see page 49)

Doronicum
Leopard's-bane
(see page 45)

How to use this book

In each chapter there are lists of plants suitable for particular problem sites, such as sandy soil, exposure to coastal winds and salt spray, or the atmospheric pollution of city gardens. There are lists of subjects suitable for acid and for alkaline (chalky) soils. These will provide a shortlist of genera (and sometimes species) from which to select. The large master chart at the end of each chapter will indicate whether the plant is suitable for shade or sun, and whether it is dependably hardy. The symbols used throughout the book are:

○ requires full sun
⊙ will thrive in full sun or partial shade
◑ prefers partial shade
● will grow in shade
★★★★ hardy throughout the British Isles
★★★ may need protection from late spring frosts or from cold winds (these plants are often hardy, but the flowers may suffer if exposed when coming into bloom)
★★ hardy only in mild districts such as the South and West, and certain other coastal areas with a mild local climate, but may be worth trying elsewhere if protection can be provided against the worst weather
★ tender – use only for seasonal planting during summer; a few may be left outdoors in particularly mild areas such as certain coastal places in the south-west

Besides details of height and a brief description of the plant, other salient aspects, such as fragrance and whether it is evergreen, are shown at a glance on the main chart. Heights must be treated with caution however, for soil and climate can have a significant effect on both growth rate and ultimate size, and those given are only a guide for average conditions.

Whenever possible, try to see any plant you intend to buy growing, and in a mature state – it is easy to be deceived when viewing young plants in a garden centre.

See page 224 for a complete list of symbols used in this book.

range available to growers, but there can be few gardeners who should not find sufficient plants of interest here to fulfil their basic planting needs. There is always scope for experimentation in gardening, but only once the 'backbone' plants are established.

The selection of species has had to be arbitrary, and can be no more than representative, otherwise it would need a book ten times the size of this one. One nursery alone lists over forty-six species of dwarf Junipers (others may stock more), out of which we have selected only a couple. Other species may be better, it depends on what you want them for, and on personal taste. But generally, though by no means always, other species will have the same requirements regarding soil, climate and aspect.

When it comes to varieties the problem of selecting representative examples is even more difficult, and nowhere more so than among popular flowers such as dahlias and roses, where new introductions can make last year's introductions sound outdated. But this is not a book for the enthusiast of a particular type of plant, and the emphasis is on old and well-proven varieties that are widely available. The specialist will be prepared to hunt the catalogues for particular species or varieties, but the object of this book is to act as a guide to the type of plant to grow to suit a particular garden.

Forsythia × intermedia
(see page 104)

Geranium dalmaticum
(see page 60)

A few groups of plants of outstanding merit as general garden plants – such as Roses and Heathers – have merited their own chapters. If these plants satisfy the garden need, there is no limit to the hours of pleasure to be derived from discovering new varieties. One nursery alone offers 290 varieties of *Calluna vulgaris*, quite apart from all the other Heaths and Heathers! Another nursery lists over 700 species and varieties of rhododendron and azalea, which demonstrates that no matter how limited the range of suitable plants for a site may seem, there are few gardens large enough to accommodate more than a fraction of the suitable plants. There is certainly no shortage of material for our gardens – whatever its soil, site, or problems.

Coping with clay

Clay soils are usually quite rich in plant foods, but that is little immediate consolation to the gardener if the soil is either so sticky or baked so hard that it is impossible to cultivate. Even when a clay soil can be worked, it is by nature wet and cold in comparison with other soils, regardless of climate. This in itself frequently means a later start to the growing season than would be the case on lighter

Eucryphia glutinosa
(see page 104)

soil in the same district. Not many plants really enjoy heavy clay — yet by routine and methodical soil improvement techniques most plants will grow satisfactorily.

The answer to clay soil improvement lies not in 'miracle cures' which are sometimes advertised, but by good drainage (and that may mean proper land drains) and regular and steady application of organic materials over the years, in the form of peat, compost, or manure. If the amount available is small, concentrate on improving one area first, instead of spreading it so thinly that nothing benefits.

Although double-digging is a chore, the act of breaking up the sub-soil will improve drainage and the general soil structure.

Liming is another traditional way of improving the structure of clay soils, but never apply lime without first testing the pH (see page 12), for if the clay overlies chalk it may already be alkaline and to

Below: Gardens can be planned to be at their best at a particular time of the year. Here, a spring garden has been formed by planting varieties of heathers, *Erica carnea* with spring-flowering bulbs. (See pages 126 to 137.)

increase it still further could add to the problems. Hydrated lime is applied at about 275g per square metre (8oz per square yard), but also be guided by the existing pH.

Green manuring is another way to provide humus and thereby improve soil structure. Quick-growing subjects such as Mustard, Rape or annual Lupins are sown on vacant ground, and the leafy crop dug in before it seeds.

Avoid walking on clay soils when they are wet – the compaction can make both growth and cultivation difficult.

Gardening on sand

Not surprisingly the gardener with sandy soil faces almost the opposite problems to those presented by clay. It can be delightfully

Rudbeckia
Black-eyed Susan
(see page 49)

Left: Many gardeners yearn for plants and settings that reflect the nature of old cottage gardens. This atmosphere has been recaptured here with a combination of shrubs, herbaceous and climbing plants, and an edging of armeria.

11

Cistus
(see page 101)

Miniature Rose
(see page 141)

Polygonum affine
(see page 49)

easy to work at all times of year, but it will be hungry and offer little in the way of food reserves. And even within days of heavy rain they can be too dry.

Liberal quantities of organic materials are the solution – and irrigation where it is practical (though this is of little help in times of water shortage). Compost, peat, spent hops and green manure will all improve the moisture- and food-holding capacity of the soil. Thick mulches applied during the spring and summer are also beneficial.

Usually it is only possible to alter the structure radically over a period of years, and then often only in a limited area, so it is best to grow mainly those plants naturally adapted to poor, dry soil, and concentrate the humus on a small area where you wish to grow other kinds.

Living with lime

Delightful gardens can be created on chalk or limy soils, using plants naturally adapted to this type of environment. It is necessary to resign oneself, however, to growing only those plants able to tolerate a high pH (the pH scale is explained below), as it is more difficult to make an alkaline soil more acid than it is the reverse.

To make the soil more acid use sulphate of ammonia or sulphur at 70g per square metre (2oz per square yard), but only where the nitrogen released will be beneficial (too much can cause unbalanced growth). Aluminium sulphate can be used at the same rate and this does not release nitrogen.

About 1·5kg (3lb) of peat or 7kg (15lb) of garden compost will have a similar effect to a dressing of the chemicals just mentioned.

Acidity or alkalinity is measured on a pH scale. The chemistry of it is not relevant here, but the scale runs from 0 at the acid end to 14 at the alkaline end. Such extremes are never encountered in horticulture, and few soils fall below 4 or are higher than 8. Chemically, 7 is neutral, but 6·5 is the best horticulturally, as the majority of plants will grow at this level.

Simple kits can be purchased for testing the pH of soils. An indicator fluid is mixed with a sample of soil and the approximate pH read off on a colour scale. It is strongly recommended that every garden soil should be tested.

It is possible to use iron chelates (Sequestrene) to 'unlock' the iron held in the soil by lime (it is the inaccessability of the iron that causes leaves to yellow), and this enables many plants to survive that would otherwise remain sickly.

Heathers, however, do not respond to this treatment. One reason they need acid soil is because of a biological relationship between the plant and a fungus that grows on and in the roots. This fungus, on which the Heathers depend to some extent for their well-being, does not grow in alkaline soil – so simply making the iron available does not restore health.

Gardening on acid soil

Acid soils are usually thought of as peaty, but that is not necessarily so. Although peat and woodland soils are almost always acid, some sands can also be acid.

Acid soils can easily be made more neutral by adding chalk or lime. Adding about 300g of limestone or 200g of hydrated lime per square metre (9oz and 6oz per square yard respectively) will increase the pH about one step on the scale, although less may be required if the soil is low on organic matter, much more if it has a high content.

Seaside gardening

Two problems beset anyone who gardens by the sea – high winds and salt spray. Both these would be death to many plants, and anyone who moves to a coastal area after gardening inland will probably have to adapt to growing a different range of plants than those to which he's become accustomed.

To compensate, there are many delightful plants, too tender to grow inland, that will thrive in the milder winter climate offered by many coastal areas, where frosts are usually much less severe. Even in Scotland there are places where the Gulf Stream maintains a warm flow of air, enabling many plants to grow that would die inland; the gardens at Inverewe are a famous example of what can be achieved.

The first essential for a coastal garden is a windbreak, and there is no reason why this should not be a living screen (see page 153). With protection from the worst effects of the wind from the sea, delightful and interesting gardens can be created.

Cissus antarctica
Kangaroo Vine
(see page 217)

Other difficult sites

Town and city gardens used to suffer badly from atmospheric pollution, much of which has been reduced in recent years. Even so, gardens adjoining busy roads have to contend with dirt and dust as well as fumes, and in these situations it is best to grow trees and shrubs able to tolerate such an assault. Suitable subjects are listed in the relevant chapters. A suitable hedge will also act as a filter of noise, dirt and litter.

Shade is another frequent problem with town gardens, where the proportion of hedges and buildings is high in relation to the growing area, and plants suitable for full or partial shade will be found in each chapter.

One of the most difficult sites is the passage between two houses. Shade is naturally a problem, but even worse is the wind-tunnel effect the buildings create. This can have a devastating effect on plants, and only the toughest kinds should be grown in this situation.

Wind has already been mentioned as a problem of coastal areas, but some sites inland are also notoriously windy, and the answer is to plant suitable hedges and screens, within which it is possible to garden successfully.

Every garden has its problem spots – but if you are prepared to search out the right plants, no corner need be dull or without interest.

Hedera
Ivy
(see page 218)

Annuals and Biennials

Many children are introduced to the joys of gardening with a packet of annuals – the results are rapid, the care and preparation minimal, and the flowers bright and gay. Those same qualities are an asset even in the most established garden, as they can be used to add colour to bare gaps, brighten shrub borders while more permanent plants become established, and supply a wonderful range of flowers for home decoration.

Summer bedding with annuals, or perennials treated as annuals, is an art in itself. For sheer flower power and dazzling brilliance there is just nothing to match a well-planted bedding scheme. Some gardeners regard such formal bedding as a trifle unnatural, and prefer the more subtle arrangement and colours of most permanent plantings – but one cannot fail to admire some of the wonderful plant combinations achieved by many parks departments. The planning of summer bedding schemes calls for a degree of artistic flair if the multitude of bright colours are to be mixed, merged and contrasted like paints on a canvas. Besides colour, there is the whole question of texture and height, and the possible permutations are almost endless.

Whether or not formal beds of flowers appeal to individual gardeners, there is every reason to set aside a piece of ground (on the vegetable plot, perhaps) to grow annuals for home decoration. Annuals can provide flowers for the home from spring to autumn at very little cost, and many have the added attraction of fragrance – the Sweet Pea and Mignonette being two examples.

Among the annuals there are some of the brightest trailers and climbers – Nasturtiums and trailing lobelia to cascade from window-boxes or hanging baskets, and Sweet Peas, Morning Glory or Cathedral Bells to climb a trellis or clothe a fence.

Even the rock garden can be made more colourful with suitable annuals once the main flush of true alpines has passed in the spring and early summer (see page 16).

Annuals and biennials also provide some useful plant associations among permanent plants. The ground beneath roses can be made more interesting in the spring with Pansies or Wallflowers, while Tulips and Wallflowers associate well together.

Treatment of annuals and biennials

Many of the plants we treat as annuals are, by nature, biennial or perennial, and some of those we treat as biennials are really

Sweet William
(see page 26)

Far left: Annuals can make an excellent and colourful edging to paths and borders. In this traditional combination, white-flowered alyssum is interplanted with blue lobelia, backed by a row of golden-flowered tagetes. (These dependable annuals are detailed on pages 25, 28 and 29.)

Nigella
Love-in-a-mist
(see page 21)

Eschscholzia
Californian Poppy
(see page 27)

ANNUALS TO SOW IN AUTUMN, FOR EARLY BLOOM
Alyssum
Bartonia
Centaurea
Clarkia
Crepis
Delphinium
Eschscholzia
Gilia
Godetia
Gypsophila
Iberis
Lathyrus
Lavatera
Leptosiphon
Limnanthes
Linaria
Nemophila
Nigella
Papaver
Scabiosa
Autumn sowing is not recommended for cold areas, but can be useful in milder districts, or where some protection can be provided.

ANNUALS TO SOW LATE, FOR AUTUMN BLOOM
Alyssum
Centaurea
Clarkia
Godetia
Iberis
Lathyrus
Lavatera
Leptosiphon
Limnanthes
Tropaeolum (Nasturtium)
Although the main sowing should be made in spring, it is worth trying a late sowing of suitable kinds to extend the season. They can be sown up to the end of June.

ANNUALS FOR CARPETING
Alyssum maritimum
Iberis
Leptosiphon
Nemophila insignis
Phacelia

ANNUALS FOR THE ROCK GARDEN
Alyssum maritimum
Bryachycome iberidifolia
Leptosiphon
Limnanthes douglasii
Linaria
Mesembryanthemum criniflorum
Nemophila
Portulaca

ANNUALS FOR SUNNY BANKS OR BORDERS
Alyssum maritimum
Arctotis grandis
Bartonia
Brachycome
Cosmea
Cucurbita (Gourds)
Dimorphotheca
Eschscholzia
Gaillardia
Iberis
Papaver
Portulaca
Salvia
Tropaeolum

ANNUALS AND BIENNIALS FOR COOL OR SHADY PLACES
Campanula
Digitalis
Hesperis
Lunaria
Nemophila
Nicotiana

ANNUALS FOR EDGING
Ageratum (dwarf)
Alyssum maritimum
Brachycome iberidifolia
Calliopsis (dwarf varieties)
Gilia (dwarf varieties)
Iberis (dwarf varieties)
Leptosiphon
Limnanthes douglasii
Matthiola bicornis
Mesembryanthemum criniflorum
Nemesia
Nemophila
Phlox drummondii
Portulaca
Tagetes patula

perennials. For example, the antirrhinum is usually treated as a half-hardy annual, even though it is a hardy perennial. And Wallflowers, which are grown as biennials, are really perennials.

In the case of some half-hardy perennials, we treat them as annuals because of the problem of overwintering them as adult plants, but in other cases, such as antirrhinums and Wallflowers, they simply produce better and more reliable plants when raised afresh each year. (Antirrhinums are illustrated on page 23.)

The plants in this chapter are included on the basis of how they are normally treated – not according to a strictly scientific definition. They will usually be found in seed catalogues on this same basis. A seed catalogue will enable you to select specific varieties and colours, which it has been impossible to deal with comprehensively in this chapter because of the vast range of forms and colours that are available. For example, one well-known catalogue alone offers forty-five varieties of French and African Marigolds — all varying in colour, height, habit or form. You are quite likely to be faced with ten or more varieties of Pot Marigold (calendula) to choose from, varying in height from 30 to 60cm (1–2ft) and in various shades of orange and yellow, some with quilted centres, many with ball-shaped flowers, and others of more traditional shape. Nowadays we are quite literally spoilt for choice. The selection of varieties is very much a personal choice.

Although individual treatment may vary slightly for specific plants, the following advice will meet the cultural requirements of most annuals and biennials.

Hardy Annuals: These are sown outdoors, and they flower and die all in the same season (although they are sometimes sown in the autumn to flower the following year — which is really biennial treatment). Almost without exception they require a sunny position to do well. The nutritional content of the soil is less critical, although a hungry one often produces a prolific crop of flowers. The ideal soil is one that has been dug during the winter or early spring, with compost added, and a sprinkling of bonemeal once it has become friable.

Most hardy annuals are sown between March and June, but the earlier the better, provided the soil is in good condition — moist and warm. If the weather is poor or the soil dry, it is best to wait a week or two.

African Marigold
(see page 29)

For sowing seeds, it is important to produce a fine tilth, which means raking the soil thoroughly and breaking down all lumps. How the seeds are sown chiefly depends on the method of growing them. When growing flowers for cutting and subsequent house decoration, straight drills taken out with a draw hoe is undoubtedly the best — it makes hoeing and weed eradication much easier. For general effect, especially in borders of mixed annuals, a less rigid approach is best. The usual way is to draw, with a stick, irregular areas in the soil, and to sow each one with a different annual. The seeds can be broadcast within each area, but it is far better to sow them in straight drills, as this makes cultivation much easier when it comes to thinning and weeding. It is important to make each area reasonably large — about 1m (1yd) square — otherwise the boldness of display is lost.

Early thinning is important, but it should be done in two stages. Second stage thinnings can sometimes be transplanted to other parts of the garden.

Tall-growing annuals, such as Larkspur, will need thin canes or twiggy sticks for support in exposed areas. These supports should be positioned while the plants are still small, and they will soon be hidden as the plants grow.

Removing faded flower heads will extend the flowering season, though obviously this is not feasible with all annuals.

Half-hardy annuals: These annuals will not normally tolerate frost, although a few hardy types, such as antirrhinums, are raised early under heat in order to achieve a sufficiently long growing season. Some half-hardy annuals, such as French Marigolds, can be sown

Sweet Pea
(see page 28)

17

outdoors in May or June. Normally, however, half-hardy annuals are raised under glass.

Those plants which need a long growing season should be sown in a greenhouse in February, March or April, but only if sufficient warmth for germination is available (a seed germination case will help), and if a temperature of about 7°C (45°F) can be maintained after germination. If a warm greenhouse is not available, sow in a cold greenhouse or frame in late March or April.

Sow in pots or boxes of seed compost, and lightly cover the seed. If the box is covered with a pane of glass to conserve moisture the seeds will soon germinate. The seedlings should be transplanted into boxes of compost as soon as they can be handled without the risk of damaging the seed leaves. This is a critical stage, for the seedlings should have room to develop into sturdy plants. Good light and freedom from cold draughts are essential.

Before setting the annual plants in the open soil in May or June, all bedding plants raised under glass must be well hardened off. A cold frame is the best staging point, the top being left open increasingly until, over a period of weeks, the plants are hardened sufficiently to be planted in the open.

It is important to keep the plants well watered until they have become established outdoors, and as with hardy annuals it is best to remove dead flower heads whenever possible.

To encourage bushiness, many plants, such as antirrhinums and salvias, should have their growing tips pinched out when the plants are a few centimetres (inches) high.

Below: African Marigolds, *Tagetes erecta*, are invaluable bedding plants. 'Cupid Yellow' is a dwarf double kind with flowers up to 7.5cm (3in) across. (African Marigolds are described on page 29.)

Biennials: These are sown one year to flower the next, after which they die. They are a little more inconvenient to grow than annuals, as they really need a nursery bed in which to grow during the summer, before being planted in their flowering positions.

To offset that inconvenience, many of them flower in the spring, when most annuals would be no more than seedlings. Forget-me-nots, Wallflowers and Double Daisies are all indispensable for a spectacular display of spring bedding plants.

Sow during late spring or early summer on a prepared seed bed in a sunny or semi-shaded position. Take out shallow drills 15–23cm (6–9in) apart and sow in these, lightly covering with soil. Very small seeds are best sown in a seedbox placed in a frame or left outdoors and protected from heavy rain. Once the seedlings can be thinned or transplanted to a nursery bed, little further attention is required until they are ready for transplanting to their flowering positions after the summer bedding has been cleared. Try to move them while there is still some warmth in the soil.

Flowers for fragrance

Fragrance is always welcome, and annuals and biennials can contribute much, whether in the form of a fragrant border, or to provide attractive scent beneath a window or for cutting.

Sweet Peas are loved as much for their scent as their lovely flowers. Indeed, in the days before plant breeders developed the wonderful colour range and size of flower that we know today, Sweet Peas were grown purely for fragrance. Sweet peas are illustrated on page 115.

The word 'sweet' in front of a common name gives a clue to fragrance, and two other 'sweet' plants are Sweet William and Sweet Sultans. Sweet Sultans are discussed under cut flowers on page 21, but Sweet Williams, although delightful when cut, and arranged in a vase, are so useful for flowering in early summer that it is almost a pity to deprive the garden of such colourful and fragrant plants. The heads have intensely rich colouring, often with

Below: Leptosiphon is a ground-hugging plant that covers itself in a mass of small but attractive flowers. A packet of mixed colours makes a bright edging to a border. (See page 28.)

Stock
(see page 28)

Nicotiana affinis
Flowering Tobacco
(see page 202)

Arctotis
(see page 25)

contrasting zones, in shades of crimson, cerise, pink and white. The fragrance is reminiscent of Pinks, the family to which they belong. Like Pinks, they thrive on chalky soil, and if necessary a dusting of lime will improve results.

There are now strains of Sweet William suitable for cultivation as half-hardy or hardy annuals, although the plants will not then flower until late in the summer.

Sweet Rocket is a biennial that produces its fragrant white or purple flowers from May to the end of June. Its perfume is most noticeable in the evening, and it looks at its best in half shade, near trees or shrubs. Its Latin name is *Hesperis matronalis*.

Sweet Alyssum is better known as a low, white edging plant rather than for its fragrance, which is not outstanding.

Wallflowers would be widely grown even if they were not fragrant – they are so welcome with their rich yellow, orange and red shades in April and May. For fragrance they are best planted beneath a window, near a door or as an edging to a path, so that their scent can be appreciated.

Dianthus tend to be a confused group when it comes to treatment, but most seed catalogues list varieties that can be treated as half-hardy or hardy annuals or biennials, and they are usually pleasantly fragrant. They appreciate a chalky soil.

One of the sweetest-scented of all garden plants is Night-scented Stock (*Matthiola bicornis*). They should be sown where their evening fragrance can be enjoyed, for it is then that the drooping flowers raise their heads and release the wonderful scent.

The ordinary Stocks, much used in summer bedding, are also fragrant, and there are many forms to be found in seed lists.

A plant that has come very much into favour in recent years is Flowering Tobacco (*Nicotiana affinis*). This is due, no doubt, to the vastly improved varieties that are now available. Besides the normal white, there are varieties with greenish-yellow, crimson, mauve, pink and yellow flowers, and they vary in height from 30 to 75cm (1–2½ft). Although there are varieties whose flowers remain open during the day, most open fully only in the evening, which is when their lovely sweet scent is at its best. If cut while open they should remain that way indoors and continue to release their fragrance.

Perhaps the sweetest-scented of all is Mignonette (*Reseda odorata*). It is not an attractive plant, the unspectacular spikes containing mainly creamy-white flowers, but the smell is so pleasant that it is still worthy of a place in the garden. It is often effective sown among other annuals.

Flowers for cutting

Annuals contain some exceedingly effective cut flowers for home decoration. Apart from the fragrant flowers already described, there is no shortage of colourful and long-lasting flowers from which to choose. The ones mentioned below are only a selection, and the tables on pages 25 to 29 offer more ideas.

Arctotis (African Daisy): A spectacular flower to grow in a dry, sunny position. The large daisy-like flowers have long stems, ideally suited for cutting. *A. grandis* has pearly-white flowers with a mauve centre, but there are hybrids in brilliant shades of orange, red, yellow, carmine, cream and white, many zoned with a contrasting colour.

Calendula (Pot Marigold): An extremely easy plant to grow, doing well on poor, sandy soil. The plants have a smell which though not unpleasant is not to everyone's taste.

Callistephus hortensis (Aster): If you pick up a good seed catalogue you may be presented with about thirty varieties and colour strains from which to choose, and most of them will be good for cutting. Some resemble chrysanthemums. Asters are especially valuable because of their late flowering season, but they really need a sheltered position and deeply dug soil for good results.

Centaurea cyanus (Cornflower): The taller forms of these popular blue, pink, red or white flowers are best for cutting. They seem to grow well in any soil, provided the position is sunny.

Centaurea moschata (Sweet Sultan): The flowers resemble Cornflowers in shape, but are pleasantly fringed and fragrant. colours include pink, lavender, purple, yellow and white. They are very easy to grow.

Chrysanthemum (annual): The annual chrysanthemum, with daisy-like flowers often brightly zoned, makes a good cut flower because it is particularly long-lasting in water. There are named varieties, but a mixed packet adds variety.

Clarkia: Long spikes bear clouds of pink, mauve, purple or red flowers, elegant when cut. Clarkia is exceedingly easy to grow, but may need the support of twiggy sticks.

Cosmea binpinnatus (Cosmos): This plant makes a striking show in a mixed border, but its crimson, rose or white flowers, like single dahlias and set among ferny foliage, are ideal for indoor decoration. To avoid the disappointment of very late flowering, it is important to sow early. They are tall-growing, compared with most annuals, and need plenty of room in which to develop.

Dimorphotheca (Star of the Veldt): These daisy-like flowers revel in a sunny position, soon coming into flower from a spring sowing as a half-hardy annual. Although the flowers only open in the sun, they do make a useful cut flower.

Larkspur (Annual Delphinium): These small versions of the border delphinium are every bit as charming. Be prepared to stake in windy or exposed positions.

Nigella (Love-in-a-mist): A favourite annual for the border, and equally good when cut to decorate a home. Because of its relatively short flowering season it is best sown in September and March, with a further sowing in May.

Scabiosa (Pincushion Flower): Although not as large as the scabious of herbaceous borders, it is nevertheless a splendid cut flower. The main colour is blue, but lavender, pink, maroon, cerise and white are among the colours now available.

Zinnia: These bright plants are rather like small dahlias and are attractive flowers to cut for floral decoration. They are not easy to grow, however, and need full sun in a warm position, a rich soil and plenty of water. They should never become cramped in seedboxes, and are best sown in pots to avoid subsequent root disturbance. Outdoor sowings are possible in mild districts, but

Petunia
(see page 28)

Sweet Sultan
(see page 25)

Cosmos
(see page 26)

Cobaea scandens
(see page 26)

should not be attempted in the North without the protection of cloches or frames.

Annual climbers

Whether grown to hide an ugly site, or for the sheer joy of their flowers, annual climbers can be very rewarding, and can often be used to brighten an area that would otherwise be lost to cultivation – their vertical dimension taking advantage of valuable growing space.

Although there are not many annual climbers, the ones commonly available are very spectacular. Pride of place must go to the Sweet Pea, not only for its fragrance, but because hybridizers have brought this flower to the peak of perfection. And varieties now vary from 30cm to 1·8m (1–6ft) or more.

For exhibition-length stems, considerable effort has to go into preparing special trenches, and constant training on the 'cordon' system of growing up canes. The result is perfect and beautiful blooms, but quite adequate flowers for cutting and screening are possible if they are simply allowed to scramble up netting or some other support. They will, however, benefit from full sun and regular

Right: Dwarf French Marigolds, *Tagetes patula*, are justifiably popular as an edging plant in beds of other annuals. They are so prolific they are often in flower before being planted out. (See page 29.)

feeding – and above all the removal of seed pods as they form. For early flowers, they are best sown in pots in autumn and over-wintered in a cold frame.

Morning Glory (*Ipomoea*) is a free-flowering climber for a sheltered position in full sun. One variety has enormous saucer-shaped flowers striped blue and white. Another has deep azure-blue trumpet-shaped blooms. (Illustrated on page 195.)

Closely related is *Convolvulus major* with trumpet-shaped flowers in blue, rose, cream or white shades. Ipomoea is best treated as tender, but the convolvulus can be cultivated as a hardy annual.

Cobaea scandens is popularly known as Cathedral Bells or Cup and Saucer Vine, which gives some indication of its appearance. The flowers are like large individual Canterbury Bell blooms, purple in colour. They can be grown in pots, overwintered in a frost-proof greenhouse, and treated as a half-hardy biennial. They can also be sown as an annual, provided an early start is made and the plants are given a warm, sheltered position. It is a very striking plant in the right position.

Nasturtiums are well-known annuals, but a careful selection of varieties is necessary for climbing plants, as many are bush-forming in habit. They are extremely effective at covering a bank, producing

Below: A mixed planting of antirrhinums is always popular, and there is a variety for almost any situation. Heights range from 15cm (6in) to 90cm (3ft). Rust-resistant varieties are available and should be sown where this disease is troublesome. (See page 25.)

Foxglove
(see page 26)

Salpiglossis sinuata
(see page 29)

Pansy
(see page 29)

a blaze of colour. The drawback is that the leaves seem to be particularly attractive to caterpillars. (Illustrated on page 195.)

A dainty-looking climber is the Canary Creeper (*Tropaeolum canariensis*), a very close relative of the Nasturtium. This has pale yellow, fringed flowers. Unlike its relatives, however, it needs a rich soil. It can be treated as a hardy annual, but often results are more certain if treated as a half-hardy plant.

Not everyone wants flowers from a climber, and there are two other annuals well worth a place in any garden – the ornamental-leaved Japanese Hop, and Ornamental Gourds, with their fantastically-shaped fruits.

The Japanese Hop (*Humulus japonicus*) will rapidly form an effective screen, but it can be made more interesting by growing the variegated form, *H. j.* 'Variegatus', which is strikingly blotched with white.

Ornamental Gourds come in some amazing shapes and forms, which understandably makes them popular for drying and varnishing for decoration. These plants are fun to grow and it is well worth finding a place for them.

Flowers for a spring display

Wallflowers, Forget-me-nots, Double Daisies and Pansies . . . some of our favourite flowers blooming in spring. And they are all raised from seed. (Double Daisies are illustrated on page 71.)

The secret of success with all these flowers is to sow at the right time, and to establish them in their flowering positions while the soil is still warm in autumn. May or June is a good time to sow, as this gives them a long season of growth before winter sets in. And if they can be sown thinly and thinned early in a position in which they can remain undisturbed for the summer, so much the better. Nipping out the growing tips of plants such as Wallflowers, when they are growing strongly, will encourage bushiness and promote a more spectacular display. Regular weeding between the plants during the summer will ensure they are not competing for food and light. If these rules are followed and the plants moved to their flowering position not later than October, the results will justify the effort.

The possibility of sowing annuals in autumn has been mentioned on page 16, and some of these can be used in spring bedding displays. Among those you can try are the bright blue *Nemophila insignis*, saponaria, which has graceful sprays of pink flowers, silene, with clusters of rose-pink flowers, and Virginian Stock.

The key to successfully flowering annuals in spring is to sow them at the correct time – they need to be strong enough to perform what is required of them, but not to be so forward that they suffer from severe winter weather. In the South, the middle of September is about right, while the middle of August is preferable for the North. In sheltered gardens, or on sandy or dry chalk soils, they can be moved to the flowering position before winter, provided sufficient growth has been made, but on heavy land or in cold districts they are best left until March, then transferred with a good clump of soil round the roots.

DEPENDABLE ANNUALS AND BIENNIALS

Species and Varieties	Height	Treatment	Colours	Cut flower	Light requirement	Fragrance	Hardiness	Description
Acroclinium	45cm (18in)	HA	W, P	✿	○		★★★★	'Everlasting' flowers on long stems. Semi-double daisy flowers with yellow centres.
Ageratum	15-45cm (6-18in)	HHA	B		○		★	Heads of small, blue powder-puff flowers. Most varieties are less than 25cm (10in) and useful as an edging plant.
Alyssum maritimum Sweet Alyssum	10-15cm (4-6in)	HA	W		○		★★★★	Small mounds covered with white flowers. Excellent edging plant or for growing between crazy-paving.
Amaranthus caudatus Love-lies-bleeding	75cm (2½ft)	HA	R, G	✿	○		★★★★	Long drooping tassels of crimson or green flowers. An impressive 'spot' plant.
Antirrhinum Snapdragon	15-90cm (6in-3ft)	HHA	W, P, R, O, Y		○		★★	These popular plants are now available in a wide range of heights and colours. Rust-resistant varieties should be used where this disease is a problem.
Arctotis African Daisy	30-60cm (1-2ft)	HHA	W, P, R, O, Y	✿	○		★	Large daisy-like flowers, superb for a hot, sunny position. Fine for cutting.
Bartonia aurea	60cm (2ft)	HA	Y		○		★★★★	A brilliant annual with golden-yellow flowers rather like St. John's Wort. Blooms over a long period.
Bellis perennis 'Flore-pleno' Double Daisy	15cm (6in)	HB	R, P, W		◉		★★★★	Large double daisies, much used in spring bedding. Flowers from March to May.
Brachycome iberidifolia Swan River Daisy	23cm (9in)	HHA	B, W		○		★	Small daisy-like flowers, covering compact plants.
Calendula officinalis Pot Marigold	30-60cm (1-2ft)	HA	Y, O	✿	◉		★★★★	Very bright annuals, with large double flowers in various shades of orange and yellow. Sturdy growth.
Calliopsis Annual Coreopsis	30-60cm (1-2ft)	HA	Y, R	✿	○		★★★★	Gay, single flowers with a contrasting centre. Nice cut flowers.
Callistephus hortensis Aster	30-60cm (1-2ft)	HHA	W, Y, P, R, B	✿	○		★	There are now varieties with many different colours and habits. Single, double, reflexed and incurving forms are available. Flowers during late August and September.
Campanula medium Canterbury Bell	45-75cm (1½-2½ft)	HB	B, P, W		◉		★★★★	Very beautiful and striking biennials, with large upward-pointing bells.
Centaurea cyanus Cornflower	45-90cm (1½-3ft)	HA	B, P, R, W	✿	○		★★★★	Once a familiar sight in our corn fields, but now more often seen grown as a flower for cutting.
C. moschata Sweet Sultan	45cm (1½ft)	HA	W, R, P, Y	✿	○	✿	★★★★	Attractive fragrant flowers with fringed petals. Excellent for cutting.
Cheiranthus allionii Siberian Wallflower	38cm (15in)	HB	Y, O		○		★★★★	Smaller flowers than most of the normal wallflowers, but very good for massed bedding. In bloom March to May.
C. cheiri Wallflower	15-45cm (6-18in)	HB	R, Y, P, O	✿	○	✿	★★★★	Indispensable spring bedding plants, and their wonderful fragrance makes them ideal for cutting. Flowering period is March to May.
Chrysanthemum (annual type)	30-60cm (1-2ft)	HA	R, Y, O, W	✿	○		★★★★	Gay plants, with a variety of colours — some attractively banded or zoned.
Clarkia elegans	60cm (2ft)	HA	P, B, R	✿	○		★★★★	Elegant spikes, with double flowers. Easy to grow.

Right: The Iceland Poppy, *Papaver nudicaule*, provides a range of soft and delicate flowers during the summer months. Although best treated as a biennial, it can be flowered as an annual by sowing early under glass. (See page 28.)

Far right: Ageratum has small heads of blue powder-puff flowers, and the dwarf varieties are fine edging plants. This variety is 'Blue Chip', an ageratum of very uniform habit. (See page 25.)

DEPENDABLE ANNUALS AND BIENNIALS Continued

Species and Varieties	Height	Treatment	Colours	Cut flower	Light requirement	Fragrance	Hardiness	Description
Cobaea scandens	3m (10ft)	HHB	B		○		★	A climbing plant with purple flowers rather like Canterbury Bells. Needs a good start and a warm summer.
Convolvulus major	3m (10ft)	HA	B, P, W		◉		★★★★	A climber to cover a trellis quickly. Bright, trumpet-shaped flowers.
C. minor	30cm (1ft)	HA	B, P, W		◉		★★★★	Bright flowers with contrasting yellow or white centres.
Cosmea bipinnatus Cosmos	60-90cm (2-3ft)	HHA	R, P, W	✿	◉		★	Large, single flowers with a centre of yellow stamens. Feathery foliage.
Crepis rubra Hawkweed	45cm (1½ft)	HA	P		○		★★★★	Soft pink Dandelion-shaped flowers carried well clear of the foliage.
Delphinium Larkspur	45cm-1.2m (1½-4ft)	HA	P, B, W	✿	◉		★★★★	Small versions of the border delphinium. Pink, blue, and white spikes.
Dianthus barbatus Sweet William	15-60cm (6in-2ft)	HB	P, R	✿	○	✿	★★★★	Very attractive plants, with zoned flowers.
D. heddewigii Annual Pinks	10-30cm (4-12in)	HHA	P, R, W		○		★★★★	An annual version of the garden Pink.
Digitalis purpurea Foxglove	90cm-1.5m (3-5ft)	HB	R, P, W, Y		●		★★★★	Handsome versions of our wild Foxglove, with magnificent spikes of bell-shaped flowers with spotted throats.
Dimorphotheca aurantiaca Star of the Veldt	23-30cm (9-12in)	HHA	Y, O, W	✿	○		★	Large, open daisy-like flowers. Appealing plants, but they require full sun.

DEPENDABLE ANNUALS AND BIENNIALS Continued

Species and Varieties	Height	Treatment	Colours	Cut flower	Light requirement	Fragrance	Hardiness	Description
Eschscholzia Californian Poppy	15-30cm (6-12in)	HA	Y, O, R, P		○		★★★★	Extremely bright annuals if given a sunny position.
Gaillardia picta	30-45cm (1-1½ft)	HHA	R, Y	✿	○		★★★★	Single or double flowers, often shaded or tipped, carried on good stems.
Gilia	30-45cm (1-1½ft)	HA	B		○		★★★★	An easily-grown plant with flower heads that resemble small lavender-blue pincushions.
Godetia	15-60cm (6in-2ft)	HA	P, R	✿	○		★★★★	Long-lasting flowers — and a fine plant for bedding in a sunny position.
Gypsophila elegans	45cm (1½ft)	HA	W, P	✿	○		★★★★	Small white or pink flowers, according to variety, very popular for cutting to mix with other flowers.
Helianthus annuus Sunflower	60cm-2.4m (2-8ft)	HA	Y		○		★★★★	The traditional tall, single sunflower is well-known, but there are now dwarf and double forms.
Hesperis matronalis Sweet Rocket	60cm (2ft)	HB	W, B		◑	✿	★★★★	Sweetly scented white or purple flowers from May to July.
Iberis coronaria Candytuft	10-30cm (4-12in)	HA	P, W		○	✿	★★★★	Flat heads of pink, red or white blooms cover the plants.
Impatiens balsamina Balsam	30-45cm (1-1½ft)	HAA	P, W,R		○		★	Showy plants with flowers resembling small camellias.
Ipomoea Morning Glory	3m (10ft)	HAA	B		○		★	A free-flowering climber for a warm, sheltered position.

DEPENDABLE ANNUALS AND BIENNIALS Continued

Species and Varieties	Height	Treatment	Colours	Cut flower	Light requirement	Fragrance	Hardiness	Description
Kochia tricophylla (See page 202)								
Lathyrus odoratus Sweet Pea	30cm-1.8m (1-6ft)	HA	R, W; B, P, O	✿	○	✿	★★★★	The Sweet Pea is normally thought of as a climber, but there are varieties that form dwarf bush shapes suitable for a window-box.
Lavatera Mallow	60cm-1.2m (2-4ft)	HA	P	✿	○		★★★★	Bushy plants, suitable for a large border or for cutting.
Leptosiphon	15cm (6in)	HA	W, P, Y, O		○		★★★★	A ground-hugging annual with bright little flowers. Useful as an edging plant.
Limnanthes douglasii	15cm (6in)	HA	Y		○		★★★★	Yellow saucer-shaped flowers edged with white. Makes a gay edging.
Linaria maroccana Toadflax	23-30cm (9-12in)	HA	R, Y, P		○		★★★★	A gay edging plant in a wide range of colours, lips or throats often contrasting. Like miniature Snapdragons.
Linum grandiflorum Flax	30-60cm (1-2ft)	HA	W, R		○		★★★★	Striking little plants — one variety has white flowers with a crimson centre another has crimson petals with a silk-like sheen.
Lobelia erinus	15cm (6in)	HHA	B, R, W		○		★	The blue varieties are traditional edging plants. Pendulous varieties are useful for window-boxes and hanging baskets.
Lunaria biennis Honesty	60cm (2ft)	HB	W, B		◑		★★★★	White or purple flowers, followed by flat, silvery seed pods, useful for winter decoration.
Matthiola annua Stock	30-45cm (1-1½ft)	HHA	R, B, P, W, Y	✿	○	✿	★★★	It is now possible to be fairly certain of double-flowers with these traditional and beautiful bedding plants.
M. bicornis Night-Scented Stock	30cm (1ft)	HA	B			✿	★★★★	Although the flowers are unspectacular they have a delicious fragrance, strongest on a warm evening.
Mesembryanthemum criniflorum Ice Plant	7.5cm (3in)	HHA	P, R, O, Y		○		★	Vivid daisy like flowers for a sunny position. Fleshy, succulent leaves.
Myosotis (See page 202)								
Nemesia	23-30cm (9-12in)	HHA	Y, O, B, R, P		○		★	Free-flowering plants, with neat compact habit. Wide range of colours.
Nemophila insignis Baby Blue Eyes	15cm (6in)	HA	B		◉		★★★★	Produces a carpet of sky-blue flowers. Needs cool, moist conditions.
Nicotiana affinis (See page 202)								
Nigella damascena Love-in-a-mist	45cm (1½ft)	HA	B, P	✿	○		★★★★	Blue, cornflower-like flowers amid a mass of feathery foliage. Pleasant when massed.
Papaver nudicaule Iceland Poppy	60-75cm (2-2½ft)	HB	P, Y, O, R		○		★★★★	Pleasant Poppy flowers, some delicately picoteed. Can be treated as a half-hardy annual.
Pentstemon Beard Tongue	45cm (1½ft)	HHA	W, P, R		○		★★	Trumpet-shaped blooms, rather like an open-throated antirrhinum.
Petunia hybrida (See page 203)								

Species and Varieties	Height	Treatment	Colours	Cut flower	Light requirement	Fragrance	Hardiness	Description
Phacelia	23-45cm (9-18in)	HA	B		◯		★★★★	Gentian-blue flowers, bought into bloom in about eight weeks from sowing. Dwarf kinds are useful for edging.
Phlox drummondii	15-30cm (6-12in)	HHA	B, P, R, W		◯		★	Masses of gay clusters of star-like flowers, in a range of colours, some with distinctly defined eyes.
Portulaca grandiflora	15cm (6in)	HHA	P, Y, W		◯		★	Easy to grow, and an excellent choice for a hot, sunny bank. There are single and double kinds.
Reseda odorata Mignonette	30cm (1ft)	HA	Y, R	✿	◯		★★★★	Lovely fragrance from the spikes of yellowish-white flowers. There is also a variety with reddish flowers, although fragrance is the main attraction.
Rhodanthe	30cm (1ft)	HHA	W, P		◯		★	One of the 'everlasting' flowers, grown to dry for winter decoration.
Salpiglossis	45-60cm (1½-2ft)	HHA	Y, R, P, B		◯		★	Fascinating flowers, each one beautifully marked with a richly coloured veining.
Salvia	15-30cm (6-12in)	HHA	R		◯		★	A blaze of scarlet when in flower, which justifiably makes it a popular bedding plant.
Scabiosa Pincushion Flower	45-75cm (1½-2½ft)	HHA	P, R, B, W	✿	◯		★★★★	An annual form of scabious, splendid for cutting.
Tagetes erecta African Marigold	30-90cm (1-3ft)	HHA	Y, O		◯		★	Gorgeous double ball-shaped flowers on sturdy plants. Many shades of orange and yellow.
T. patula French Marigold	13-30cm (5-12in)	HHA	Y, O		◯		★	Invaluable bedding plants, ideal for edging formal beds. Usually in flower before they are planted out.
T. signata Tagetes	15-23cm (6-9in)	HHA	Y, O		◯		★	Plants form mounds covered with yellow or orange small single flowers. Very effective for edging or bedding.
Tropaeolum canariensis Canary Creeper	3m (10ft)	HA	Y	✎	◉		★★★★	A climber with elegantly fringed pale yellow flowers resembling Nasturtiums.
T. majus Nasturtium	30cm-1.8m (1-6ft)	HA	Y, O		◯		★★★★	Too well known to need description. Be careful to choose a variety with the right growth habit — some are climbers, others are compact.
Verbena	15-45cm (6-18in)	HHA	B, P, R		◯		★	Useful for bedding or edging. Clusters of small bright flowers, usually with a white eye.
Viola Pansy	15-23cm (6-9in)	HB	R, O, Y, B, W		◑		★★★★	Invaluable plants — they have a wonderful colour range, and can be had in flower from spring till late autumn.
Zinnia elegans	15-60cm (6in-2ft)	HHA	R, O, Y, P, W	✿	◯		★	In the right climate, these colourful flowers, resembling small dahlias, can be most impressive.

Key to colours:
B, blue (including purples and mauves); O, orange; P, pink; R, red; W, white; Y, yellow

Key to treatment:
HA, hardy annual; HB, hardy biennial; HHA, half-hardy annual; HHB, half-hardy biennial

Herbaceous Plants

This chapter is about the plants normally found in an herbaceous border – but it would be inaccurate to be too narrow in definition. Many of the plants described can be used in many parts of the garden – from containers on the patio to formal beds for cutting or exhibition. And the so-called herbaceous border frequently contains plants that are not strictly herbaceous, but retain some growth above ground all year round. For that reason, the plants sold for herbaceous borders are often termed 'hardy perennials', which could, of course, include trees and shrubs, but by common usage implies border plants.

Perovskia is one example of a plant that really belongs with the shrubs (in this book it is included in the shrub section, on page 106). However, it is a plant often treated as a border perennial. It makes 60–90cm (2–3ft) of new growth each summer, which bears the flowers. If this shrub is pruned back to about 45cm (18in) high in spring, it will be stimulated to send up another season's flowering shoots. For that reason, it can look as much in place in the herbaceous border as among shrubs.

Whatever the precise definition of our border plants, they are the mainstay of most gardens, and are among the most diverse of plants in shape, form, habit and colour. Leaving aside those plants which qualify for the rock garden, they range in height from about 20cm (8in) in the case of the Marsh Marigold (*Caltha palustris*) and Lung-wort (*Pulmonaria angustifolia*) to the 2·4m (8ft) or so of the Foxtail Lily (*Eremurus robustus*). Some of these border plants bloom prolifically for months, such as the Catmint (*Nepeta mussinii*), while others have a brief but spectacular display, like the Oriental Poppy (*Papaver orientale*). A few have deliciously fragrant flowers, such as Pinks and Carnations (dianthus) and Lily-of-the-valley (*Convallaria majalis*), and others aromatic foliage, like Bergamot (*Monarda didyma*) or Majoram (*Origanum vulgare*). (*Caltha palustris* is illustrated on page 58, and *Monarda didyma* on page 35.)

The era of long, wide borders devoted solely to herbaceous plants has long since gone. Splendid though they looked, these borders needed a large garden and plenty of time – two things that modern gardeners lack.

The plants, however, are as desirable as ever, and only their setting needs to be modified. The trend during recent years has been away from the conventional wide border backed by a hedge or a wall, towards island beds, with a path or lawn surrounding them. The tallest plants are placed in the middle, instead of at the

Dicentra
Bleeding Heart
(see page 45)

Far left: Herbaceous plants can often be enhanced by setting them amid shrubs with coloured foliage. Here, a dark-leaved form of the Smoke Bush, *Cotinus coggygria*, is set behind nepeta and Lamb's Ears, *Stachys lanata*. (Shrubs with coloured foliage are listed on page 85.)

Aquilegia
Columbine
(see page 44)

Coreopsis
Tickseed
(see page 45)

Papaver orientale
Oriental Poppy
(see page 48)

HERBACEOUS PLANTS FOR CHALKY SOIL

Acanthus	Helleborus
Achillea	Hemerocallis
Aconitum	Heuchera
Agapanthus	Hosta
Alchemilla	Incarvillea
Alstroemeria	Iris
Anaphalis	Kniphofia
Anchusa	Liatris
Anemone japonica	Ligularia
Anthemis	Linum
Aquilegia	Lobelia
Artemisia	Lychnis
Aster	Lysimachia
Astrantia	Macleaya
Campanula	Mertensia
Centaurea	Monarda
Chelone	Nepeta
Chrysanthemum	Oenothera
Cimicifuga	Omphalodes
Coreopsis	Origanum
Crambe	Paeonia
Dianthus	Papaver
Dicentra	Platycodon
Dictamnus	Polemonium
Doronicum	Polygonum
Echinops	Potentilla
Epimedium	Pulmonaria
Erigeron	Rudbeckia
Eryngium	Salvia
Euphorbia	Scabiosa
Gaillardia	Sedum
Geranium	Sidalcea
Geum	Solidago
Gypsophila	Stokesia
Helenium	Thalictrum
Helianthus	Verbascum
Heliopsis	Veronica

HERBACEOUS PLANTS FOR HEAVY OR CLAY SOIL

Achillea	Lychnis
Alchemilla	Lysimachia
Aster	Macleaya
Centaurea	Mertensia
Coreopsis	Oenothera
Crambe	Omphalodes
Epimedium	Platycodon
Eupatorium	Polemonium
Geranium	Polygonum
Heliopsis	Potentilla
Helleborus	Pulmonaria
Hemerocallis	Rudbeckia
Hosta	Salvia
Ligularia	Sidalcea

HERBACEOUS PLANTS FOR COASTAL PLANTING

Achillea	Iris unguicularis
Agapanthus	Kniphofia
Anchusa	Linum
Catananche	Lupinus
Centranthus	Lychnis
Chrysanthemum	Macleaya
Crambe	Oenothera
Dianthus	Papaver
Echinops	Salvia
Erigeron	Sedum
Eryngium	

HERBACEOUS PLANTS FOR WINDY, EXPOSED SITUATIONS

Achillea (dwarf kinds such as 'Moonshine')
Alchemilla
Anaphalis
Anemone japonica
Artemisia
Aster (dwarf hybrids)
Centaurea
Chelone
Coreopsis
Eryngium
Geranium
Gypsophila
Hemerocallis
Heuchera
Kniphofia
Liatris
Linum
Lychnis
Oenothera
Origanum
Platycodon
Polygonum (dwarf kinds such as 'Lowndes Variety')
Potentilla
Scabiosa
Sedum
Stokesia
Veronica

HERBACEOUS PLANTS FOR A HOT, DRY SITE

Acanthus	Heuchera
Achillea	Incarvillea
Alstroemeria	Kniphofia
Anaphalis	Liatris
Anchusa	Lupinus
Anemone japonica	Morina
Anthemis	Nepeta
Artemisia	Oenothera
Catananche	Origanum
Centaurea	Papaver
Centranthus	Platycodon
Chelone	Polemonium
Coreopsis	Potentilla
Dictamnus	Salvia
Echinops	Scabiosa
Erigeron	Sedum
Eryngium	Stokesia
Geum	Veronica
Gypsophila	
Heliopsis	

HERBACEOUS GROUND COVER

Alchemilla mollis	Geranium
Anaphalis triplinervis	Heuchera
Bergenia cordifolia	Hosta
Dianthus	Nepeta mussinii

PLANTS FOR A MOIST SITUATION

Aruncus	Ligularia
Astrantia	Lobelia cardinalis
Caltha palustris	Lychnis chalcedonica
Cimicifuga	Lysimachia
Eupatorium	Mimulus luteus
Hosta	Polygonum
Iris kaempferi	Thalictrum
I. sibirica	Trollius

back, and the bed can be appreciated from whichever angle it is viewed.

Such beds need not be very large, but 1·5m (5ft) is about the minimum width. As an approximate guide, the height of the tallest plants should be about half the width of the border, so this will give some idea of the scope offered by a border of a particular width.

Even if a traditional one-sided border is established, it is sensible to position a path of about 45cm (18in) wide between the back of the border and the wall or fence, to allow easy access.

It is usual to arrange a border to produce bloom from the dawn of spring to the last throes of autumn, and by careful selection of plants this is possible, even in the smallest border. A couple of Christmas and Lenten Roses (*Helleborus niger* and *H. orientalis*) will provide flower from Christmas until April, when Elephant's Ears (*Bergenia cordifolia*) and Leopard's-bane (doronicum) take over until midway through the year. June and July sees so many border flowers in bloom that the choice is wide open, the pyrethrums being only one example. Black-eyed Susan (*Rudbeckia deamii*) is an excellent plant and will flower from July to September, when either Dragon's Head (*Physostegia virginica*) or that most excellent of plants the Ice Plant (*Sedum spectabile*) will take over until the end of October.

With perhaps half a dozen or so plants it is possible to span the normal growing season. But the choice is infinitely wider than the arbitrary selection just mentioned, and there is no reason why there should not be a new plant coming into flower practically every week during spring and summer, even if space is limited.

The use of bulbs should never be overlooked when planning a flower border – there is no taboo about mixing them with herbaceous plants, and indeed the flower border is an excellent setting for Lilies, Crown Imperial, irises and some of the larger alliums.

Occasionally, gardeners plant a border to be at its best at one time of the year only – perhaps spring, autumn, or mid-summer. There is no doubt that such borders look spectacular when in full bloom; where there is enough room to have these borders, and provided they do not dominate the garden, they are an excellent idea. In a small garden, however, it is usually desirable to have the colour and interest spread over as long a period as possible.

Planning and planting a border

Careful planning, with due regard to height and ultimate spread of the plants to be used, is essential before a spade or garden fork is put into the soil. Organize and plan the border on graph-paper first, balancing colours, heights and flowering periods. The chances are you won't get it right first time, but even after the border has been planted you can make notes about minor colour clashes, plants that are not doing as well as they should and which may need a change in conditions, for replanting in the autumn. There will always be combinations or spacings that just don't work, despite even the most careful planning.

Without forethought, however, it is more difficult, for combinations and associations call for an intimate knowledge of plants and years of experience. For that reason, it is always useful to make a

Bergenia cordifolia
Elephant's Ears
(see page 44)

Physostegia virginica
Dragon's Head
(see page 49)

Helleborus niger
Christmas Rose
(see page 47)

33

note of pleasing plant associations when you see them in other gardens.

The ground should be prepared thoroughly, deeply dug and have as much compost or organic material as possible incorporated, as border plants will remain undisturbed for at least three years. If planting is being done in the spring, this is the time to apply a general garden fertilizer.

Once the soil has been broken down and the fertilizer applied, position labels where each plant is to be placed. Then, when the plants arrive, and even if they arrive in instalments, you will know exactly where each is to be planted.

Planning and marking in advance also avoids the temptation to plant too closely when the plants are seen. Planting at the right spacing for a year or two's time inevitably means the newly-purchased plants look sparse, but it does not appear that way once they are in full growth, and any bare patches the first season can be peppered with annuals, bedding plants or bulbs.

Most subjects can be planted in either September and October or March and April. There are, however, a few plants which are less accommodating in this respect, and they need to be planted at specific times for the best results. Pyrethrums and Bearded Iris are best transplanted once the flowers fade. Spring-flowering subjects are moved in autumn, while autumn-flowering kinds such as stokesia and physostegia are transplanted in spring.

Plants with fleshy roots, such as *Acanthus mollis* and platycodons are also best moved in spring.

Plants grown in containers can, of course, be planted in spring or autumn without hesitation, and throughout the summer provided they are well watered until they become established.

Plants with straight, carrot-like roots should be planted in holes sufficiently deep to take them without bending, and the soil needs to be firmed in round the length of the root as planting progresses. With other kinds, spread the roots out in a natural manner. Avoid planting too deeply, but do not let the crown stand proud of the soil.

Never plant single specimens, despite the temptation to economize or to grow a wider range of plants within the space available. At least three of a kind should be allowed, to ensure a bright display without patchiness. In a large border, five of a kind would not be amiss.

It goes without saying that they should be arranged in groups or clusters and never in straight lines.

Some good border plants

The range of hardy border plants is vast. There are so many that it would be impossible to grow but a small fraction of those in cultivation, even in a large garden. The chart on pages 44 to 49 contains about 100 border flowers, which is representative of some of the best, but few gardeners could grow them all, and there are many other delightful plants besides those mentioned. It is assumed that most gardeners are familiar with more popular subjects such as chrysanthemums, dahlias, delphiniums and lupins, so the following

Below: Japanese Anemone, *Anemone japonica* 'September Charm' is a late-flowering beauty for the herbaceous border, and is useful for a chalky soil or a hot, dry site. (See page 35.)

list deals with those groups that are sometimes overlooked yet are merit-worthy and deserve a place in the border.

Achillea: This is an extensive family, with plants ranging from a few centimetres to more than a metre. They are all easy to grow and are a good choice for chalky soil or stony gravel. Dwarf species, in particular, are unsuitable for wet clays.

Not all achilleas are good garden plants, but a justifiably popular species is *A. filipendulina*, which grows to about 1·2m (4ft) and has an erect habit and wide, flat heads of bright yellow flowers.

Even more gardenworthy is 'Moonshine', a dwarfer variety, with feathery silvery foliage of interest for the whole season, and neat heads of canary-yellow flowers on 60cm (2ft) stems.

Anemone: Another large genus, with some members being small spring-flowering tuberous plants growing only a few centimetres high, to autumn-flowering herbaceous plants 90cm (3ft) tall. Species grown from tubers are described on pages 72 and 79.

Perhaps the finest border anemone, especially useful because of its late flowering period, is *A. japonica*, the Japanese Anemone. Easy to grow, and not invasive, it will thrive in sun or partial shade. There are several good varieties to be found, including 'Bressingham Glow', a rosy-red, semi-double, 45cm (1½ft); 'Lady Gilmour', large pink flowers, branching stems, 60cm (2ft); 'Louise Uhink', white, 90cm (3ft); and 'September Charm'. This variety has lovely soft pink flowers with a golden centre, each about 10cm (4in) across, and carried on neat plants of about 45cm (1½ft). The flowers of all the varieties resemble lavateras in shape, and are extremely attractive.

Below: Bergamot or Bee Balm, *Monarda didyma*, is an interesting plant, and one that will do well on chalk. The aromatic foliage is topped by attractive thistle-like flowers from July to September. The variety illustrated is 'Cambridge Scarlet'. (See pages 31 and 48.)

The nomenclature of these plants is a little confused, as some botanists consider some of the varieties of *A. japonica* to be more accurately *A. hupehensis*, which was once a variety of *japonica*. However, as most of the varieties are hybrids it is only of academic interest. (*Anemone japonica* is illustrated on page 34.)

Aster: There are a few weedy asters, and some superb asters, with sterling qualities. The Michaelmas Daisy is one of the latter kind – though only because so much has been done by plant breeders in the last twenty years or so, transforming it from the rather pathetic race seen growing wild or in neglected gardens into a plant of spectacular beauty in September and October. It is important not to be put off the good varieties by memories of the inferior kinds. Michaelmas Daisies are likely to be found listed under *A. novi-belgii*, although the term is sometimes applied to other, similar, asters flowering at this time. They are all easily grown, but respond to a little extra care. It is important not to plant them too closely, and to thin the shoots if they become crowded. They make good plants for all gardens.

A good nursery will be able to supply many fine varieties, and the following is only a representative selection: 'Ada Ballard', large mauve-blue, 90cm (3ft); 'Blandie', pure white, semi-double, 1·2m (4ft); 'Carnival', cherry red, semi-double, 60cm (2ft); 'Freda Ballard', rich red, semi-double, 75cm (2½ft); 'Mistress Quickly', dark blue, 1·2m (4ft); 'Patricia Ballard', large, pink, semi-double, 90cm (3ft); and 'Sonata', large sky-blue, 90cm (3ft). There are also dwarf kinds such as; 'Dandy', purple-red, 30cm (1ft); 'Lady in Blue', blue, semi-double, 25cm (10in); 'Little Pink Beauty', pink, semi-double; and 'Snowsprite', white, 30 cm (1ft).

Campanula: This is yet another diverse family, and one of great importance to the gardener – its members contribute to the rock garden as well as to the border, and of course there are the biennials, such as Canterbury Bells, and greenhouse delights like *C. isophylla* 'Alba'. Most campanulas are extremely easy to grow, the only exceptions being some of the rock garden species.

Among those suitable for the herbaceous border, *C. lactiflora* is one of the best. This plant is a strong-grower, but it dislikes disturbance and is best transplanted while young. The individual blue flowers are about 2·5cm (1in) across, and are set in graceful spikes which are in bloom for a couple of months. The shade of blue and ultimate height depends on variety, of which there are several good ones, such as 'Prichard's Variety', and 'Loddon Anna' which is pink. 'Pouffe' is quite different in habit, spreading outwards instead of upwards.

C. lactiflora will succeed well in sun or semi-shade, but likes shelter from strong winds.

For the front of the border, *C. carpatica* is a good candidate. The plants are low-growing, sending up flower spikes to about 30cm (1ft). The light or dark blue, or white, open bells face upwards.

Cimicifuga: A beautiful and distinctive genus, with graceful spikes of small pearly-white flowers. They prefer some shade and plenty of moisture. Species such as *C. cordifolia*, *C. dahurica* and *C. japonica* are all good plants, but perhaps the best are *C. racemosa*, 'Elstead Variety' and 'White Pearl'.

Campanula lactiflora
Bell Flower
(see page 44)

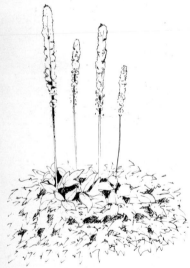

Cimicifuga racemosa
Bugbane
(see page 45)

Dicentra: Some of this genus are of little note for their flowers, although all have attractive fern-like foliage rendering them useful as an edging plant. There is, however, one outstanding member of the family – *D. spectabilis*, popularly known as Bleeding Heart. It is a superb plant for a position sheltered from cold winds, possibly protected by a wall or evergreens as the tips of early growth are liable to be damaged.

Ideally they like a warm position with a sheltered root-run. Despite this, and the fact that the thongy roots do not divide well, the plant will give years of trouble-free flower once established, blooming from late April to mid-June.

The locket-shaped flowers with a white protrusion hanging from the pink 'heart' are carried on graceful long arching stems.

Geranium: The geraniums of the border are not to be confused with bedding geraniums, more correctly called pelargoniums. Many of the true geraniums are vigorous, spreading plants, and usually thrive in dry, stony conditions. Good drainage is essential for these plants, but otherwise they will grow in a wide range of soils, including those with a high lime content.

They are useful plants that will put up a good show even in poor, starved soils, and grow well in sun or semi-shade.

One of the best is *G. psilostemon* (sometimes known as *G. armenum*). It is one of the tall-growing species, reaching between 60cm (2ft) and 1·1m (3½ft), depending on whether the soil is moist or dry. The magenta flowers are about 2·5cm (1in) across, borne over a long period from June to August.

'Johnson's Blue' is covered with deep blue saucer-shaped flowers in early summer. It grows about 45cm (18in) high, and is best cut back after flowering to tidy the plant and produce a fresh crop of attractive leaves.

G. sanguineum is a popular favourite, but tends to outgrow its alloted space. Nevertheless, it is a nice plant, about 30cm (1ft) high but sprawling, and for this reason is a useful ground-cover subject. The neatly cut foliage is topped by a long succession of magenta flowers from May to September. There are forms of this plant with pink or white flowers, including 'Holden Variety' and 'Lancastriense' (pink), and the white 'Album'.

Heliopsis: Yellow daisy-like flowers of the Sunflower tribe, but a merit-worthy plant in some of the good varieties now available. They are well-behaved plants, making strong growth but not becoming invasive, and flower for eight weeks or more, from July onwards. One of the best varieties is 'Golden Plume', a rather stiff plant with spear-shaped leaves and double yellow flowers, particularly good for cutting.

Hemerocallis: The Day Lilies are so called because their blooms last only a single day – but as there is usually a succession to follow, this scarcely matters. They are good garden plants, being strong, healthy growers but not invasive, and will grow in sun or partial shade, although a moist, fertile soil is required for best results.

Two dwarf species are the orange-yellow *H. middendorffii*, which grows about 30cm (1ft), and *H. minor*, a slender plant with grass-like foliage to 30cm (1ft) and small, sweetly scented pale yellow flowers. But it is among the garden hybrids that the widest

Heliopsis
(see page 47)

Hemerocallis
Day Lily
(see page 47)

Polygonatum multiflorum
Solomon's Seal
(see page 49)

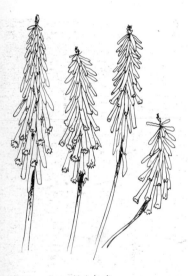

Kniphofia
Red Hot Poker
(see page 47)

range and most spectacular flowers are to be found, mainly in shades of yellow, red, and pink. There are so many good named varieties that it would be an invidious task to select just a few names. (Illustrated on page 46.)

Hosta: These are wonderful foliage plants, particularly useful for a moist, shady part of the border. They have justifiably been the centre of an upsurge of interest in recent years, and no border seems complete without one of two species.

Twenty years ago very few kinds would be found in a nursery catalogue, yet today there are many delightful species and varieties from which to choose, and some are described on page 199.

Kniphofia: The Red Hot Pokers are a familiar autumn sight, but they are not the easiest of plants to grow. Good drainage is vital, and in cold, damp areas some winter protection may be needed, although leaving the foliage uncut until spring may be sufficient in most areas. During the growing season, plenty of moisture is appreciated. They are such magnificent border plants once established that they are well worth a little care. (Illustrated on page 38.)

Among the species, *K. galpinii* is a particularly good plant of small stature, up to 90cm (3ft), and is especially valuable because it flowers so late – October and sometimes into November.

Right: Red Hot Pokers, kniphofias, are spectacular plants by any standard, and live up to their common name, with fiery spires of bloom. This variety is 'Jenny Bloom'. (See above and 47.)

Left: Herbaceous potentillas are trouble-free border plants. Varieties such as 'Fire-dance' are sure to brighten any border. (See pages 40 and 49.)

Below: Rudbeckia 'Goldsturm' is a key border plant, its gold petals contrasting strikingly with the dark central disc. (See pages 41 and 49.)

Verbascum
Mullein
(see page 49)

Omphalodes cappadocica
(see page 48)

Lysimachia punctata
Yellow Loosestrife
(see page 48)

There are numerous named garden hybrids, most of them well worth growing, but for a creamy-white one instead of the more usual oranges and yellows, try 'Maid of Orleans'. It reaches about 1·1m (3½ft) and flowers over a long period. 'Samuel's Sensation' is one of the best orange-flame varieties.

Oenothera: One of the most well-known Evening Primroses, *O. biennis*, is a biennial, as its name implies, but there are good perennial species too. One of these is *O. cinaeus*, which produces a brilliant display of yellow flowers, with the bonus of very attractive spring foliage tinted purple, red, buff and pink.

O. missouriensis is a dwarf, prostrate plant, with bright red creeping stems and narrow, pointed leaves coated with soft, silvery hair. The clear yellow flowers are sometimes 12·5cm (5in) wide. It will trail over the ground and is especially good for a sunny bank.

Most of the garden hybrids can be recommended as good, trouble-free plants.

Omphalodes: These plants are especially useful for a dark corner, which they soon fill with dense foliage. *O. cappadocica* is a good species to grow, the whole plant only being 15cm (6in) in height, and is covered with dozens of small sprays of tiny bright blue flowers in April and May.

Polygonum: This is another genus that demonstrates the diversity of habit and growth within a group of plants. Some members are rock garden plants, while at the other extreme there is the Russian Vine, *P. baldschuanicum* (see page 117), a really rampant climber.

In the herbaceous border, one of the smallest is *P. affine*, growing to about 25cm (10in). It makes a carpet of growth with tufts of narrow leaves, which have a reddish tinge in autumn and winter. Stumpy 20cm (8in) spikes of deep pink or red flowers appear throughout summer and autumn. The variety 'Darjeeling's Red' is good, quickly forming wide mats, but its flowers are more pink than red. 'Lowndes Variety' is one of the best.

P. amplexicaule is another good border plant, having masses of thin 60cm (2ft) spikes of rich red flowers. This strong and sturdy plant is deep ruby-red. There are also pale pink and salmon-red varieties.

P. carneum (once listed as *P. bistora* 'Superbum'), is a leafy plant, but less inclined to run out of control than *P. bistorta*. The stumpy spikes, carried on plants that reach about 60cm (2ft), are bright pink – not spectacular individually but effective viewed in a mass, which they usually are.

Most polygonums prefer a moist soil, though in other respects are undemanding and very easy to grow.

Potentilla: It is important to understand that the herbaceous potentillas are discussed here, not the shrubby kind, which are on page 97. Both types are extremely valuable garden plants.

The herbaceous potentillas require a rich, well-drained soil, preferably in sun, but they will also be happy in semi-shade. Waterlogged soil in winter can be fatal, but plenty of moisture is required during the growing season. A mulch is usually beneficial, and flowering is extended if dead heads are removed. As a group they are low-growing, trouble-free plants with a long flowering period. (Illustrated on page 39.)

It is among the garden hybrids that some of the best will be found, including 'Gibson's Scarlet', which has brilliant single red flowers, 'Glory of Nancy', orange-crimson, semi-double flowers often 5cm (2in) across, and greyish foliage; and 'Wm Rollisson', bright orange-red. They all have attractive and appealing strawberry-type foliage.

Rudbeckia: This genus includes many almost indispensable border plants. Most have a plain yellow ring of petals surrounding a cone-shaped disc. Although partial shade will be tolerated, they are really sun-lovers. A well-drained, nutritious soil will bring the best results, but they are not fastidious. Water is always appreciated during the growing season. Among the species, *R. deamii* is especially free-flowering. Good garden hybrids are 'Goldquelle' (double, chrome yellow, bushy growth), and 'Goldsturm' (gold, black centre). ('Goldsturm' is illustrated on page 39.)

Salvia: Many of the hardy salvias are not outstanding plants, but *S. superba* will contribute to any border. It has deep violet flowers on branching spikes. The whole plant forms a sturdy bush of about 90cm (3ft) with sage-like foliage. There are some dwarf varieties suitable for the front of the border — 'East Friesland', which only grows to 45cm (18in), and 'May Night', which also has the advantage of flowering as early as May.

Sedum: Most sedums are rock garden plants, but there are also some outstanding border plants. Being succulent in nature, they love a sunny position and do not mind drought conditions. A wide range of soils will suit them, including difficult ones such as sand, gravel or chalk. They are also good seaside garden plants.

Best-known, and undoubtedly one of the finest border plants, certainly in autumn, is *S. spectabile*, so loved by butterflies. It makes an erect plant between 30–60cm (1–2ft), with clasping heart-shaped succulent leaves. It is attractive out of flower, but in bloom it is superb, crowned with dense heads that almost meet to cover the plant. Among the varieties to grow are 'Autumn Joy' (salmon-pink), 'Carmen' (deep pink), and 'Ruby Glow' (rosy-red).

Stokesia: There is only one species to interest the gardener — *S. laevis*, an interesting plant with lavender-blue daisy-shaped flowers in autumn. It requires sun and a well-drained soil. Although it is hardy, late blooms may be damaged by bad weather. 'Blue Star' is the best to grow, having fine, lavender-blue flowers about 7·5cm (3in) across on branching stems.

Veronica: Yet another very diverse group of plants, though the shrubby species are now known as hebes. Veronicas are easy to grow. They prefer a sunny situation, but will grow satisfactorily in partial shade, and provided there is a good humus content in the soil they will grow well on sandy or limy soil. The most prevalent colours are blue and white. If the selection has to be confined to two species, *V. teucrium* and *V. virginica* are among the best. *V. teucrium* 'Blue Fountain' has sheaves of blue flower spikes on small, compact plants. Two other fine varieties are 'Crater Lake Blue', a deep blue, 30cm (1ft), and 'Shirley Blue', which grows to 20cm (8in).

Among the *V. virginica* varieties, 'Alba' is particularly attractive, with slender spikes of white flowers towering up to 1·5m (5ft).

Salvia superba
(see page 49)

Convallaria majalis
Lily-of-the-Valley
(see page 45)

Veronica
(see page 49)

Decorative Dahlia

DECORATIVE DAHLIAS

Varieties	Height	Colour	Size of blooms	Description
Ann Hilary	1m (3½ft)	Pink to apricot	10-15cm (4-6in)	A free-flowering variety, producing flowers on long stems — ideal for flower arrangers.
Cyclone	1.2m (4ft)	Lilac-pink	15-20cm (6-8in)	A strong growing variety that is good for exhibition.
Evelyn Rumbold	1.2m (4ft)	Purple	25cm (10in)	One of the largest flowers.
Hamari Boldness	1.2m (4ft)	Lavender-pink	25cm (10in)	A large flower produced on straight stems — ideal for exhibition.
Jo's Choice	1m (3½ft)	Scarlet	7.5-10cm (3-4in)	A popular variety for exhibitors.
Lavengro	1.2m (4ft)	Lilac and bronze	25cm (10in)	An old and well established variety for garden display.
Mrs. MacDonald Quill	1.2m (4ft)	Blood-red, with white-tipped petals	25cm (10in)	A very spectacular variety.
Nijinsky	1m (3½ft)	Purple	10-15cm (4-6in)	A small ball variety, excellent for exhibition.
Suffolk Punch	1.2m (4ft)	Wine-red	15-20cm (6-8in)	A variety with attractive bronze foliage.
Trelawney	1.2m (4ft)	Bronze-red	25cm (10in)	A strong-growing variety producing large blooms.
Vigor	1.2m (4ft)	Pale yellow	10-15cm (4-6in)	A free flowering water-lily variety.
White Fire	1.2m (4ft)	White, with a hint of pink	10-15cm (4-6in)	An outstanding variety.

Cactus Dahlia

CACTUS AND SEMI-CACTUS DAHLIAS

Varieties	Height	Colour	Size of blooms	Description
Beauty of Aalsmeer	1.3m (4½ft)	Deep salmon	15-20cm (6-8in)	A semi-cactus variety with long stems.
Cheerio	1m (3½ft)	Deep cerise, tipped white	10-15cm (4-6in)	An old and established small semi-cactus variety.
Golden Glitter	1.2m (4ft)	Bright gold	15-20cm (6-8in)	A vigorous semi-cactus variety with unusual fern-like foliage.
Hamari Bride	1.2m (4ft)	White	15-20cm (6-8in)	An excellent semi-cactus dahlia, good for garden display and exhibition.
Jescot Jane	1.2m (4ft)	Soft pink	10-15cm (4-6in)	A delicate semi-cactus variey with feathered edges to the petals.
Klankstad Kerkrade	1.2m (4ft)	Pale yellow	10-15cm (4-6in)	A well established cactus dahlia for garden display.
Paul Crichley	1.3m (4½ft)	Lilac to pink	20-25cm (8-10in)	A superb large cactus dahlia.
Polar Sight	1.3m (4½ft)	Pure white	25cm (10in)	A giant cactus variety that is a must for the exhibitor.

Ball Dahlia

COLLERETTE, POMPON AND DWARF BEDDING DAHLIAS

Varieties	Height	Colour	Description
Amusing	90cm (3ft)	Scarlet and gold	A very free-flowering miniature ball variety, ideal for floral arrangement enthusiasts.
Butterball	45cm (1½ft)	Yellow	A miniature-decorative dwarf-bedding variety.
Clair de Lune	1m (3½ft)	Pale sulphur-yellow with a creamy collar.	A collerette variety with strong stems — ideal as a dahlia to provide blooms for the home.
Dazzler	30cm (1ft)	Bright scarlet	A miniature-decorative dwarf-bedding variety — one of the smallest bedding dahlias.
Fascination	60cm (2ft)	Rosy-purple	A paeony-flowered dwarf-bedding variety which look wonderful in a group of three or five plants.
Little Con	1m (3½ft)	Crimson-scarlet	A delightful pompon variety, ideal for flower arrangement.
Rothesay Castle	45cm (1½ft)	Cream-pink	A miniature-decorative dwarf-bedding variety with a compact habit.
Wee Joy	1m (3½ft)	Orange	A pompon variety, ideal for flower arrangers.
Yellow Hammer	60cm (2ft)	Yellow	A single dwarf-bedding variety with attractive foliage.

Single-flowered Dahlia

Below: The Flea Bane, erigeron, resemble dwarf Michaelmas Daisies, and come in a similar range of colours. This variety is 'Foerster's Liebling'. (See page 46.)

HERBACEOUS PLANTS FOR BEDS AND BORDERS

Species and Varieties	Height	Flowering period	Light requirement	Fragrance	Staking not required	Hardiness	Description
Acanthus longifolius Bear's Breech	75cm (2½ft)	7-9	◉		NS	★★★★	Deeply lobed shiny leaves. Tall lilac-rose flower spikes.
A. spinosus Bear's Breech	1.2m (4ft)	7-9	◉		NS	★★★★	Bold spikes of mauve-purple flowers. Deeply cut foliage.
Achillea 'Moonshine' Yarrow	60cm (2ft)	6-8	○		NS	★★★★	Silvery fern-like foliage. Flat heads of bright yellow flowers.
Aconitum 'Blue Sceptre' Monkshood	60cm (2ft)	7-8	◉		NS	★★★★	An easily grown plant with helmet-shaped blue and white flowers.
Agapanthus campanulatus 'Profusion' African Lily	90cm (3ft)	7-8	○		NS	★★★	Blue lily-like flowers and green strap-shaped foliage. Flowers freely in a warm position.
Alchemilla mollis Lady's Mantle	45cm (1½ft)	6-8	○		NS	★★★★	Downy rounded foliage above which is carried many sprays of sulphur-yellow flowers.
Alstroemeria 'Ligtu Hybrids' Peruvian Lily	90cm (3ft)	6-8	◉		NS	★★★★	Attractive flowers like small lilies at the top of leafy stems. Do not disturb once established.
Anaphalis triplinervis	30cm (1ft)	7-9	◉		NS	★★★★	Greyish woolly leaves, topped with clusters of white star-like 'everlasting' flowers.
Anchusa 'Loddon Royalist' Alkanet	90cm (3ft)	5-7	○			★★★★	Among the most brilliant blue border flowers. A tall plant with hairy stems.
Anemone japonica Japanese Anemone	45-90cm (1½-3ft)	8-10	◉		NS	★★★★	Useful plants for late summer and autumn flower. Usually pink. Spreading but not invasive.
Anthemis tinctoria Ox-eye Chamomile	75cm (2½ft)	6-8	○		NS	★★★★	Yellow, marguerite-like flowers, excellent for cutting.
Aquilegia 'McKana Hybrids' Columbine	75cm (2½ft)	5-6	◉		NS	★★★★	Fascinating spurred flowers in a wide range of colours. Best planted as a clump.
Artemisia lactiflora Wormwood	1.2m (4ft)	8-10	◐		NS	★★★★	Strong stems and plumes of creamy-white flowers make this an imposing plant.
Aruncus sylvester Goat's Beard	1.2m (4ft)	6-7	◉		NS	★★★★	Broad, fern-like leaves and large ivory-white plumes of minute flowers make this a handsome plant.
Aster novi-belgii Michaelmas Daisy	60cm-1.2m (2-4ft)	9-10	◉			★★★★	Invaluable plants for autumn colour. Masses of daisy-like flowers in a wide range of colours.
(Dwarf Hybrids)	30-45cm (1-1½ft)	9-10	◉		NS	★★★★	Bushy plants of compact habit, but with the same attractive flowers as the taller Michaelmas Daisies.
Astrantia maxima Masterwort	90cm (3ft)	6-8	●		NS	★★★★	Flattish heads of light rose flowers and light green deeply divided leaves.
Bergenia cordifolia Elephant's Ears	25cm (10in)	4-5	◉		NS	★★★★	Large green leaves, forming an attractive ground cover, and sprays of rose-pink flowers.
Caltha palustris Marsh Marigold	20cm (8in)	5-6	◉		NS	★★★★	Delightful yellow flowers, especially happy by the waterside.
Campanula lactiflora Bell Flower	1.2m (4ft)	6-8	◉			★★★★	Light blue bells, about 2.5cm (1in) across, carried on tall leafy stems.
Catananche coerulea 'Major' Cupid's Dart	60cm (2ft)	6-8	○		NS	★★★★	Blue cornflower-like flowers with a rather papery texture.

Species and Varieties	Height	Flowering period	Light requirement	Fragrance	Staking not required	Hardiness	Description
Centaurea dealbata 'Steenbergii' Knapweed	45cm (1½ft)	6-8	○			★★★★	Deep rose thistle-like flowers. Jagged grey-green leaves.
C. macrocephala	1.2m (4ft)	6-8	○			★★★★	Large golden-yellow flowers on stout, branched stems.
Centranthus ruber 'Coccineus'	45cm (1½ft)	6-9	○		NS	★★★★	Branching heads of bright red flowers. Good border plant or for growing on walls.
Chelone obliqua Shell-flower	60cm (2ft)	8-10	◉		NS	★★★★	Stiff stems with deep green, pointed leaves, and spikes of reddish-pink flowers. Likes a light soil.
Chrysanthemum maximum Shasta Daisy	90cm (3ft)	7-9	◉		NS	★★★★	A large-flowered Marguerite 'Wirral Supreme' is a double variety.
Cimicifuga racemosa Bugbane	1.2m (4ft)	8-9	◐			★★★★	An effective plant in autumn when its slender spikes of creamy-white flowers tower above the foliage.
Convallaria majalis Lily-of-the-Valley	15cm (6in)	4-5	●	✿		★★★★	Exquisitely scented white flowers. Roots can also be lifted to force for early flower and fragrance.
Coreopsis verticillata Tickseed	60cm (2ft)	7	○		NS	★★★★	Plants are decked with starry yellow flowers over 4cm (1½in) across. There are also dwarf varieties. Useful for cutting.
Cortaderia argentea Pampas Grass	1.5m (5ft)	8-10	●		NS	★★★★	A giant grass with elegant silvery plumes on stiff stems.
Crambe cordifolia Flowering Seakale	1.8m (6ft)	5-7	○			★★★★	Broad heart-shaped leaves on branching stems. Produces an almost cloud-like display of white flowers.
Dahlia (see pages 42, 43)							
Dianthus caryophyllus Carnation	45-60cm (1½-2ft)	6-8	○	✿	NS	★★★★	Carnations have always been popular plants, with the fragrant pink, white, red or yellow flowers, set against a foil of grey leaves.
Dicentra spectabilis Bleeding Heart	60-75cm (2-2½ft)	4-6	◉		NS	★★★★	Fascinating rosy-red and white heart-shaped flowers that hang from graceful arching sprays over feathery foliage. Requires a cool soil.
Dictamnus fraxinella Burning Bush	75cm (2½ft)	6-8	◉		NS	★★★★	Erect spikes of lilac flowers, but the novelty of the plant lies in the leaves. These give off a volatile gas which can be ignited on a warm, still day to give a brief flash.
Doronicum 'Harper Crewe' Leopard's-bane	90cm (3ft)	4-5	◉			★★★★	Yellow, daisy-like blooms, making a cheerful sight in spring.
Echinacea purpurea 'The King' Purple Cone Flower	90cm (3ft)	7-9	◉			★★★★	Large, magenta-purple rayed flowers with drooping petals and dark centres.
Echinops 'Taplow Blue' Globe Thistle	1.2-1.5m (4-5ft)	6-8	○		NS	★★★★	A large plant with grey-green leaves and spherical steel-blue thistle heads. Useful for cutting.
Epimedium grandiflorum Barrenwort	25cm (10in)	4-5	◑		NS	★★★★	An excellent ground cover for semi-shaded areas, the practically evergreen foliage often being attractively tinted. Flowers are white, pink or violet.

Right: Day Lilies, hemerocallis, have trumpet-shaped blooms that are short-lived but constantly replaced by fresh ones. 'Linda' is one of the many varieties. (See pages 37 and 47.)

HERBACEOUS PLANTS FOR BEDS AND BORDERS Continued

Species and Varieties	Height	Flowering period	Light requirement	Fragrance	Staking not required	Hardiness	Description
Eremurus robustus Foxtail Lily	1.8-2.4m (6-8ft)	6	○	✿		★★★★	A giant of the herbaceous border. Massive spikes of starry pale pink flowers. Not easy to grow successfully.
Erigeron (Garden Hybrids) Flea Bane	60cm (2ft)	6-8	○		NS	★★★★	Useful plants for massing towards the front of the border. Resemble dwarf Michaelmas Daisies, and come in similar colours.
Eryngium oliverianum Sea Holly	90cm (3ft)	6-8	○		NS	★★★★	A reliable plant with jagged-edged leaves and bright blue teasel-like flower heads. Can be dried for winter decoration.
Eupatorium purpureum Joe-Pye Weed	1.5m (5ft)	8-9	○		NS	★★★★	Heads of mauve-pink flowers on strong stems.
Euphorbia polychroma Spurge	45cm (1½ft)	4-5	◉		NS	★★★★	A trouble-free plant with sulphur-yellow flowers on mounds of fresh green leaves.
Festuca glauca	15-23cm (6-9in)		◉		NS	★★★★	A pretty grass with tufted habit and slender, glaucous leaves. A useful edging plant.
Gaillardia (Garden Hybrids) Blanket Flower	15-90cm (6in-3ft)	6-8	◉			★★★★	Produces abundant supply of yellow, orange or red daisy-like flowers, good for cutting. Prefers a light soil.
Geranium Cranesbill	15-90cm (6in-3ft)	6-8	◉		NS	★★★★	There are many good species for the border, usually in shades of pink or blue. They normally thrive in any soil, and are a useful group of plants.
Geum 'Mrs. Bradshaw' Avens	45cm (1½ft)	5-8	○		NS	★★★★	The geums are free-flowering plants with a long season. 'Mrs. Bradshaw' is red, but other varieties are orange or yellow.
Gypsophila 'Bristol Fairy' Chalk Plant	90cm (3ft)	6-7	○		NS	★★★★	A shimmering mass of small double white flowers, excellent for cutting. There is also a pink form. Needs a chalky soil.
Helenium autumnale Sneezeweed	60cm -1.5m (2-5ft)	7-8	○		NS	★★★★	A showy plant. Useful for cutting. Mainly yellow or red flowers on long, straight stems.

HERBACEOUS PLANTS FOR BEDS AND BORDERS Continued

Species and Varieties	Height	Flowering period	Light requirement	Fragrance	Staking not required	Hardiness	Description
Helianthus 'Loddon Gold' Sunflower	1.5m (5ft)	8-9	○		NS	★★★★	A double, golden-yellow form of the perennial sunflower. Nice strong stems, and an excellent cut flower.
Heliopsis scabra 'Golden Plume'	1.2m (4ft)	7-9	○		NS	★★★★	Rather stiff plants, resembling helianthus. Spear-shaped leaves. Double yellow flowers, suitable for cutting.
Helleborus niger Christmas Rose	30-45cm (1-1½ft)	12-3	●		NS	★★★★	An invaluable winter flower. Although hardy, protection prevents the blooms becoming damaged. White flowers.
H. orientalis Lenten Rose	30-45cm (1-1½ft)	2-3	●		NS	★★★★	Similar to the Christmas Rose, but the flowers vary from white to purple. Always a welcome sight at the end of winter.
Hemerocallis (Garden Hybrids) Day Lily	60-90cm (2-3ft)	7-9	◉		NS	★★★★	Clusters of trumpet-shaped flowers, which are short-lived but constantly replaced.
Heuchera (Garden Hybrids) Alum Root	30-60cm (1-2ft)	6-9	◑		NS	★★★★	A graceful plant with dainty flowers Carried over basal clumps of attractive leaves. Flowers are pink or red.
Hosta Plantain Lily	30-60cm (1-2ft)	7-8	◑		NS	★★★★	Stately sprays of Lily-like flowers but its main attraction lies in the leaves. The various species have beautiful variegation and some are described in the text.
Incarvillea delavayi Trumpet Flower	60cm (2ft)	6-7	○		NS	★★★★	Gloxinia-like rose-carmine flowers, and dark green foliage resembling that of Mountain Ash.
Iris (see page 76)							
Kniphofia (Garden Hybrids) Red Hot Poker	90cm-1.8m (3-6ft)	8-9	○		NS	★★	Always popular, these striking plants with their grass-like foliage and stiff spikes of red or yellow flowers, are hardy if protected with straw during winter in cold areas.

Left: The thistle-like Sea Holly, eryngium, looks equally in place in a true herbaceous border or a mixed border containing shrubs. (See page 46.)

HERBACEOUS PLANTS FOR BEDS AND BORDERS Continued

Species and Varieties	Height	Flowering period	Light requirement	Fragrance	Staking not required	Hardiness	Description
Liatris spicata Gay Feather	60cm (2ft)	8-9	⊙		NS ·	★★★★	Rigid spikes of rosy-purple flowers. These open from the top of the spike first, unlike most spiky plants. Likes a moist soil.
Ligularia clivorum 'Desdemona'	1.2m (4ft)	7-9	○			★★★★	Large purplish leaves and large vivid orange daisy heads. An excellent waterside plant in the wild garden.
Linum narbonnense Flax	45cm (1½ft)	6-9	○			★★★★	Large brilliant blue flowers on a graceful plant.
Lobelia cardinalis 'Queen Victoria' Cardinal Flower	90cm (3ft)	7-10	◐		NS	★★★★	Beetroot-coloured foliage and tall, elegant spikes of vermilion flowers. Sometimes used as a 'spot' plant for summer bedding.
Lupinus (Garden Hybrids) Lupin	60-105cm (2-3½ft)	6-7	○		NS	★★★★	Too well known to need description. There are many excellent named varieties. Lupins do not like lime.
Lychnis chalcedonica Campion	90cm (3ft)	6-8	○			★★★★	Bright scarlet flowers on stiff stems. A most striking plant.
Lysimachia punctata Yellow Loosestrife	90cm (3ft)	6-8	⊙		NS	★★★★	Stiff spikes of bright yellow, star-shaped flowers.
Macleaya cordata Plume Poppy	1.2m (4ft)	8-9	⊙		NS	★★★★	Pretty grey-green leaves on upright stems. Spikes of numerous small ivory flowers.
Mertensia virginica Virginia Blue Bells	45cm (1½ft)	4-6	◐			★★★★	Sprays of dangling violet-blue tubular flowers. A useful woodland plant.
Mimulus luteus Musk	15-23cm (6-9in)	5-8	●		NS	★★★★	Golden-yellow tubular flowers, the large lower lips being blotched with mahogany. Useful plant for the waterside or a damp position.
Monarda didyma Bergamot	90cm (3ft)	7-9	⊙	🍃		★★★★	Aromatic foliage topped by red, pink, violet or white, somewhat thistle-like, flowers.
Morina longifolia Whorl Flower	75cm (2½ft)	6-9	◐			★★★★	An unusual plant. Spikes of curiously-shaped pink and white flowers, and thistle-like foliage. Prefers light soil.
Nepeta mussinii Catmint	30cm (1ft)	5-9	○	🍃	NS	★★★★	An excellent edging plant for a warm, dry position. Fragrant grey foliage and spikes of mauve-blue flowers.
Oenothera 'Yellow River' Evening Primrose	45cm (1½ft)	6-8	○			★★★★	Large yellow flowers; glossy green foliage.
Omphalodes cappadocica	15cm (6in)	4-5	●		NS	★★★★	Useful ground cover for a shady area. Rich blue Forget-me-not-like flowers. Glaucous foliage.
Origanum vulgare 'Aureum' Marjoram	25cm (10in)		○	🍃	NS	★★★★	Golden, almost evergreen, aromatic foliage. Useful for ground cover or edging.
Paeonia (Garden Hybrids) Peony	75-90cm (2½-3ft)	6-7	○		NS	★★★★	Spectacular plants with flowers that resemble large open roses. Shades of pink, red and white are usual.
Papaver orientale Oriental Poppy	25-90cm (10in-3ft)	5-6	○			★★★★	Large and spectacular blooms, in brilliant red, orange or pink. Most varieties are about 75cm (2½ft). Prefers light soil.
Penstemon barbatus Bearded Tongue	90cm (3ft)	6-9	⊙			★★★★	Graceful branching spikes of rose-red tubular flowers.
Phlox paniculata (Garden Hybrids)	90cm (3ft)	7-9	⊙		NS	★★★★	Outstanding border plants if the stock is free of disease.

Species and Varieties	Height	Flowering period	Light requirement	Fragrance	Staking not required	Hardiness	Description
Physostegia virginica 'Vivid' Dragon's Head	60cm (2ft)	8-10	◉		NS	★★★★	Rigid spikes of rosy-crimson flowers. Spreads easily but is useful for autumn interest.
Platycodon grandiflorum 'Mariesii' Chinese Balloon Flower	45cm (1½ft)	7-8	◉		NS	★★★★	Balloon-shaped flower buds open into large blue stars.
Polemonium 'Blue Pearl'	25cm (10in)	5-6	○		NS	★★★★	Clusters of bright blue cup-shaped flowers.
Polygonatum multiflorum Solomon's Seal	75cm (2½ft)	5-6	●		NS	★★★★	Arching stems with pairs of leaves along their length, and clusters of pendant white bells.
Polygonum affine 'Lowndes Variety' Knotgrass	25cm (10in)	6-9	◉		NS	★★★★	A fine ground cover plant. Dense mats of narrow leaves, which turn copper-coloured in autumn. Red flower spikes.
Potentilla 'Gibson's Scarlet'	30cm (12in)	6-8	◉		NS	★★★★	Potentillas are low-growing trouble-free plants, in bloom for many weeks. Other varieties have orange or yellow flowers.
Pulmonaria angustifolia Lung-wort	20cm (8in)	3-5	◐		NS	★★★★	A valuable spring-flowering plant with blue trumpet-shaped flowers.
Pyrethrum (Garden Hybrids)	60-75cm (2-2½ft)	5-7	○		NS	.★★★★	Beautiful plants, good for cutting. There are single and double varieties in shades of pink, red and white.
Rudbeckia deamii Black-eyed Susan	90cm (3ft)	7-9	◉			★★★★	Large orange-yellow flowers with dark centres. An excellent, bushy border plant.
Salvia superba	45-90cm (1½-3ft)	7-9	◉		NS	★★★★	Branching spikes of violet-purple flowers. Sage-like leaves.
Scabiosa caucasia 'Clive Greaves' Scabious	75cm (2½ft)	6-9	○		NS	★★★★	Large deep blue flowers, popular for cutting. There are also pink and white varieties.
Sedum spectabile Ice Plant	30-60cm (1-2ft)	8-10	○		NS	★★★★	A plant of outstanding merit. The whole plant becomes a compact mound of long-lasting colour. Colours include shades of pink and red.
Sidalcea 'Rose Queen'	1.2m (4ft)	6-8	◉		NS	★★★★	A charming plant of excellent habit. Tall spikes of lovely pink flowers rise from a neat basal clump of leaves.
Solidago (Dwarf Hybrids) Golden Rod	45-75cm (1½-2½ft)	8	◉		NS	★★★★	These plants produce a cloud of yellow flowers, on plants with a much better habit than the old forms of Golden Rod.
Stipa pennata Feather Grass	75cm (2½ft)		◉		NS	★★★★	Densely tufted grass with green leaves and large feathery flower plumes.
Stokesia 'Blue Star' Stokes Aster	45cm (1½ft)	7-9	○		NS	★★★★	Large blue flowers, resembling those of the Cornflower, carried on branching stems.
Thalictrum 'Hewitt's Double' Meadow Rue	90cm (3ft)	7-8	◐			★★★★	Clouds of double mauve flowers, held well clear of graceful fern-like foliage.
Trollius Globe Flower	45-60cm (1½-1ft)	5-6	◉		NS	★★★★	Large buttercup-like flowers in various shades of yellow, depending on variety. Prefers a moist situation.
Verbascum Mullein	1.2-1.8m (4-6ft)	6-8	○			★★★★	Thick woolly leaves and tall spikes of yellow, white or pink flowers.
Veronica teucrium Speedwell	25-60cm (10-24in)	6-8	◉		NS	★★★★	Useful, compact plants of neat habit. Spikes of small blue flowers.

Rock Garden and Water Plants

The rock garden and garden pool are often regarded as specialized areas of gardening, and indeed a true alpine specialist will grow many rare and difficult plants. But both these garden features are well within the scope of most gardeners, and in each case there are easy and reliable plants to enhance them. It is these 'backbone' plants that are discussed in this chapter.

A well-planned rock garden or a nicely balanced pool can be the focal point of a garden, and greatly expands the range of plants that can be cultivated.

The rock garden

Rock gardens used to be called rockeries, but for some reason the expression has fallen out of favour – probably because the true alpine specialists wanted to put a distance between a well-constructed rock garden and the often ill-placed and badly sited heaps of rocks that were once thrown together in the hope that nothing more would be required. It takes considerably more effort to construct a good rock garden than it does an inferior one.

Most garden centres can supply suitable rocks, and this is one aspect that must not be skimped – do not be tempted to use up pieces of rock or stone that just happen to be around.

The site is vitally important. Avoid dark, draughty corners, and beneath the shade and drip of trees. The ideal site is a gentle slope facing south or west, with well-drained soil. As few gardens can ever offer ideal conditions, it has to be a matter of compromise; the priorities should be sloping ground, but not facing due east, and good drainage. If a slope isn't available the plants will grow satisfactorily on a flat site if soil drainage is provided, although the feature is seldom as pleasing aesthetically.

If a suitable site seems impossible to provide, the delights of miniature rock garden plants need not be denied. Many will grow between crazy-paving, or planted in a dry wall in a sunny place.

If the soil is not naturally well drained, incorporate coarse material, including gravel, in the base of the site, ideally making a sump about 60cm (2ft) deep. Prepare the site thoroughly by removing all perennial weeds. If the soil is heavy, make a special compost of three parts soil to two parts of peat and one-and-a-half parts of sand or grit. Add 3kg of bonemeal to each cubic metre of compost (5lb to each cubic yard). This mixture will suit the vast majority of alpine plants, but if you wish to grow lime-haters ensure

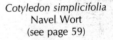

Cotyledon simplicifolia
Navel Wort
(see page 59)

Far left: Raised beds provide the drainage so necessary for rock garden plants. Covering the soil with a scree of small chippings provides additional drainage and helps to set off the plants. (See pages 58 to 60.)

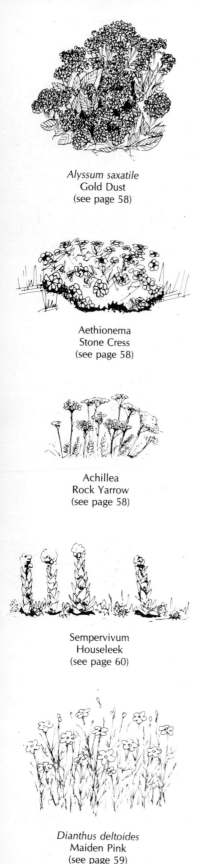

Alyssum saxatile
Gold Dust
(see page 58)

Aethionema
Stone Cress
(see page 58)

Achillea
Rock Yarrow
(see page 58)

Sempervivum
Houseleek
(see page 60)

Dianthus deltoides
Maiden Pink
(see page 59)

PLANTS FOR DRY WALLS	SUBJECTS TO PLANT BETWEEN CRAZY- PAVING
Acaena microphylla	Acaena microphylla
Aethionema 'Warley Rose'	Achillea 'King Edward'
Alyssum saxatile	Antennaria dioica 'Minima'
Arabis 'Rosabella'	Armeria maritima
Armeria maritima	Campanula garganica
Campanula garganica	Hypsella longiflora
Cotyledon simplicifolia	Phlox douglasii
Dianthus deltoides	Saxifraga (Mossy types)
Phlox douglasii	Sedum (types such as S. dasyphyllum,
Polygonum vacciniifolium	S. lydium, S. spurium, and S.
Saponaria ocymoides	spathulifolium)
Saxifraga	Sempervivum
Thymus serphyllum	Thymus serpyllum

the loam is not limy. As a guide, every tonne (ton) of stone may need 0.76 cubic metre (1 cubic yard) of soil on a flat site.

It is almost impossible to give precise instructions for arranging the stones, as every piece of rock is different. The most valuable rule is to position them with the long side in the soil, and not set them end-on in the compost. They should also follow natural tiers, and be inclined back slightly to form pockets for the soil. Pack the compost or soil well into the crevices and around the rocks to ensure there are no air pockets.

Alpines should be planted very firmly. They will arrive from the nursery in pots, and if the root-ball is very firm, press it to break it up slightly, but avoid crumbling it or losing too much compost from the roots. The compost in the pot, and the planting site, should both be nicely moist, but not waterlogged, before starting. Unless it is raining, the plants should always be watered in with a fine-rosed can as this helps to settle the soil around the roots.

Autumn is the best time to plant, provided the soil is still warm enough for some root growth to be made, in which case they will be settled in for the spring display; otherwise spring should be chosen. However, because they are grown in pots, planting may take place through the summer, provided they are watered and shaded a little until the roots become established.

Plants for crazy-paving

All the plants mentioned in this section can also be grown in the rock garden — but not all rock garden plants are suitable for using between crazy-paving. Plants growing in a paved area are inevitably going to come in for rougher treatment than those snugly protected between the crevices of rocks.

Crazy-paving plants need the same good drainage for their roots as they would if planted in the rock garden.

New Zealand Burrs (acaena) can be invasive for the rock garden, but A. microphylla is ideal for the crevices between paving. This species is mat-forming and compact. A sun-lover, it carries dense heads of scarlet flowers over purple-bronze evergreen leaves.

Another sun-lover is Rock Yarrow. Achillea 'King Edward' has beauty of leaf and flower, the soft grey-green, divided foliage making a pleasant background for the pretty heads of primrose-yellow flowers. A well-drained site is required.

A carpet of dense, silvery evergreen foliage is provided by *Antennaria dioica*. The small, hoary leaves, which grow in rosettes, are covered with white or pink flowers, depending on variety, in May and June.

Campanulas are indispensable plants for the border and rock garden, and some of them are equally useful for planting between paving. *C. garganica* has stems that cling closely to the paving stones and send up a multitude of small Ivy-like leaves and open-petalled blue flowers with a white centre. There are several varieties, each a different shade of blue or white.

Most crazy-paving plants require full sun, but an ideal subject for partial shade is *Hypsela reniformis*, which has lilac-pink tubular flowers nestling among a mat of dark green leaves. It will not grow well in a dry and parched position.

For a really bright carpeter that will grow well in sun or semi-shade, *Phlox douglasii* 'Rosea' is one of the best. It has a cushion-forming habit, and the plants are covered with almost stemless lilac-rose flowers in May and June.

Very different in appearance are the grass-like tufts of foliage made by Thrift (*Armeria maritima*). Although it does not creep in the manner of many other paving plants, the rather erect armerias are cheerful little plants with rounded heads of pink, white, crimson or purplish flowers, carried well clear of the leaves.

Saxifraga is a large genus with many excellent and varied plants for the rock garden, but some of the best for paved areas are found among the so-called Mossy types. Two varieties typical of this group are 'Gaiety', a warm pink, and 'Sprite', which has crimson-rose flowers. They will succeed in sun but prefer semi-shade, and dislike very dry conditions. (Illustrated on page 55.)

Sedums are also a diverse group of rock garden plants, and many of them will thrive in crevices between paving. Some of those suitable for this are *S. dasyphyllum*, a plant of about 5cm (2in) with pinkish flowers in July; *S. lydium*, about 5cm (2in) with pinkish flowers in June; *S. spurium*, pink flowers in July (there are also white and red varieties), and *S. spathulifolium*, which grows to 7·5cm (3in) and has yellow flowers in June. *Sedum acre* is a bright yellow-flowered carpeter that grows and spreads itself freely, but tends to become something of a weed.

No planting should be without some of the Thymes, which are efficient carpeters, as well as being aromatic when crushed. *Thymus serpyllum* has several good varieties, with flowers in shades from pale to deep pink; there is also a white-flowered form. They grow little more than 2·5cm (1in) high and thrive in full sun or semi-shade.

Plants for dry walls

Many of the plants suitable for crazy-paved areas are also excellent for dry walls — including acaena, armeria, *Campanula garganica*, *Phlox douglasii*, saxifraga and thymus. In addition, there are gems such as *Saponaria ocymoides*, which will trail down from a ledge or crevice and cover itself with a sheet of bright pink flowers in May and June. It is easily grown in light shade. (Illustrated on page 54.)

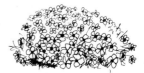

Phlox
Moss Phlox
(see page 60)

Armeria
Thrift
(see page 59)

Gentiana sino-ornata
Autumn Gentian
(see page 60)

Aubrieta
Coloured Rock Cress
(see page 59)

Primula vialii
(see Primulas on page 60)

The Alpine Knotweed (*Polygonum vacciniifolium*) is especially valuable because it flowers late – from August to October. The vigorous, creeping growth forms dense mats of bronzy-green leaves, ablaze with small deep pink flower spikes when in bloom.

Another vigorous plant that will cascade prolifically and create a golden sheet of flowers in late spring or early summer is *Alyssum saxatile* – the Gold Dust plant. It associates well with aubrieta and arabis. These lime-loving plants need a sunny position and benefit from being cut back after flowering.

Arabis is another lime-lover, and not unlike aubrieta in appearance, but coarser. Besides those with single or double white flowers there is a pink-flowered form growing in neat hummocks, known as 'Rosabella'.

Aethionema is a dwarf shrubby plant. 'Warley Rose' is a daphne-like form with deep rose flowers, which cover the low bushy growth for weeks.

The Maiden Pink (*Dianthus deltoides*) is a lime and sun lover. It produces a sheet of pink flowers, which are sweetly fragrant. There is a white variety as well as various shades of pink.

Totally different in form is the succulent Navel Wort (*Cotyledon simplicifolia*). Drooping stems bearing heads of yellow flowers arise amidst fleshy leaves.

Above: Saxifragas are a diverse group of plants, the flowers usually being in shades of pink, red or yellow. The plant illustrated is one of the Mossy saxifragas. (See pages 53 and 60.)

Other dependable rock plants

All the plants mentioned so far will enhance the rock garden proper, but the scope is naturally increased and there are many delightful plants to be included.

Aubrieta has to be high on any list. Established plants make a bold splash of colour, and there are many excellent varieties, in shades of pink, red, purple and blue. The named varieties, propagated vegetatively, are usually superior to plants raised from seed. These plants require a limy soil and a position in full sun. Trim them back after flowering.

One of the excellent campanulas has already been mentioned on page 53, but another that should form part of a basic collection is *C. carpatica*. This has large open bells, almost saucer-shaped, blue or white according to variety.

Hypsela
(see page 60)

Thymus serphyllum
Thyme
(see page 60)

Erinus alpinus is an easy plant, readily propagated from seeds. The flowers are white or pink, according to variety, carried on sprays from neat green hummocks.

Even gardeners with no particular interest in alpine plants usually have a special affection for the Gentians, with their large, blue trumpet-shaped flowers staring up from a low mound of green foliage. By selecting the right species they can be had in bloom in spring and autumn. One of the spring Gentians (*Gentiana acaulis*) is particularly impressive. Although this one will grow in semi-shade it will bloom in full sun too, and requires a good loamy soil. The Autumn Gentian (*G. sino-ornata*), which flowers in September and October, demands a lime-free soil and a cool, semi-shaded site.

Some of the Crane's Bills are fine rock plants, and *Geranium dalmaticum* is a charming species with shapely pink flowers carried on 10cm (4in) stems. The glossy leaves colour in autumn.

Gypsophila, the Chalk Plant, has several species suitable for the rock garden, but one of the best is *G. repens*, which bears masses of white or clear pink flowers. Its somewhat trailing habit makes it another candidate for planting in a dry wall.

For a magnificent display of white flowers, the spreading evergreen Perennial Candytuft is difficult to better. It follows on from the spring-flowering plants and blooms all summer. It is at its best in a sandy loam in full sun.

A useful plant for lime-free soil is the prostrate *Lithospermum diffusum* 'Heavenly Blue'. It loves a hot sunny position, and if given the right conditions will produce myriads of gentian-blue flowers all summer. If old plants become bare at the base, topdress them with leafy soil.

If a cool, semi-shaded position can be found, preferably with deep, moist loam, there are many beautiful primulas to grow. Among the suitable species are *P. auricula*, 15cm (6in), ideal for a sunny crevice with its fragrant yellow flowers; *P. frondosa*, 10cm (4in), a robust species with rosy-lilac flowers; *P. minima*, 2·5cm (1in) a minute species with large pink flowers. *P. rosea* produces deep pink flowers on 15cm (6in) stems, but it needs a moist position; *P. denticulata* is another charming species for a moist place, where it will produce large crimson, purple or white heads on 30cm (1ft) stems. *P. vialii* has purplish spiks up to 45cm (18in).

Many delightful subjects for the rock garden can also be found among the bulbs, and many possibilities are suggested on pages 63 to 81.

Annuals should not be ignored either, for they can brighten bare areas while more permanent plants become established. Some suitable annuals are listed on page 16.

Water gardening

The days when making a pond was a major construction job have long since gone. Not only do pond liners and pre-shaped pools make the job much easier, they also permit more interesting shapes, which allows more imaginative planting. The pre-formed type have ledges for marginal plants, and even quite a small pool will support a Water-lily and a small collection of marginal plants.

The depth for planting some of the popular aquatic and marginal plants is given on page 61. That table can be used to determine which plants are suitable for the particular depth of water you have available for planting.

Some good aquatic plants

Aponogeton distachyus (Water Hawthorn): This is one of the few fragrant aquatics. Its leaves float on the water and the white flowers, appearing just above the surface, smell of Hawthorn or vanilla, depending on interpretation. It is particularly useful because it flowers in spring and again in autumn.

Calla palustris 'Plena': White and green arum-like flowers are followed later by clusters of scarlet berries.

Caltha palustris 'Plena': This is a plant for marshy ground around the edge of a pond. The large, globular double yellow flowers are freely produced in late spring. (Illustrated on page 58.)

Iris: Two irises are commonly associated with the waterside – *I. kaempferi*, which has single or double flowers in a range of colours, and *I. laevigata*, which is an excellent aquatic. Flowers are usually violet-blue but sometimes white.

Mimulus luteus (Water Musk): The bright yellow flowers of the Water Musk bloom throughout summer. It will grow in the water or in soil besides the pond.

Nymphaea (Water-lily): The Queen of the garden pool. From June onwards Water-lilies majestically expose their beauty for all to admire. There are dozens from which to choose, ranging from miniatures that need only 7·5cm (3in) of water, to large and vigorous kinds that really need a lake. Colours include red, carmine, crimson, copper, orange, yellow, pink, rose, and white. Some are fragrant. A shortlist of dependable varieties is given on page 61, but there are many more excellent kinds from which to choose.

Ranunculus lingua: The Buttercup family provides several aquatic and marsh plants, the Greater Spearwort being one of them. It will grow in 7·5–45cm (3–18in) of water, and sends up erect, dark green spear-shaped leaves and large glistening yellow Buttercup flowers, reaching to 75cm (2½ft).

Sagittaria sagittifolia (Japanese Arrowhead): No pond is complete without this plant, with its attractive, glossy, arrow-shaped leaves. Spikes of large white flowers are carried about 30cm (1ft) above the water. Very deep water is not conducive to flowering. Therefore, the tubers, which are set 2.5–4cm (1 to 1½in) deep in compost, should not be more than 7.5-13cm (3-5in) below the surface of the crater.

Scirpus tabernaemontani 'Albescens': This is a striking Bulrush reaching about 90cm (3ft), with fat round stems, most attractively zoned with alternate bars of green and white. Propagation may be by division during the spring.

Typha minima (Reed Mace): This is a miniature Reed Mace, growing only to about 45cm (1½ft). The flower spikes resemble a Bulrush. It is a very dainty and free-flowering aquatic plant, and may be increased by division. It is best when planted in containers.

Iris kaempferi
(see page 61)

Draba aizoides
Whitlow Grass
(see page 59)

DEPENDABLE ROCK GARDEN PLANTS

Species and Varieties	Height	Flowering period	Light requirement	Hardiness	Description
Acaena microphylla New Zealand Bur	5cm (2in)	8-10	○	★★★★	A compact, mat-forming evergreen with bronze leaves and crimson flowers.
Achillea 'King Edward' Rock Yarrow	10cm (4in)	6-8	○	★★★★	Pretty, flatish heads of sulphur-yellow flowers, carried over greyish foliage.
Aethionema 'Warley Rose' Stone Cress	15cm (6in)	5-7	○	★★★★	Low, bushy growth and deep rose flowers. Glaucous foliage.
Alyssum saxatile 'Compactum' Gold Dust	15cm (6in)	4-6	○	★★★★	A mass of golden yellow flowers. Greyish foliage.
Androsace sarmentosa Rock Jasmine	5cm (2in)	5-6	○	★★★★	Woolly rosettes which tend to form mats. Pink flowers.
Antennaria dioica Cat's Ears	10cm (4in)	5-6	○	★★★★	Forms a dense carpet of silvery evergreen foliage. White, pink or rose flowers.
Arabis 'Rosabella' Rock Cress	15cm (6in)	4-5	○	★★★★	Easily grown and long-lived, it forms green hummocks covered with pink flowers. There is also a white-flowered arabis.

Below: The Marsh Marigold, *Caltha palustris*, looks especially attractive when its yellow Buttercup-like flowers are reflected in water. (See pages 57 and 61).

DEPENDABLE ROCK GARDEN PLANTS Continued

Species and Varieties	Height	Flowering period	Light requirement	Hardiness	Description
Armeria maritima Thrift	15cm (6in)	6-8	○	★★★★	Neat tufts of grass-like foliage and white or pink pompon flower heads.
Aubrieta Coloured Rock Cress	15cm (6in)	3-5	○	★★★★	One of the most beautiful rock garden plants, spreading to form a carpet of pink, red, purple or blue flowers.
Campanula carpatica Bellflower	15-25cm (6-10in)	6-8	◉	★★★★	Large, open, bell-shaped flowers — blue or white depending on variety.
C. garganica Bellflower	7.5cm (3in)	6-8	◉	★★★★	Soft grey foliage, forming compact tufts. Open-petalled pale blue flowers in profusion.
Cotyledon simplicifolia Navel Wort	15cm (6in)	6-7	◉	★★	Rosettes of serrated succulent leaves, and arching sprays of yellow flowers.
Dianthus deltoides Maiden Pink	15cm (6in)	6-8	○	★★★★	A gay plant with pink or red single 'pink' flowers.
Draba aizoides Whitlow Grass	7.5cm (3in)	4	◉	★★★★	Tufted plants, with tiny yellow flowers.
Erinus alpinus	10cm (4in)	5-7	○	★★★★	Sprays of white flowers over neat hummocks of foliage.

Below: Water-lilies are an indispensable element in any water garden. There are varieties to suit pools of all sizes and depths. (See pages 57 and 61.)

Calla palustris
Bog Arum
(see page 61)

Aponogeton distachyus
Water Hawthorn
(see page 61)

Nymphaea 'Escarboucle'
Water-Lily
(see page 61)

DEPENDABLE ROCK GARDEN PLANTS Continued

Species and Varieties	Height	Flowering period	Light requirement	Hardiness	Description
Gentiana acaulis Gentian	10cm (4in)	4-5	◑	★★★★	Large deep blue trumpet-shaped flowers. Very impressive in bloom.
G. sino-ornata Autumn Gentian	10cm (4in)	9-10	◑	★★★★	Brilliant blue trumpet-type flowers. Requires lime-free soil.
Geranium dalmaticum	10cm (4in)	5-7	⊙	★★★★	A charming plant, with hummocks of glossy leaves and clear pink flowers with conspicuous anthers.
Gypsophila repens Chalk Plant	10cm (4in)	5-6	○	★★★★	Masses of clear pink flowers. Bluish-grey leaves and almost trailing habit.
Hypsela longiflora	5cm (2in)	6-8	◑	★★★★	A mat-forming plant, tiny lilac-pink flowers nestling among the leaves.
Iberis sempervirens Perennial Candytuft	23cm (9in)	5-7	○	★★★★	Leaves form an evergreen mat, above which a mass of ivory-white flowers are borne.
Lithospermum diffusum 'Heavenly Blue' Gromwell	7.5cm (3in)	5-8	○	★★★★	Long-lasting gentian-blue flowers. Prostrate habit. Requires lime-free soil.
Phlox douglasii 'Rosea' Moss Phlox	10cm (4in)	5-6	⊙	★★★★	A superb plant — free-flowering and long-lived. Lilac-rose flowers; creeping habit.
Polygonum vacciniifolium Alpine Knotweed	15cm (6in)	8-10	⊙	★★★★	Deep pink flowers. Vigorous creeping growth.
Primula	10-30cm (4-12in)	3-7	◑	★★ ★★★ ★★★★	There are many good species available for the rock garden. Colours vary according to species.
Saponaria ocymoides Soap Wort	15cm (6in)	5-7	◑	★★★★	A gay plant, trailing its growth and masses of deep pink flowers over rocks or a wall.
Saxifraga Rock Foil	10-15cm (4-6in)	4-6	⊙	★★★★	A very diverse group of plants containing many excellent rock plants. Usually pink, red or yellow flowers.
Sedum Stonecrop	5-15cm (2-6in)	5-9	◑	★★★★	There are many good species for the rock garden. Attractive foliage — flowers usually pink, yellow or white.
Sempervivum Houseleek	10-20cm (4-8in)	6-7	⊙	★★★★	Grown for the attractive rosettes of foliage, often surrounded by clusters of smaller rosettes. Flowers are usually pink.
Silene schafta Catchfly	15cm (6in)	6-8	○	★★★★	Low tufts of green foliage with magenta-pink flowers.
Thymus serpyllum Thyme	2.5-5cm (1-2in)	6-8	⊙	★★★★	Aromatic low mat-forming plant. Pink, red or white flowers.

GOOD AQUATIC AND MARGINAL PLANTS

Species and Varieties	Height	Planting depth	Flowering period	Description
Aponogeton distachyus Water Hawthorn	Floa-ting	30cm (12in)	4 and 10	An excellent aquatic, with freely produced vanilla-scented white flowers, and shiny oval, leaves.
Calla palustris Bog Arum	15cm (6in)	5cm (2in)	6	White flowers like miniature Arum Lilies.
Caltha palustris 'Plena' Marsh Marigold	15cm (6in)		4	Freely produced globular double yellow buttercup-like flowers.
Cyperus longus	90cm (3ft)	10cm (4in)		A rush with tufts of grass-like foliage. Reddish-brown plumes.
Iris kaempferi	60cm (2ft)		7	Single or double flowers in a range of colours.
I. laevigata	45cm (1½ft)	5cm (2in)	5-7	An excellent aquatic iris. Violet-blue or white flowers.
Juncus ensifolius	30cm (1ft)	10cm (4in)		A rush with iris-like foliage and dainty brown flowers.
Menyanthes trifoliata Bog Bean	23cm (9in)	7.5cm (3in)	3-6	Foliage like broad bean leaves. Clusters of pinkish flowers.
Mimulus luteus Water Musk	30cm (1ft)	10cm (4in)	6-8	Bright yellow flowers with blotched lips.
Pontederia cordata Pickerel	60cm (2ft)	7.5cm (3in)	6-8	Glossy spear-shaped leaves and crowded spikes of blue flowers.
Ranunculus lingua Spearwort	75cm (2½in)	7.5-45cm (3-18in)	7-9	Narrow, lance-shaped leaves and buttercup-like flowers.
Sagittaria sagittifolia Japanese Arrowhead	30cm (1ft)	5cm (2in)	6-7	Spikes of large white flowers and deeply arrow-shaped leaves.
Scirpus tabernaemontani 'Albescens'	90cm (3ft)	10cm (4in)		A Bulrush with fat, round stems alternately barred green and white.
Typha minima Reed Mace	45cm (1½ft)	10cm (4in)	7	A miniature Reed Mace with Bulrush-like flower spikes.

SIX GOOD WATER-LILIES

Species and Varieties	Planting depth	Description
Nymphaea 'Escarboucle'	30-75cm (1-2½ft)	Large ruby-red flowers. Free-flowering and long-lasting.
N. 'Froebeli'	20-38cm (8-15in)	Wine-red. Free-flowering. Ideal for small pools. Fragrant.
N. 'Graziella'	20-38cm (8-15in)	Reddish-orange fading to apricot-yellow. Good for a small pool.
N. 'James Brydon'	25-60cm (10in-2ft)	Rich carmine, paeony-shaped flowers. Purplish leaves.
N. pygmaea 'Helvola'	15-25cm (6-10in)	A pale yellow miniature Water-lily with mottled leaves.
N. 'Rene Gerard'	25-60cm (10in-2ft)	Large, star-shaped rosy-pink flowers, splashed crimson.

Planting depth means the depth of water above the crown.

Pontederia cordata
Pickerel
(see this page)

Sagittaria sagittifolia
Japanese Arrowhead
(see this page)

Nymphaea 'James Brydon'
Water-lily
(see this page)

Bulbs, Corms and Tubers

The term 'bulb' is often used rather loosely as a collective term for corms and tubers, as well as true bulbs. As they are usually bought from the same source, and in many respects are treated in the same way, the convention has been followed in this book, although dahlias are included under herbaceous plants on pages 42 and 43.

A true bulb is formed like an onion, of layers, which are modified leaves. In the centre is an embryo shoot, and if the bulb is of flowering size an embryo flower too. For this reason, bulbs can often be planted in poor soil and still produce a reasonable display the first year (as the flower is already present in the bulb), but for continued health and prolific flowering good soil and site are essential.

Corms are really thickened stems, and appear solid throughout when cut, instead of forming layers as with a bulb. The thin papery scales on the outside serve only as protection, not a food reserve.

Tubers are thickened underground stems or roots, again organs of storage. They are often less symmetrical in shape than corms, and unlike the corms do not have a papery outer covering.

Rhizomes are underground stems, usually growing horizontally, which throw up shoots some distance away from the parent plant. Bearded irises are an example of plants with rhizomes, although some other species of irises are bulbs.

Galanthus nivalis
Snowdrop
(see page 80)

The role of bulbs

Bulbs have three main applications — they can be used for forcing, in which case they are usually bought afresh each year; as seasonal bedding plants (being lifted to make room for the next season's flowers); or as permanent plantings.

Bulbs are usually forced indoors, but great care must be taken to choose suitable varieties. Some traditional bulbs are ideal for forcing into early flower (hyacinths or daffodils, for example) but even so not all varieties are suitable.

For very early bloom, prepared bulbs may be necessary. These will have been chilled to about 5°C (41°F) for several weeks, which breaks their dormancy and enables them to grow quickly. It is possible to do this yourself by placing the bulbs in a refrigerator in ventilated paper bags for six to nine weeks before planting.

Some bulbs, particularly the small-flowered kinds such as Snowdrops and chionodoxa, do not force well. To enjoy these charming plants indoors, plant them in pots or pans and plunge under peat

Far left: The Snakeshead Fritillary, *Fritillaria meleagris*, is an intriguing flower, with delicate chequered nodding flowers. (See pages 68 and 80.)

63

Chionodoxa
Glory of the Snow
(see page 79)

Zephyranthes candida
Flower of the West Wind
(see page 81)

Allium triquetrum
(see page 76)

**BULBS FOR USE
AS CUT FLOWERS**
Allium aflatunense
A. albopilosum
A. flavum
A. moly
A. triquetrum
Alstroemeria
Amaryllis
*Anemone coronaria (St Brigid & De
  Caen)*
Brodiaea
Camassia
Galanthus
Gladiolus
Iris (Dutch, English, Spanish)
Ixia
Ixiolirion
Lilium 'Mid Century Hybrids'
Muscari
Narcissus
Nerine
Ornithogalum pyramidale
O. thyrsoides
Ranunculus
Scilla nutans
Tulipa

BULBS FOR THE SEASIDE
Amaryllis belladonna
Crinum
Tulipa

BULBS FOR SHADE
Anemone
Cyclamen coum
C. europeum
C. neapolitanum
Endymion
Eranthis
Erythronium
Fritillaria
Galanthus
Leucojum
Lilium giganteum
L. henryi
Muscari
Narcissus
Ornithogalum nutans
Scilla

BULBS FOR SANDY SOIL
Allium moly
Alstroemeria
Amaryllis belladonna
Brodiaea
Chionodoxa
Colchicum
Crocus
Croscosmia masonorum
Endymion hispanicus
Galtonia candicans
Gladiolus
Ipheion uniflorum
Iris (not English)
Ixia
Muscari
Nerine
Scilla
Zephyranthes candica

BULBS TO NATURALIZE IN GRASS
Camassia esculenta
Colchicum autumnale
C. byzantinum
C. speciosum
Crocus speciosus
Eranthis hyemalis
Erythronium dens-canis
Fritillaria latifolia
F. meleagris
Galanthus
Muscari
Narcissus
Ornithogalum nutans
O. umbellatum
Scilla

BULBS FOR CHALKY SOIL
Allium
Crocus
Cyclamen neapolitanum
Erythronium
Narcissus
Sternbergia
Tulipa

outdoors, and bring them indoors only when there are signs of flower buds.

Bulbs used for forcing are seldom likely to bloom the following year, and may be planted in a sheltered corner to build up reserves again to flower outdoors in future years.

A large number of bulbs are bought each year to plant after the summer bedding has finished, to provide spring display before being lifted again to make room for bedding plants. This is an effective way to achieve a bright and impressive spring display, but if the quality of the blooms is not to deteriorate rapidly, the bulbs must be replanted in a spare piece of ground until the foliage dies down naturally (it is sufficient to take out a shallow trench and lay the bulbs close together in this, with the foliage exposed, and to eplace the soil). Such lifted bulbs will need a slow-acting general fertilizer incorporated in the soil at planting time.

Permanent plantings are often much more satisfactory. Although here will be years when the size of bloom is not as large as the first year, this is only the cyclic effect of the old bulbs dividing and new ones reaching a good flowering size. Generally, the blooms will be larger and earlier — and they will form clumps, which in most situations looks far more effective than single bulbs coming up in a regular pattern.

There is a golden rule with permanent flower beds — you must be prepared to let the foliage die down naturally, even though the bed would look tidier with the foliage trimmed. And they must be fed once a year, using a slow-acting balanced fertilizer applied after flowering or before the new growth appears the next season.

Naturalized bulbs in grass or woodland need very little attention, but grass mowing will have to wait until the foliage has withered.

Although most gardeners cut a few Daffodils from the garden for indoor decoration, bulbs are rather neglected as a cut-flower — apart from those grown commercially for the florist trade. Where there is room to grow suitable kinds for this purpose, the result will be well worthwhile. The flowers will be much less expensive than those bought at the shops, and because the bulbs will last for many years, and increase steadily, they are not an expensive investment for the return they yield over the years. Apart from the narcissi, there are many delightful cut-flowers, from the popular anemones and Tulips to Lilies and alliums. Ideas for bulbs to grow for cutting are given on page 64.

Spring-flowering bulbs can be planted effectively in beds on their own, but they often generate more interest if inter-planted with other subjects. Daffodils look superb planted between lines of Wallflowers, especially if the Wallflowers are deep red. May-flowering Tulips are most effective sharing a bed with Forget-me-nots.

Hyacinths would be wasted among Wallflowers, where they would become lost. Also, it is far better to keep scented flowers apart and enjoy the fragrance in separate parts of the garden.

Hyacinths are usually most effective in a bed on their own, though an edging of crocuses looks nice. Daffodils also lend themselves to single-subject beds, but more interest can be created by planting with Tulips, which increases the flowering period of the bed.

Aconites, crocuses, Grape Hyacinths, even Snowdrops, make pretty edgings, but their beauty can be short-lived.

If a bed is to be devoted to spring-flowering bulbs, a planting of mixed subjects will be most effective, and extends the period of interest.

A long, narrow bed, for instance, could have a double row of Daffodils at the back, with a row of bedding Hyacinths or May-flowering Tulips set in front of them, and an edging of crocuses or Snowdrops.

It is usually better to have a small area well planned and planted, rather than to dot the bulbs about the garden, where much of the impact is lost.

Alstroemeria
Peruvian Lily
(see page 79)

Leucojum aestivum
Summer Snowflake
(see page 81)

Ipheion uniflorum
Spring Starflower
(see page 81)

Above: The Autumn Crocus, *Colchicum speciosum*, flowers in October or November, before the leaves appear. The large flowers are impressive by any standards, but especially valuable at that time of year. (See page 75.)

It would be a mistake, however, to think of bulbs only in terms of spring flowers. There are delightful and charming subjects to be had in flower at most times of the year. Lilies and irises are obvious examples, but there are autumn-flowering crocuses and cyclamen and summer-flowering Chincherinchees and Summer Hyacinths, to name but a few.

Although they are not often seen, it is possible to make a permanent bed of bulbs, using subjects that flower at various times of the year, and this is a trouble-free way to provide interest and colour from spring till autumn. The only work involved in a bed of this kind is keeping it free of weeds — but a suitable ground cover plant will rectify that. Bulbs will easily push their way through a carpeter such as Thyme.

Soil and site

If you are prepared to plant afresh each year, most true bulbs will give a magnificent display whatever the soil or site, provided it is not waterlogged. Good drainage is essential for all bulbs.

If you want the bulbs to live and to flower another year, then some attention has to be paid to the soil. Although most bulbs will grow happily in sand or clay, provided there is drainage, a friable soil with plenty of humus is best. And as many species have extensive and penetrating roots, it should be dug deeply before planting. Peat will improve a sandy soil, and sand a clay soil. Rather than spread peat or sand throughout the entire planting area, they may be more effective when localized to the area of planting. Sand or grit in the base of a planting hole can be particularly beneficial for subjects such as Lilies and gladioli. If your soil is sandy, however, concentrate on those plants most suited to a light soil, which are listed on page 64.

The majority of bulbs prefer neutral or slightly acid soils, although hyacinths and certain other bulbs, listed on page 64, prefer one that is slightly chalky. Lilies can have strong preferences, some requiring lime-free conditions while others will grow perfectly satisfactorily where there is lime. Examples of both types are given on page 77.

Winter-flowering bulbs

Most of the winter-flowering bulbs bloom at the end of winter, from the end of January onwards, though the weather has a significant effect on flowering time from season to season. But whether they flower in January or February, the bold little flowers that force their way into bloom at this time of year are welcome for the promise of things to come, as well as for their own intrinsic beauty.

Chionodoxa luciliae (Glory of the Snow): This dainty flower is not the earliest of the winter flowers, but makes a welcome appearance about the end of February with loose heads of pale blue star-shaped flowers with white centres. It enjoys sun, but does not object to some shade, particularly after the leaves have withered. Plant 5cm (2in) deep, then leave undisturbed until they are too crowded. A useful bulb for naturalizing in the garden.

Crocus
(see page 80)

Crocus chrysanthus: Although these and other early-flowering species are much smaller than the large-flowered Dutch type, they are more in keeping with a rock garden setting, and what they lack in size they make up for in daintiness and the fact that they appear ·at the end of winter.

Above: Winter-flowering crocuses bring early colour to the garden. They are easy to grow yet bring colour when it is scarce. (See page 67.)

There are many varieties, including 'Blue Bird' (purple and white), 'E.A. Bowles' (yellow, striped bronze), 'Snow Bunting' (lilac and white), and 'Zwanenburg Bronze' (deep yellow with a bronze flush outside). Plant up to 2·5cm (1in) deep, not more.

Cyclamen coum: At the mention of cyclamen, most people think of the large-flowered florist's type, and overlook their hardy and miniature relatives. It is a pity because these delightful plants include some that flower in the worst months of the year — from December to March. Other species flower in the autumn, but among the winter-flowering species is *C. coum*. This thrives beneath deciduous trees, and carries its pink, carmine or white, reflexed flowers on short stalks about 7·5m (3in) long. They are best massed beneath trees or grouped in a shady part of the rock garden. Just cover the corms with sieved leafmould or peat.

Eranthis hyemalis (Winter Aconite): These look gorgeous planted in drifts beneath deciduous trees and shrubs. An attractive ruff of green bracts frame the buttercup-yellow flowers. Plant 5cm (2in) deep. This species will also spread by seed. Leave undisturbed, if possible, and ensure they do not become dry in spring.

Erythronium dens-canis
Dog's Tooth Violet
(see page 80)

Sternbergia lutea
Yellow Star Flower
(see page 81)

Ornithogalum balansae
(see page 81)

Galanthus nivalis (Snowdrop): Most people have an affection for this plant, which is among the first to flower and always greeted with a feeling of joy. There are several species, but *G. nivalis* is the most common one. The white bells with green markings are normally single, but there is a double-flowered variety. Snowdrops thrive in heavy, preferably moist, soil, in sun or shade. Plant 7·5cm (3in) deep.

Spring-flowering bulbs

Allium: The alliums deserve to be planted more often, for the various species can provide flowers from May to August, and colours range from white to yellow, lilac, pink or red, and heights from less than 30cm (1ft) to more than 1·2m (4ft). Species to flower in May include *A. aflatunense* (purple-lilac), *A. neapolitanum* (white), *A. rosenbachianum*, and *A. triquetrum* (white).

Crocus (large-flowered): Among the best-known spring-flowering plants, with a wide range of colours. Useful for edging beds and for naturalizing in grass. Plant 2·5cm (1in) deep.

Endymion hispanicus (Giant Bluebell): A large-flowered version of the woodland Bluebell. It has stiffer, more substantial-looking flower spikes than the Bluebell, and colours include blue, white and pink.

These plants resent disturbance, and are best naturalized in grass or beneath trees. Plant 10cm (4in) deep.

Erythronium dens-canis (Dog's Tooth Violet): These delicate-looking flowers, with small heads of slightly nodding pink or white flowers, need a sheltered spot, preferably with some shade. They will do well on chalky soil and naturalize well in light woodlands. They need to be planted in groups for best effect. Plant 7·5cm (3in) deep.

Fritillaria imperialis (Crown Imperial): This is the most imposing of all spring bulbs, with stout stems rising to 90cm (3ft), topped with a crown of orange or yellow hanging bells set amid a cluster of leaves. (Illustrated on page 70.)

Plant 20cm (8in) deep. Because the bulbs sometimes rot, it is advantageous to set them on their sides.

Fritillaria meleagris (Snakeshead Fritillary): Much smaller than the Crown Imperial, but equally interesting. The quaint flowers, on stems of about 30cm (1ft), are interestingly marked, and often chequered. Markings include deep red, violet and purple. Plant 10cm (4in) deep. (Illustrated on page 62.)

Hyacinthus (Hyacinth): Too well known to require detailed description. Outdoors they require a rich soil, and should be planted 13cm (5in) deep in October or November. Do not use prepared bulbs outdoors. Fresh bulbs will need to be planted each year for formal bedding, but the old bulbs can be left to naturalize and form small clumps.

Ipheion uniflorum (Spring Starflower): This is a bulb for well-drained soil and a sunny spot, although it will grow in semi-shade. A bright little South African plant, with white funnel-shaped flowers tinged pale violet, borne above a mass of grass-like leaves. Plant 4cm (1½in) deep.

Leucojum aestivum (Summer Snowflake): Despite its name, this plant appears in late spring, during April and May, when it bears its head of white bells, marked with green, on 45cm (1½ft) stems. It soon makes a fairly large clump if left undisturbed in the damp soil that it likes. Plant 13cm (5in) deep.

Muscari armeniacum (Grape Hyacinth): Rather stiff-looking plants, with tight clusters of small blue flowers on stout stems, rather like miniature hyacinths. Very effective as an edging to formal beds.

Narcissus (Daffodils): There are few gardens without a clump of Daffodils, yet all too often they are rather run-down examples of the all-yellow trumpet kind. Beautiful though these are, and they are one of the traditional sights of spring, there are many more delightful kinds to be grown.

There are two broad groups – the large-flowered and the small species. The large-flowered kinds are again divided into further groupings, according to the size of the cup and whether the stems have single blooms or clusters of flowers. The range of types, shapes and colours is wide, and a good bulb catalogue will provide excellent suggestions for varieties.

No rock garden would be complete without some of the miniature narcissi, and a selection of species is given on page 76. A good bulb catalogue will provide more suggestions.

All Daffodils are narcissi, but usually it is the large-cupped varieties that are called Daffodils, the others being known as narcissi.

Large-flowered kinds have large bulbs, and sometimes they are sold as single-nosed or double-nosed. The latter will have more than one flower stem to each bulb. Although single-nosed bulbs can be planted with a bulb planter, the multiple-nosed kinds should be planted with a trowel, to ensure they do not become stuck in the hole with an air pocket beneath. Plant 10cm (4in) deep.

The small-flowered species naturally have much smaller bulbs, and these are best planted 5cm (2in) deep.

Narcissi need planting early, before Tulips and Hyacinths. They are undemanding regarding soil, and will grow satisfactorily in sun or shade. They are, of course, one of the best bulbs for naturalizing.

Ornithogalum: *O. nutans* is a good subject for partial shade. The greenish-white flowers are borne on loose spikes up to 38cm (15in). It is attractive when naturalized between shrubs. Plant 7·5cm (3in) deep. *O. balansae* has numerous white star-shaped blooms, striped green on the reverse, in March or April.

Puschkinia scilloides (Striped Squill): These resemble the scillas, but the flowers are pale blue with a darker stripe. They look most at home in the rock garden, and are useful for heavy soils. Plant 5cm (2in) deep.

Scilla non-scripta (Bluebell): A popular native woodland plant needing no introduction. It is most effective naturalized in a shady area. Plant 10cm (4in) deep.

Scilla sibirica (Siberian Squill): A popular and easily grown spring flower, with nodding blue bells. Each bulb produces several stems and a group planted in a rock garden looks very pretty. They are also suitable for planting in short turf, and can be grown in indoors. Plant 10cm (4in) deep. (Illustrated on page 79.)

Muscari armeniacum
Grape Hyacinth
(see page 81)

Narcissus cyclamineus
Miniature Narcissus
(see page 76)

Scilla sibirica
Siberian Squill
(see page 81)

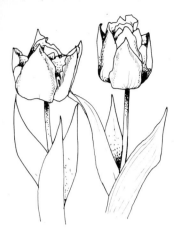

Early-double Tulip
(see page 77)

Tulipa (Tulip): Superb cut flowers, and always popular. The only problems in the garden are wind (with the tall-growing varieties) and their reluctance to flower dependably after the first year. There are, fortunately, varieties to solve both problems.

In windy sites the solution lies in planting low-growing types such as Single Early or Double Early varieties (page 78), or some of the species tulips listed on page 77. Tulips will flower best in succeeding years after planting if left in the ground to multiply and grow undisturbed, but if the soil is heavy they should be lifted. If lifted and dried, plant in a different position the next year to reduce the chance of Tulip Fire, a serious disease, becoming a problem. If left unlifted, a fungicide such as quintozene will help with the control of this disease. Most of the species kind flower well each year.

Tulips are particular about soil, and best results will be obtained from a sandy, well-drained loam, in a sunny position.

Plant Tulips late, from mid-autumn to early winter. October is the earliest for April-flowering kinds, November for May-flowering varieties. Plant 10–15 cm (4–6 in) deep, according to the size of the bulb.

Right: The Crown Imperial, *Fritillaria imperialis*, is one of the most impressive of all spring-flowering bulbs. They appreciate a limy soil enriched with a liberal quantity of compost or manure. (See page 68.)

Summer-flowering bulbs

It is during the summer months that bulbs tend to be neglected – there is so much competition from the herbaceous plants. Yet there are many fine bulbs which contribute in no small way to the delights of the summer garden.

Some of the bulbs included here are often regarded primarily as herbaceous border plants – alstroemeria and crocosmia are examples – but they are perpetuated by underground storage organs (fleshy tubers in first example, corms in the second). Dahlias, however, have been included with herbaceous plants.

Allium: Some of the spring-flowering species have already been described, but there are others to carry these plants well into summer. June sees *A. albopilosum* (silvery-lilac), *A. caeruleum* (blue), *A. moly* (yellow), *A. oreophilum* (purple-lilac or violet), and *A. sphaerocephalum* (crimson-maroon), coming into flower. *A. flavum* (yellow) and *A. pulchellum* (rose-pink) will bloom in July and August. (*Allium moly* is illustrated on page 78.)

Alstroemeria (Peruvian Lily): These are notoriously difficult to establish, but once settled are lovely plants with tubular Lily-like flowers, in a range of soft colours – including pinks, oranges, and

Below: Because many spring bulbs are upright in growth, the overall effect can be enhanced by interplanting with other spring-flowering plants to provide interest at ground level. Here, Tulip 'Queen of the Bartigons' has been interplanted with a form of Double Daisy, *Bellis perennis*. (Tulips are discussed on pages 77 and 78.)

Lilium amabile
(see page 73)

Tulipa saxatilis
(see page 77)

Lilium chalcedonicum
(see page 73)

coral. Plant the tubers 15cm (6in) deep in well-drained soil, preferably on the sunny side of a sheltered wall, and do not delay planting once they have been received from the nursery. They can also be grown from seed, in which case it is easier to establish them. Do not disturb once planted, and as they are not totally hardy it is best to afford protection *in situ* by applying a thick mulch for the winter.

Anemone coronaria (Windflower): This plant could equally well have been included under spring or autumn flowers, because they can be had in flower from February to October by adjusting planting time and providing protection. They are well-known as cut flowers, 'De Caen' having single blooms, 'St. Brigid' semi-double. Plant 5cm (2in) deep in rich, moist soil.

Brodiaea laxa: These are good plants for the wild garden and for cutting. The violet-purple flowers are carried on wiry stems. Plant 10cm (4in) deep.

Camassia (Bear Grass): A short but impressive display is provided by this plant, with its graceful spikes of blue-purple or white flowers with narrow petals and prominent stamens. Plant 10cm (4in) deep in good soil. (Illustrated on page 74.)

Crinum x powellii: Heads of delicate pink trumpet-shaped Lily-like flowers are borne on long stems. It is not hardy, and if planted outside must have the protection of a sunny wall and a mild district.

Crocosmia masonorum: Brilliant orange-scarlet blooms make this a showy plant for the border. It produces sprays of flowers like montbretia, and will last two weeks when cut and placed in water. Plant 7·5cm (3in) deep.

Cyclamen europaeum: Similar to *C. coum* (page 67), but with crimson flowers from July to September.

Galtonia candicans (Summer Hyacinth): A decorative plant, best planted in groups in the flower border or amongst shrubs. Each spike carries thirty or more sweetly-scented white bell-shaped flowers. Plant 15cm (6in) deep in well-drained soil.

Gladiolus (large-flowered): Well-known plants, valuable for cutting or planting in beds and borders. They prefer a medium or light loam, deeply dug and with moisture-retaining humus incorporated. Good drainage is also important.

There are many excellent varieties, and most seed or bulb catalogues offer a comprehensive range. Choose high-crowned corms with a small plate (root scar) beneath, and plant about 10cm (4in) deep.

Iris: This very diverse family has members from a few centimetres to a metre in height, some with rhizomes, others with bulbs.

Largest are the Bearded iris, forms of *I. germanica*. Flowering in late May and June, these majestic plants fill the gap between Tulips and the main flush of border plants. They are undemanding plants, ideal for a limy soil, which should also be well-drained. The site should be in full sun. It is important to plant shallowly but firmly — the rhizome should barely be covered.

Some representative varieties of Bearded Iris are given on page 76, reflecting the colour range available.

Spanish, English and Dutch bulbous iris are excellent planted in clumps in the herbaceous border. These names signify types, not the country in which the bulbs have been grown. These are the iris usually sold by florists. First to flower are the Dutch varieties in early June, followed by the Spanish in late June, and then the larger English in late June and early July. There are several good varieties of each kind, and some of these appear on page 76. Plant 7·5cm (3in) deep.

There are also two charming rock garden iris – *I. reticulata* (violet with a yellow tongue, although there are several varieties) and *I. danfordiae*, a real charmer with fragrant yellow flowers spotted brown. Both are also excellent grown in pans for indoor decoration.

Ixia (African Corn Lily): Sadly not a hardy subject, but can be tried against a warm wall in mild districts. Star-shaped flowers in many bright colours, often with a contrasting centre, but unfortunately they close in dull weather. Plant 5cm (2in) deep.

Ixiolirion montanum: Another slightly tender species, only suitable for trying outside in the most favourable areas. Blue flowers resemble chionodoxa on lax stems.

Lilium (Lily): These are among the most exotic-looking bulbs likely to be planted outdoors – yet they are quite easy to grow if given the right conditions.

There are many species and varieties on the market, and a selection is given on page 77 – lime-tolerant species being indicated. Lilies can be grown on acid or alkaline soils, but it is important to select suitable species.

Three other species not listed in the table, but worth a place in any garden, are *L. amabile* (red, spotted black), *L. chalcedonicum* (bright scarlet with olive-brown base), and *L. hansonii* (golden yellow, spotted brown; fragrant). Like most Lilies they flower in July. Mid-century Hybrids come in a wide range of colours and are among the best Lilies to grow in a mixed border.

Most Lilies require a situation where they can have their heads in the sun (for part of the day at least), but their roots in shade provided by low-growing shrubs or ground-cover plants.

Lilies should normally be planted as soon as received, as the scaly bulbs may dry out and the plants suffer. If they are received when the ground is not suitable for planting, pot up and plant out later. Most Lilies are stem-rooting (the stem above the bulb sends out roots at intervals) and these need planting about 20cm (8in) deep; plant base-rooting species about 10cm (4in) deep.

Light soil will benefit from plenty of peat worked into the planting area. In all but the most well-drained soils, place some sand or grit at the bottom of the planting hole.

Ornithogalum: The Chincherinchee (*O. thyroides*) is famous as a long-lasting cut-flower, with its packed spikes of creamy-white flowers. It is not hardy, but can be grown in most areas if lifted after flowering, like gladioli.

A hardy relative, the Star of Bethlehem (*O. umbellatum*), spreads rapidly, and is effective in front of shrubs with its white star-like flowers. Another useful summer-flowering species is *O. pyramidale*, which has large white flowers like *O. nutans* (see page 69).

All these species can be planted about 10cm (4in) deep.

Ranunculus: Few plants produce a more gorgeous effect in the border in May or early June than the ranunculus bought as small

Lilium hansonii
(see this page)

Amaryllis belladonna
Belladonna Lily
(see page 79)

Lilium pardalinum
(see page 77)

73

claw-shaped tubers. The large, double flowers are available in shades of yellow, pink, orange and red.

A sunny position is essential, and a rich, well-drained soil is required for good results. Plant the tubers claws down after soaking for twenty-four hours.

Autumn-flowering bulbs

Plants that flower late in the season can be just as valuable as spring-flowering kinds. They extend the period of colour and help to make winter seem less long.

Amaryllis belladonna (Belladonna Lily): Although a slightly tender plant, these bulbs can be planted under a south or south-west wall if the soil is well drained and rich. Heads of fragrant, trumpet-shaped flowers are carried in a cluster at the top of the stems. The large bulbs should be planted just below the surface, and a thick mulch used to provide protection during winter. They will be better left undisturbed if it is possible to overwinter them.

Colchicum: C. autumnale (Autumn Crocus) is probably the best-known autumn-flowering bulb. The large crocus-like mauve flowers appear before the leaves. C. byzantinum has bright mauve

Below: Summer-flowering bulbs should not be overlooked; subjects such as Camassia leichtlinii 'Flore-plena' always add interest to a rock garden or border. (See page 72.)

owers like a loose crocus, and *C. speciosum* is similar, but with
iolet or rose-purple flowers with a white throat. They all do well in
limy soil. (Illustrated on page 66.)

Crocus speciosus: This is one of the true crocuses, with violet-blue
lowers. Useful to naturalize in grass.

Cyclamen neapolitanum: A miniature cyclamen similar to
C. coum, described on page 67, but flowering from August to
November. It has mauve to pale pink or white flowers, and marbled
eaves. (Illustrated on page 75.)

Nerine bowdenii: This is one of the most beautiful autumn-
flowering bulbs, with clusters of delicate pink flowers, resembling
tubular Lilies. Sadly, they are not fully hardy, and can only be
planted against a warm, sunny wall in mild areas.

Plant at least 15cm (6in) deep. The bulbs will work their way
towards the surface in time. (Illustrated on page 79.)

Sternbergia lutea (Yellow Star Flower): A very striking bulb with
bright yellow crocus-like flowers. Plant 10cm (4in) deep in a sunny
position.

Zephyranthes candica (Flower of the West Wind): White crocus-
like flowers, useful as an edging plant in warm areas. Leaves persist
the whole year. It may need winter protection.

Below: *Cyclamen neapolitanum* produces
its dainty miniature cyclamen flowers
from August to November, and unlike the
florist's form is quite hardy. (This and
other species are described above and on
pages 67, 72 and 80.)

IRISES

Types and varieties	Height Range	Flowering Time	Representative Varieties
Bearded Irises (dwarf)	15-30cm (6-12in)	5-6	'Burgundy' (claret-purple); 'Keepsake' (golden-yellow with orange beard); 'Primus' (yellow standards with mahogany-red falls edged yellow).
Bearded Irises (tall)	75cm-1m (2½-3½ft)	5-6	'Aline' (azure-blue); 'Gudrin' (creamy-white with brilliant orange beard); 'Lothario' (lavender-blue standards, with pansy-blue falls).
Bulbous-rooted Irises (Dutch)	45-60cm (1½-2ft)	Early 6	'Blue Champion' (clear blue with yellow blotches); 'Golden Harvest' (deep yellow); 'Lemon Queen' (yellow, with sulphur-yellow falls).
Bulbous-rooted Irises (Spanish)	45-60cm (1½-2ft)	Late 6	'Cajanus' (clear yellow); 'King of the Blues' (deep blue, with yellow blotches); 'Queen Wilhelmina'' (pure white, with small yellow blotches).
Bulbous-rooted Irises (English)	60cm (2ft)	Late 6 and early 7	'Delft's Blue' (dark blue with pale blue falls); 'Mont Blanc' (pure white).
Iris kaempferi	60-90cm (2-3ft)	7-8	'Adonis' (purple-blue on a grey ground colour); 'Moonlight Waves' (white); 'Purple Splendour' (deep violet-purple).
Iris sibirica and Iris orientalis	75cm-1.2m (2½-4ft)	6	'Eric the Red' (purplish-red, with reticulated falls); 'Heron' (deep ultramarine, white blotches); 'Snowy Egret' (pure white, flushed yellow).

MINIATURE NARCISSI FOR THE GARDEN

Varieties	Colour	Flowering Time	Height	For naturalizing light grass	Light Requirement	For the Wild Garden	For the Rock Garden	Description
Narcissus bulbocodium	Yellow	3-4	15cm (6in)	Yes	⊙	Yes	Yes	This narcissus is known as the 'Yellow Hoop Petticoat'.
N. caniliculatus	White with yellow cups	4	15-20cm (6-8in)	—	⊙	Yes	—	A narcissus that needs a sunny position.
N. cyclamineus 'Peeping Tom'	Deep yellow	3	32cm (13in)	—	⊙	Yes	—	Flowers for three to four weeks.
N. triandrus 'Albus'	Creamy-white	4	15cm (6in)	Yes	⊙	Yes	Yes	Produces two to three small flowers to each stem.
N. triandrus 'April Tears'	Yellow	4	20cm (8in)	Yes	⊙	Yes	Yes	Thr trumpets are slightly deeper in colour than the petals.

ALLIUMS FOR GARDEN DECORATION

Species	Height	Flower Colour	Flowering Time	Good for cut flowers	Ideal for the wild garden	Description
Allium aflatunense	75-90cm (2½-3ft)	Purple-lilac	5-6	Yes	Yes	Strikingly attractive in full sun.
A. albopilosum	60cm (2ft)	Silvery-lilac	6	Yes	Yes	A highly recommended species.
A flavum	25-30cm (10-12in)	Yellow	7-8	Yes	Yes	An allium which is easy to grow.
A. giganteum	90cm-1.2m (3-4ft)	Violet	7	—	Yes	A spectacular plant for the flower border.
A. moly	25cm (10in)	Golden-yellow	6	Yes	Yes	Grows well in the flower or shrub border.
A. oreophilum	1.2-1.8m (4-6ft)	Carmine-red	6	—	Yes	Good for the rock garden.
A. triquetrum	45-60cm (1½-2ft)	White, striped green	May	Yes	Yes	Good for semi-shade.

Note: Most of these alliums, except where mentioned, like a well-drained and sunny position. These attractive plants do well in limy soil

TULIPA SPECIES FOR THE GARDEN

Species and Varieties	Colour	Flowering Time	Height	Light Requirement	Description
Tulipa biflora	White, with a bright yellow centre.	3-4	10cm (4in)	○	In sheltered areas it may flower in February.
T. chrysantha	Yellow and red	4	15-20cm (6-8in)	○	Its wavy leaves are set low down on the stem, close to the ground.
T. clusiana	Violet centre, with cherry striped outer petals	4	30cm (12in)	○	This tulip is often known as 'The Lady Tulip', and displays a dainty and feminine air.
T. eichleri	Flame-red	4	25cm (10in)	○	When grouped together they are very spectacular.
T. hageri	Brownish-red, with a yellow-edged centre	5	15-20cm (6-8in)	○	T. hageri 'Splendens' is a good type of this species to try.
T. maximowiczii	Red, with bluish-black centre	4-5	10-15cm (4-6in)	○	A tulip species that does well in the rock garden.
T. saxatilis	Lilac, with yellow centre	4	15-23cm (6-9in)	○	Up to three flowers are borne on each stem.
T. sylvestris	Golden-yellow	4	23-30cm (9-12in)	○	A good species for naturalizing in grass.

Lilium auratum (see this page)

GARDEN LILIES

Species and Varieties	Height	Flowering Period	Stem Rooting	Soil Type	Light Requirement	Fragrance	Description
Lilium auratum	1.5-1.8m (5-6ft)	8-9	Yes	Peaty and lime free soil.	○	✿	Popularly known as the 'Golden-rayed Lily of Japan'. Pure white and covered with brown and crimson spots.
L. canadense	90cm-1.8m (3-6ft)	7	—	Moist.	●	✿	Yellow to red-orange flowers, spotted brown.
L. candicum	90cm-1.2m (3-4ft)	6	—	Tolerates lime in the soil.	○	✿	Beautiful pure white flowers. This is the Madonna Lily.
L. davidii	1.2-1.8m (4-6ft)	7-8	Yes	Peaty soil, with some lime.	◑		Orange Turks-cup flowers spotted purple and black.
L. giganteum	1.8-3.6m (6-12ft)	6-8	—	Moist	◑	✿	Large funnel-shaped flowers, coloured white on the inside with red markings, and green on the outside.
L. henryi	1.5-1.8m (5-6ft)	8-9	Yes	Tolerates lime in the soil	◑	✿	Deep orange-yellow flowers, spotted brown.
L. pardalinum	1.2-1.8m (4-6ft)	7	—	Moist, lime-free soil	◑		The Californian Lily. Deep orange flowers, shading to crimson with maroon spots.

Right: *Allium moly* is ideal for planting in a shrub border, where its golden-yellow flowers blend well with dark-foliaged shrubs. (See pages 71 and 76.)

Far right: The Siberian Squill, *Scilla sibirica*, is an extremely popular spring-flowering bulb, at home in a rock garden in sun or semi-shade. (See pages 69 and 81.)

Extreme right: *Nerine bowdenii* is a very attractive autumn-flowering bulb, but needs the protection of a wall and is hardy only in favourable districts. (See pages 75 and 81.)

TULIPS FOR THE GARDEN

Types	Description	Height	Spread	Flowering Time	Colour	Planting Depth	Planting Time	Soil
Cottage Tulips	Tall stems, with rounded flowers.	60-90cm (2-3ft)	15-20cm (6-8in)	4-5	White, yellow, pink, green, bi-coloured.	15-20cm (6-8in)	11-12	Plant on a sunny and sheltered site. Will grow in alkaline soil.
Darwin Hybrids	Large and brilliant flowers.	60-75cm (2-2½ft)	15-20cm (6-8in)	5	Yellow, red, orange, cream combinations.	15-20cm (6-8in)	11-12	Plant in a sunny and sheltered site. Will grow in alkaline soil.
Darwin Tulips	Strong stems. Large and rounded flowers.	60-75cm (2-2½ft)	15-20cm (6-8in)	5	Orange, red, yellow, pink, violet and white.	15-20cm (6-8in)	11-12	Plant in a sunny and sheltered site. Will grow in alkaline soil.
Double Early Tulips	Paeony-like, sometimes frilled.	30-37cm (12-15in)	15cm (6in)	4	Yellow, pink, orange, white and scarlet.	15-20cm (6-8in)	11-12	Plant in a sunny and sheltered site. Will grow in alkaline soil.
Fosteriana Hybrid Tulips	Large flowers which are blunt-pointed and brilliant in colour.	30-43cm (12-18in)	15cm (6in)	4	Vivid red, deep golden-yellow.	15-20cm (6-8in)	11-12	Plant in a sunny and sheltered site. Will grow in alkaline soil.
Greigii Tulips	Blunt, pointed petals which open to show brown or black centres.	18-35cm (7-14in)	13cm (5in)	4-5	Orange, red, scarlet, yellow, pink, bi-coloured.	15-20cm (6-8in)	11-12	Plant in a sunny and sheltered site. Will grow in alkaline soil.
Kaufmanniana Hybrid Tulips	Flowers opening into six-pointed stars.	15-25cm (6-10in)	13cm (5in)	3	Yellow, salmon, pink, white and red.	15-20cm (6-8in)	11-12	Plant in a sunny and sheltered site. Will grow in alkaline soil.
Lily-flowered Tulips	Long waisted flowers, with pointed petals that bend outwards at their tips.	45-60cm (1½-2ft)	15cm (6in)	4-5	White, yellow, red, pink, lavender, bi-coloured.	15-20cm (6-8in)	11-12	Plant in a sunny and sheltered site. Will grow in alkaline soil.
Parrot Tulips	Large fringed flowers, sometimes with twisted bi-coloured petals.	60cm (2ft)	20cm (8in)	4-5	Pink, red, mauve, orange, white, yellow, bi-coloured.	15-20cm (6-8in)	11-12	Plant in a sunny and sheltered site, but they may need protection from cold winds.
Single Early Tulips	The flowers open out flat.	20-36cm (8-14in)	10-15cm (4-6in)	4	White, yellow, red, violet and bi-coloured.	15-20cm (6-8in)	11-12	Plant in a sunny and sheltered site. Will grow alkaline soil.
Triumph Tulips	Sturdy stems, with angular flowers.	40-50cm (16-20in)	15cm (6in)	4-5	Orange, red, pink, white and bi-coloured.	15-20cm (6-8in)	11-12	Plant in sunny and sheltered site. Will grow in alkaline soil.

BULBS FOR THE GARDEN

Species and Varieties	Height	Spread	Flowering period	Fragrance	Suitable for the rock garden	Light requirement	Hardiness	Description
Allium (see page 76)								
Alstroemeria Peruvian Lily	60cm (2ft)	30cm (1ft)	6-8			○	★★	Clusters of trumpet-like flowers, mainly in shades of pink and salmon. Difficult to establish.
Amaryllis belladonna Belladonna Lily	60cm (2ft)	30cm (1ft)	9	✿		○	★★	Fragrant rose-red star-like blooms in a small group at the top of each stem. Best at base of south-facing wall.
Anemone coronaria Windflower	23cm (9in)	15cm (6in)	2-10			◉	★★★★	Excellent and popular cut flowers. The flowering period depends on planting time, and whether protection is available. De Caen type are single, the St Brigid semi-double.
Brodiaea laxa	60cm (2ft)	7.5cm (3in)	7			○	★★★★	Violet-purple flowers top strong, wiry stems. Very useful for cutting.
Camassia Bear Grass	45cm (1½ft)	30cm (1ft)	6-7		▲	◉	★★★★	Graceful spikes of blue-purple or white flowers with narrow petals and prominent stamens.
Chionodoxa luciliae Glory of the Snow	15cm (6in)	7.5cm (3in)	2-3		▲	◉	★★★★	Easily grown, and always welcome when they open their blue and white flowers in February. There is also a pink variety.
Colchicum autumnale Autumn Crocus	15cm (6in)	23cm (9in)	9-11			◉	★★★★	The flowers, like a large crocus, appear before the leaves. Mauve flowers. Nice planted in groups in grass.
C. byzantinum	15cm (6in)	23cm (9in)	9			◉	★★★★	Bright, mauve flowers like a loose crocus. Best in small groups.

Species and Varieties	Height	Spread	Flowering period	Fragrance	Suitable for the rock garden	Light requirement	Hardiness	Description
C. speciosum	15cm (6in)	23cm (9in)	10-11			⊙	★★★★	Similar to previous two, but violet or rose-puple with a white throat.
Crinum x powellii	60cm (2ft)	30cm (1ft)	7-9			○	★	Clusters of rose-pink lily-shaped flowers on long stems. Protect young shoots from frost.
Crocosmia masonorum	60cm (2ft)	15cm (6in)	7-8			○	★★★★	Flame-orange trumpet-shaped flowers — like montbretia but with the blooms facing upwards.
Crocus (large-flowered)	10cm (4in)	10cm (4in)	3		▲	⊙	★★★★	Too well-known to need description. Plant in groups for best effect.
C. chrysanthus	7.5cm (3in)	7.5cm (3in)	2-3		▲	⊙	★★★★	There are many named varieties of this and other species crocus, and all the usual crocus colours are present. Small but attractive flowers.
C. speciosus	13cm (5in)	7.5cm (3in)	9-10		▲	⊙	★★★★	The rich violet-blue of this autumn-flowering crocus looks nice among autumn cyclamen. Seeds and spreads easily.
Cyclamen coum	7.5cm (3in)	15cm (6in)	12-3		▲	◐	★★★★	Miniature, and perfectly hardy, versions of the popular houseplant. Flowers pink to carmine, sometimes white.
C. europaeum	10cm (4in)	15cm (6in)	7-9	❀	▲	◐	★★★★	Similar to C. coum, but with crimson flowers in the autumn.
C. neapolitanum	10cm (4in)	15cm (6in)	8-11		▲	◐	★★★★	Another miniature cyclamen. Nicely marbled foliage. Flowers mauve to pale pink. There is also a white variety.
Endymion hispanicus Giant Bluebell	30cm (1ft)	15cm (6in)	4-6			●	★★★★	A large-flowered version of our woodland Bluebell. There are white forms and pink, besides various shades of blue.
Eranthis hyemalis Winter Aconite	10cm (4in)	7.5cm (3in)	2-3		▲	●	★★★★	Vivid yellow flowers rather like buttercups. Excellent naturalized.
Erythronium dens-canis Dog's Tooth Violet	15cm (6in)	10cm (4in)	4-5		▲	◐	★★★★	Dainty pink, purple, rose or white flowers that nod on slender stems.
Fritillaria imperialis Crown Imperial	90cm (3ft)	38cm (15in)	4			⊙	★★★★	A stately plant with a head of bell-shaped flowers surrounding a stout stem, topped with a crown of leaves.
F. meleagris Snakeshead Fritillary	30cm (1ft)	15cm (6in)	4-5			⊙	★★★★	An unusual plant with bell-shaped drooping flowers, in various shades that form a chequered pattern.
Galanthus nivalis Snowdrop	10cm (4in)	10cm (4in)	1-2		▲	⊙	★★★★	One of the delights of late winter, when the nodding white bells make an appearance.
Galtonia candicans Summer Hyacinth	1m (3½ft)	23cm (9in)	7-9	❀		○	★★★★	An easy plant to grow. Each spike carries 30 or more white bell-shaped flowers.
Gladiolus (large-flowered)	1.2m (4ft)	15cm (6in)	7-9			○		Too well known to need detailed description. There are also small-flowered species, some of which are hardy.
Hyacinthus Hyacinth	23cm (9in)	15cm (6in)	4-5	❀		⊙	★★★	Although hyacinths are seen at their best indoors, they can also be bedded out with good effect.

Species and Varieties	Height	Spread	Flowering period	Fragrance	Suitable for the rock garden	Light requirement	Hardiness	Description
Ipheion uniflorum Spring Starflower	15cm (6in)	10cm (4in)	3-5	✿	▲	☉	★★★	Gay little flowers, white tinged with pale violet. Plant in a large group.
Iris (See page 76)								
Ixia African Corn Lily	45cm (1½ft)	10cm (4in)	5-6			○	★	Gay and colourful star-shaped flowers carried as spikes on a rather flimsy stem. Best to lift and store for the winter.
Ixiolirion montanum	30cm (1ft)	10cm (4in)	6			○	★★	Blue flowers the shape of chionodoxa on lax stems; good for cutting. If grown outside, provide a sheltered position.
Leucojum aestivum Summer Snowflake	45cm (1½ft)	15cm (6in)	4-5			◑	★★★★	White nodding bells tipped yellowish-green. Requires a damp, peaty soil.
Lilium (See page 77)								
Muscari armeniacum Grape Hyacinth	20cm (8in)	10cm (4in)	4-5	✿	▲	☉	★★★★	Tightly clustered small blue flowers on stout stems. There is also a double-flowered form, which resembles a miniature hyacinth.
Narcissus (See page 76)								
Nerine bowdenii	60cm (2ft)	15cm (6in)	9-11			○	★★	Clusters of delicate pink flowers, resembling some lilies. Attractive planted near a sunny wall.
Ornithogalum nutans	38cm (15in)	15cm (6in)	4-5			☉	★★★★	White and pale green, satin-like blooms carried in loose spikes. Useful naturalized between shrubs.
O. pyramidale	60cm (2ft)	15cm (6in)	6			☉	★★★★	Similar to *O. nutans*, but with large white flowers. Seeds freely.
O. thyrsoides Chincherinchee	45cm (1½ft)	10cm (4in)	5-7			☉	★	White to cream flowers on packed spikes. Last well when cut. Can be grown in most areas if lifted.
O. umbellatum Star of Bethlehem	20cm (8in)	10cm (4in)	5-6			☉	★★★★	White star-like flowers. Spreads rapidly, and looks nice in front of shrubs.
Puschkinia scilloides Striped squill	10cm (4in)	7.5cm (3in)	3-5		▲	☉	★★★★	Pale blue scilla-like flowers with darker blue stripes.
Ranunculus Crowfoot	30cm (1ft)	15cm (6in)	6-7			○	★★★	Beautiful double and semi-double flowers, about 3in (7.5cm) across. In shades of crimson, scarlet, pink, salmon, orange and yellow.
Scilla non-scripta Bluebell	18cm (7in)	10cm (4in)	4-5			●	★★★★	A popular native woodland plant. Useful in a natural setting.
S. sibirica Siberian Squill	15cm (6in)	10cm (4in)	3		▲	◑	★★★★	A popular spring-flowering bulb. Blue nodding flowers.
Sternbergia lutea Yellow Star Flower	10cm (4in)	10cm (4in)	9-10			○	★★★★	This autumn-flowering bulb has very striking bright yellow blooms.
Tulipa (See page 77)								
Zephyranthes candida Flower of the West Wind	15cm (6in)	10cm (4in)	9-10			○	★★	Pure white crocus-like flowers. Has leaves present the whole year. May need winter protection.

Shrubs For Foliage, Flowers and Berries

In Victorian days, shrubs tended to be planted in dense shrubberies, which were often dark and dusty and certainly did not allow the plants to be seen at their best. Often, they were planted too close together, and insufficient consideration was given to their ultimate height and habit.

Happily, shrubs now tend to be planted with more feeling – perhaps partly due to many gardeners being better informed, but also because gardens are now smaller, so people have to choose their shrubs more carefully and use space wisely and effectively.

In many respects it is better to have a few well-chosen shrubs carefully positioned than a whole border of ill-chosen plants. Often, a shrub is planted as a specimen in a lawn, or against a house wall (wall shrubs are discussed on page 111), and these can look superb when in flower or fruit. Certainly no garden is too small for a choice shrub of some kind.

Where there is space for a proper shrub border it is not difficult to have interest and colour the whole year, with the minimum of effort. There is no reason why there should not be a shrub in flower every month of the year. Even in the bleak months of December and January the fragrant chimonanthus and eye-catching hamamelis can be in flower at the back of the border, with sweet-smelling mahonia in front, and an edging of colourful heathers. By using the charts on pages 99 to 108 shrubs can be selected for year round flowers.

The effect of colourful or interesting barks and twigs should not be overlooked when planning for winter interest. On page 88 there are suggestions for shrubs with red, yellow, green, and white winter twigs, and on page 85 there are listed two shrubs with fascinating branch formation, seen at their best when the bushes are out of leaf – the Wire Netting Bush (*Corokia cotoneaster*) and the Corkscrew Hazel (*Corylus avellana* 'Contorta'). And on page 87 there is a list of shrubs with notable berries, most of which are present for at least part of the winter.

It will soon become apparent that there need be nothing dull about a shrub border, at any time of the year.

Planning a shrub border

Plan for an ever-changing picture, and unity without patchiness. Flowering season and colour are most important in this respect, but do not overlook height – and if necessary use a tree to provide it. Trees such as the beautiful upright-growing *Prunus* 'Amanogawa'

Hypericum
Rose of Sharon
(see page 105)

Far left: Potentillas are indispensable shrubs, providing colour over a long period. *Potentilla fruticosa* 'Red Ace' is a fairly recent introduction and the best red shrubby potentilla. (See page 97.)

83

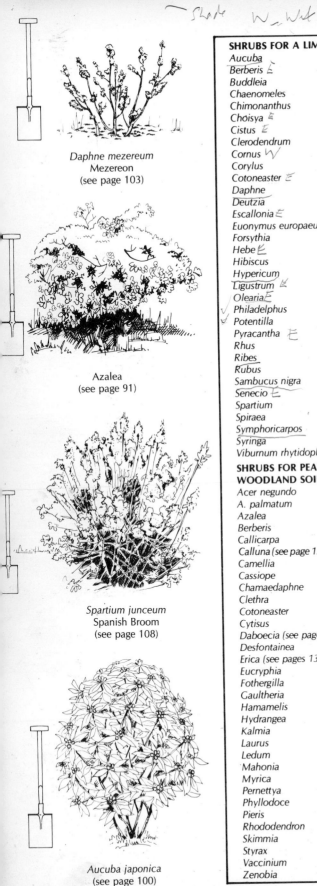

Daphne mezereum
Mezereon
(see page 103)

Azalea
(see page 91)

Spartium junceum
Spanish Broom
(see page 108)

Aucuba japonica
(see page 100)

SHRUBS FOR A LIMY SOIL

Aucuba
Berberis E
Buddleia
Chaenomeles
Chimonanthus
Choisya E
Cistus E
Clerodendrum
Cornus W
Corylus
Cotoneaster E
Daphne
Deutzia
Escallonia E
Euonymus europaeus
Forsythia
Hebe E
Hibiscus
Hypericum
Ligustrum E
Olearia E
Philadelphus
Potentilla
Pyracantha E
Rhus
Ribes
Rubus
Sambucus nigra
Senecio E
Spartium
Spiraea
Symphoricarpos
Syringa
Viburnum rhytidophyllum E

SHRUBS FOR PEATY OR WOODLAND SOIL

Acer negundo
A. palmatum
Azalea
Berberis
Callicarpa
Calluna (see page 137)
Camellia
Cassiope
Chamaedaphne
Clethra
Cotoneaster
Cytisus
Daboecia (see page 134)
Desfontainea
Erica (see pages 133-137)
Eucryphia
Fothergilla
Gaultheria
Hamamelis
Hydrangea
Kalmia
Laurus
Ledum
Mahonia
Myrica
Pernettya
Phyllodoce
Pieris
Rhododendron
Skimmia
Styrax
Vaccinium
Zenobia

SHRUBS FOR SANDY SOIL

Abelia x grandiflora
Artemisia abrotanum
Berberis
Buddleia (not davidii)
Buxus sempervirens
Calluna (see page 137)
Caryopteris
Ceratostigma
Chaenomeles
Choisya ternata
Cistus
Clerodendron
Colutea
Cornus mas
Cotinus
Cotoneaster
Cytisus
Elaeagnus
Daphne
Erica (see pages 133-137)
Escallonia
Euonymus
Fatsia japonica
Fuchsia
Genista
X Halimiocistus sahucii
Halimium
Hebe
Hedysarum
Helianthemum
Helichrysum
Hippophae rhamnoides
Hyssopus aristatus
Lavandula
Leycesteria
Ligustrum ionandrum
Lupinus arboreus
Mahonia aquifolium
Olearia
X Osmarea burkwoodii
Pachysandra
Perovskia atriplicifolia
Philadelphus
Phlomis
Phormium tenax
Potentilla
Pyracantha
Rhus
Romneya
Rosmarinus
Ruscus
Salvia
Santolina
Senecio
Spiraea x vanhouttei
Symphoricarpos
Tamarix
Thymus
Ulex
Yucca

SHRUBS FOR WET PLACES

Betula nana
Cornus alba
Hippophae rhamnoides
Salix hastata
S. lanata
Viburnum opulus 'Sterile'

SHRUBS FOR CLAY SOIL

Abelia
Aucuba
Berberis
Buddleia
Chaenomeles
Choisya
Colutea
Cornus
Corylus
Cotinus
Cotoneaster
Deutzia
Escallonia
Euonymus
Forsythia
Hypericum
Laurus
Mahonia
Osmanthus
Philadelphus
Potentilla
Pyracantha
Ribes
Rosa
Salix
Senecio
Spiraea
Symphoricarpos
Syringa
Viburnum
Vinca
Weigela

SHRUBS WITH ATTRACTIVE FOLIAGE

Acer negundo 'Elegans'
A. n. 'Variegatum'
Artemisia abrotanum
Aucuba japonica
Berberis thunbergii*
Buxus sempervirens 'Aureovariegata'
B. s. 'Elegantissima'
Calluna (see page 137)
Cornus alba 'Sibirica Variegata'
Cotinus coggyria 'Royal Purple'
Cotoneaster
Elaeagnus pungens 'Maculata'
Enkianthus campanulatus*
Eucryphia glutinosa*
Fatsia japonica
Fothergilla monticola*
Helichrysum splendidum
Ilex aquifolium 'Aureo-marginata'
Ligustrum ovalifolium 'Aureum'
Lonicera nitida 'Baggessen's Gold'
Mahonia
Pachysandra terminalis
Phlomis fruticosa
Phormium tenax
Pieris
Rhus typhina 'Laciniata'*
Sambucus nigra 'Aurea'
Santolina chamaecyparissus
Senecio greyi
Weigela florida 'Variegata'
Yucca
* good autumn colour

WINTER FLOWERING SHRUBS

Abeliophyllum
Chimonanthus
Cornus mas
Corylopsis
Daphne mezereum
Erica (see pages 133-137)
Garrya
Hamamelis
Jasminum nudiflorum
Lonicera x purpusii
Mahonia
Viburnum fragrans
V. tinus

SHRUBS FOR SHADY PLACES

Acer palmatum*
Aucuba*
Azalea*
Berberis
Buxus*
Camellia
Chaenomeles
Choisya
Cornus alba
C. kousa
Corylus
Cotoneaster conspicuus 'Decorus'*
C. horizontalis*
C. simonsii
Danae*
Daphne*
Enkianthus
Fatsia japonica
Forsythia
Garrya
Gaultheria*
Hamamelis
Hedera*
Hydrangea
Hypericum*
Leycesteria
Ligustrum*
Lonicera
Mahonia*
Osmanthus
Pachysandra*
Pernettya*
Prunus laurocerasus
P. lusitanica
Pyracantha
Rhododendron*
Ribes*
Rubus
Ruscus*
Sambucus*
Sarcococca*
Skimmia*
Symphoricarpos*
Viburnum tinus
Vinca*
* will live happily under trees

SHRUBS WITH INTERESTING BRANCH FORMATION

Corokia cotoneaster
Corylus avellana 'Contorta'

Fuchsia
(see page 104)

Hamamelis mollis
Witch Hazel
(see page 104)

Mahonia
(see page 106)

Lavandula
Lavender
(see page 105)

Far right, top: Camellias are superb shrubs for an acid soil, and add a touch of stateliness to a garden in March and April. The variety illustrated is 'Beauté de Nantes'. (See pages 92 and 196.)
Far right, bottom: *Hydrangea macrophylla*, a trouble-free shrub for mild districts. (See page 95.)

SHRUBS FOR COASTAL AREAS
Atriplex halimus
Aucuba*
Berberis buxifolia*
B. darwinii*
B. x stenophylla
B. thunbergii
Buddleia
Cistus*
Colutea
Corokia cotoneaster
Cotoneaster (most species: not simonsii)
Cytisus albus
C. x kewensis
Elaeagnus*
Escallonia*
Euonymus japonicus*
Fatsia japonica*
Fuchsia
Garrya elliptica*
Genista
Griseliria*
X Halimiocistus sahucii*
Halimium*
Hebe*
Hippophae rhamnoides
Hydrangea
Ilex aquifolium*
Lavandula*
Lonicera nitida*
Lupinus arboreus
Lycium
Mahonia aquifolium*
Olearia x haastii*
Osmanthus delavayi*
X Osmarea burkwoodii*
Phlomis fruticosa*
Phormium tenax*
Potentilla fruticosa
Ribes sanguineum
Rosemarinus*
Rubus cockburnianus
Salvia officinalis*
Santolina chamaecyparissus*
Senecio*
Spartium junceum
Tamarix
Ulex*
Viburnum tinus*
Vinca minor*
Yucca*
* evergreen

SHRUBS FOR MOIST SITUATIONS
Clethra alnifolia 'Paniculata'
Cornus alba*
C. stolonifera*
Hippophae*
Hydrangea (not hortensis)
Leycesteria
Philadelphus
Salix*
Sambucus
Spiraea x bumalda
Viburnum opulus
Weigela
* will tolerate swampy ground

SHRUBS FOR HOT, DRY SITES
Artemisia
Atriplex
Berberis
Buxus
Caryopteris
Chaenomeles
Cistus
Colutea
Cotinus
Cotoneaster
Cytisus
Elaeagnus
Erica
Euonymus
Genista
Hebe
Hedysarum
Helichrysum
Hippophae
Hypericum
Lavandula
Olearia
Pernettya
Perovskia
Phlomis
Potentilla
Rhus
Rosmarinus
Rubus
Santolina
Senecio
Spartium
Spiraea
Tamarix
Ulex
Vinca
Yucca

SHRUBS WITH DECORATIVE FLOWERS
Azalea
Buddleia
Camellia
Caryopteris
Ceratostigma
Chaenomeles
Chimonanthus
Cistus
Cytisus
Deutzia
Escallonia
Forsythia
Fuchsia
Genista
Hamamelis
Hibiscus
Hydrangea
Philadelphus
Potentilla
Prunus (see page 173)
Rhododendron (see page 98)
Ribes
Romneya
Rosa (see pages 148 and 149)
Spartium
Spiraea
Syringa
Viburnum
Weigela
Yucca

SHRUBS THAT GROW WELL IN TOWNS	SHRUBS WITH ATTRACTIVE FRUIT OR BERRIES
Berberis	*Aucuba*
Buxus	*Berberis*
Chaenomeles	*Callicarpa*
Cotoneaster	*Chaenomeles*
Deutzia	*Clerodendron*
Euonymus	*Colutea*
Fatsia japonica	*Cotoneaster*
Forsythia	*Euonymus*
Hamamelis	*Gaultheria*
Hypericum	*Hippophae*
Olearia x haastii	*Leycesteria*
Osmanthus delavayi	*Mahonia*
Philadelphus	*Pernettya*
Rhus typhina	*Pyracantha*
Rosa	*Rosa (species)*
Symphoricarpos	*Sambucus*
Syringa	*Symphoricarpos*
Viburnum	*Viburnum*
Weigela	

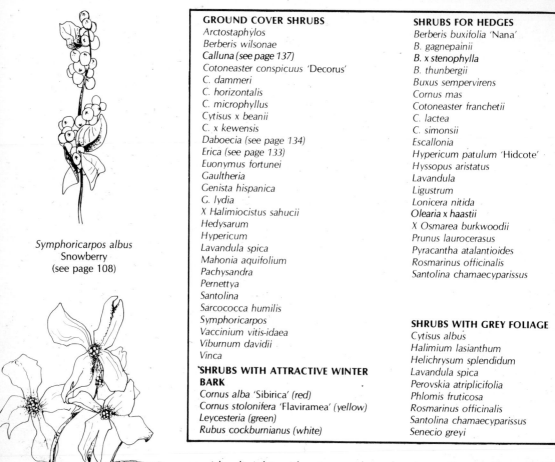

GROUND COVER SHRUBS	SHRUBS FOR HEDGES
Arctostaphylos	Berberis buxifolia 'Nana'
Berberis wilsonae	B. gagnepainii
Calluna (see page 137)	B. x stenophylla
Cotoneaster conspicuus 'Decorus'	B. thunbergii
C. dammeri	Buxus sempervirens
C. horizontalis	Cornus mas
C. microphyllus	Cotoneaster franchetii
Cytisus x beanii	C. lactea
C. x kewensis	C. simonsii
Daboecia (see page 134)	Escallonia
Erica (see page 133)	Hypericum patulum 'Hidcote'
Euonymus fortunei	Hyssopus aristatus
Gaultheria	Lavandula
Genista hispanica	Ligustrum
G. lydia	Lonicera nitida
X Halimiocistus sahucii	Olearia x haastii
Hedysarum	X Osmarea burkwoodii
Hypericum	Prunus laurocerasus
Lavandula spica	Pyracantha atalantioides
Mahonia aquifolium	Rosmarinus officinalis
Pachysandra	Santolina chamaecyparissus
Pernettya	
Santolina	
Sarcococca humilis	
Symphoricarpos	SHRUBS WITH GREY FOLIAGE
Vaccinium vitis-idaea	Cytisus albus
Viburnum davidii	Halimium lasianthum
Vinca	Helichrysum splendidum
SHRUBS WITH ATTRACTIVE WINTER BARK	Lavandula spica
	Perovskia atriplicifolia
Cornus alba 'Sibirica' (red)	Phlomis fruticosa
Cornus stolonifera 'Flaviramea' (yellow)	Rosmarinus officinalis
Leycesteria (green)	Santolina chamaecyparissus
Rubus cockburnianus (white)	Senecio greyi

Symphoricarpos albus
Snowberry
(see page 108)

Cornus florida
Flowering Dogwood
(see page 101)

Rosmarinus officinalis
Rosemary
(see page 108)

provides height without spread, and masses of magnificent pink blossom in spring. Ground cover is equally important, and prostrate, ground-hugging types should be used beneath larger specimens. They are attractive in their own right, but also help by smothering weeds and reducing maintenance.

Do not overlook evergreens, which can be an effective foil for other shrubs, as well as being attractive themselves. But avoid too many conifers in a shrub border — their very different outlines can cause them to look out of place.

It is often difficult to visualize the final height of shrubs when they are bought, but this must be taken into account when planning and planting. The heights mentioned in this chapter are only averages, and can vary considerably according to soil and site. The *rate* of growth is a further problem, as some shrubs grow rapidly while others take many years to reach a significant size. This may mean the border has gaps for several years, although the problem can be overcome by planting two or three specimens instead of one, and gradually thinning as the space is filled. It's an expensive solution, but an effective one — and sometimes the thinned shrubs can be moved to another part of the garden. Another idea is to plant non-shrubby subjects among them for a season or so. Mixed borders can be very effective.

The final choice of shrubs must be a matter of personal taste, but with something as permanent as a shrub or tree it should never be a hasty decision, and always match the plants to the soil and site.

Fortunately, most shrubs are tolerant of quite widely differing soils, and it is only when extremely alkaline (chalky) or acid (peaty or thin, sandy) soils are encountered that particular care must be taken when selecting species. Even then, some genera are notably tolerant of extremes — cotoneaster and berberis are examples, which is very fortunate as these are two indispensable groups.

Buying shrubs

Most shrubs are probably bought from a garden centre, but many are still purchased from specialist nurseries, and often ordered by post. The roots may be bare, contained in a wrapped ball of soil, or growing in a container.

Without doubt the container-grown plant is likely to continue growing with the least check. Balled plants, which have been lifted with a soil-ball, enable many subjects to be lifted and transplanted successfully that would otherwise be difficult as bare-root plants. Bare-root plants are an attraction in terms of labour and carriage, and many plants will transplant successfully this way if treated properly on arrival. But only buy them if you are reasonably sure the roots have not been allowed to dry out.

When buying a container-grown plant, try lifting it by the stem — if the full weight of pot and compost is not held firmly it is not established and is best avoided.

Do not be influenced by size — often a small specimen will transplant more readily and grow more quickly than a larger one.

Preparation and planting

Like trees, shrubs will remain on the same site for many years, and there is only one chance to get the preparation right. Always dig the ground thoroughly, ideally two spits (spade depths) deep, and be as generous as possible with compost or other organic material. This is also the time to clear the ground of deep-rooted perennial weeds. The ground should always be left for a month or two between digging and planting, and any annual weeds that have germinated can be hoed off if they appear.

Dig a hole large enough to accommodate all the roots without cramping, and spread them out as naturally as possible. If the plant is balled, however, try not to disturb the ball.

Cover bare-root plants with a damp sack or cloth to protect them from cold, drying wind while preparing the planting holes. Fill round the roots with a mixture of damp peat and soil. Ease bare-rooted shrubs up and down a little to ensure that soil dribbles between the roots.

The hessian around balled plants can be left on as it will decay in the soil, but plastic wrapping must be removed.

Tread the soil firmly, but fork out footprints so that the soil structure is not affected.

Delay planting if the ground is waterlogged or frozen. Leave bare-root plants in the wrapping in a frost-free place and keep them damp, but if they arrive much before the ground is ready place the roots in a shallow trench and cover them with moist soil.

Leycesteria formosa
Pheasant Berry
(see page 105)

Cornus mas
Cornelian Cherry
(see page 101)

Weigela
(see page 109)

89

Make holes for container-grown plants fractionally larger than the container, then fill in with peat and fine soil.

The best time to plant deciduous shrubs and trees is mid-October and until the end of March, provided the ground is not frozen or waterlogged. Evergreens are best planted in either September and October or April and May. Naturally, container-grown plants can be planted at any time the ground is not frozen, although regular watering will be necessary in dry summer weather.

Some specimen shrubs may need staking, in which case use the methods described for trees on page 169.

Pruning

Pruning is not a mysterious art, and should not be approached with the apprehension it sometimes generates. There are a few basic rules, and fortunately most shrubs need little regular pruning; often it is sufficient to remove dead flower heads and simply trim to a good shape.

Spring-flowering shrubs, such as forsythia and Flowering Currants, should be pruned immediately after flowering. Cut back flowered shoots to fresh young growths on the main branches, and thin out weak and crowded shoots.

Shrubs which flower in late summer and early autumn and blooming on the current year's growth, are best pruned hard in early spring. Examples are fuchsias, potentillas, hibiscus and *Buddleia davidii*.

Bottom: Fothergillas require a neutral or lime-free soil. Both *F. major* (illustrated) and the similar *F. monticola* have striking autumn colour. (See page 104.)

Below: The Wood Olive, *Elaeagnus pungens* 'Maculata', is a useful variegated evergreen for a hot, dry site or for sandy soil. (See page 95.)

Winter-flowering shrubs can have weak growth and diseased branches cut out in spring, otherwise just shape the plant as necessary.

Evergreens should be pruned in April, so that any unsightly cuts are quickly hidden by new growth. Only weak, straggly or diseased shoots need to be cut out. If Box, Lavender, rhododendrons or Lavender Cotton have become bare at the base or have grown too large, cut back hard in spring.

Some good garden shrubs

Acer negundo: This can be grown as a large shrub or small tree, and is described on page 170.

Aucuba japonica: A particularly useful evergreen for town gardens, and one that does well in shade. The variegated varieties, however, have better marking in some sun. It is also a good plant for tubs or urns (see pages 100, 196 and 204) and even indoors as a house-plant (see page 213).

Female plants may produce bright scarlet berries. Prune in May or June to restrict its size.

Azalea: There are two distinct groups of azalea – deciduous and evergreen (Japanese Azalea). Deciduous azaleas tend to grow taller than the evergreen kind – about 1·5m (5ft) instead of 90cm (3ft) – and the flowers are larger.

Because some flowers fade in strong sunlight, and late spring frosts can damage flower buds, plant azaleas in a position sheltered

Bottom: *Acer palmatum* 'Dissectum' has a spreading appearance, and looks at its best when arching over stones or a dry wall. (See page 99 and 194.)

Below: Skimmias are useful plants for shade or industrial areas, but male and female plants will be required for the production of red berries. *S. reevesiana* has both sexes on the same plant, but this species is not suitable for chalky soils, although *S. japonica* varieties will grow on acid or chalk soil. (See page 97.)

Rhododendron 'Mistake'
(see page 97)

Buddleia davidii
Butterfly Bush
(see page 100)

Hibiscus syriacus
Tree Hollyhock
(see page 105)

from early morning sunshine. Remove the dead flower heads from the larger-flowered deciduous kinds.

Azaleas can be grown successfully in tubs (see page 196), but they must be given lime-free water.

Berberis (Barberry): This useful group of plants will tolerate a wide range of soils, and is suitable for many purposes. Some species make excellent flowering hedges (see pages 156, 157, 161, 162, 163 and 165), though their sharp spines also make them functional.

There are both deciduous and evergreen species. Two popular evergreen kinds are B. darwinii and B. x stenophylla.

B. darwinii is an excellent plant, having pleasant, small, dark green, shiny leaves, and large bunches of small deep yellow flowers in April, with a bonus of purple berries in early autumn. B. x stenophylla has long arching sprays of yellow flowers in April, and is often seen used as a hedging plant.

One of the most popular deciduous varieties is B. thunbergii, which has pale yellow flowers speckled with red in spring, and bright red fruits to follow. The normal type has green leaves with red autumn tints, but B. t. 'Atropurpurea' has colourful dark bronze leaves during spring and summer, turning to a vivid red in autumn. There is also a dwarf version, B. t. 'Atropurpurea Nana' which only grows to about 45cm (1½ft).

Buddleia (Butterfly Bush): A useful and attractive shrub, easy to grow – as the number of davidii type naturalized on railway embankments and derelict sites in cities testifies. B. davidii is the one usually seen, having long terminal flower spikes on arching stems. The fragrant flowers are particularly attractive to butterflies. Colours are usually shades of blue, purple or red, and various named varieties are available. The plants are a delight in July and August. B. globosa, the Orange Ball Tree, is totally different in appearance – having orange ball-shaped flower heads. It will grow to about 3m (10ft) and only needs to be pruned to shape after flowering. It is only really hardy and floriferous in the South. B. davidii, however, will benefit from hard pruning in March, cutting back to within about 5cm (2in) of the old wood.

Calluna (Heather): See pages 127 to 137.

Camellia: A superb shrub for an acid, peaty soil. Despite the exotic appearance of their large, almost rose-like blooms, which are produced in winter or early spring, these are hardy plants. In northern areas, however, they need some sun to allow the wood to ripen sufficiently for the formation of flower buds. Otherwise a shady site is required. Camellias can be grown in tubs or pots (see page 196), but they should be watered regularly with lime-free water. (Illustrated on page 87.)

Ceanothus: This splendid blue-flowered shrub, ideal for a sunny wall, is described on page 119.

Chaenomeles (Japanese Quince): Another outstanding wall shrub, once known as cydonia. See page 118.

Chimonanthus (Winter Sweet): A delightful shrub, especially useful because it bears its fragrant yellow flowers from December to February. A well-drained sheltered site on chalky soil suits it best, and it responds well to the protection of a south or west facing wall.

These plants take some time to become established.

Choisya (Mexican Orange Blossom): Although not fully hardy, the Mexican Orange Blossom is a good shrub for mild districts, and its white, heavily fragrant flowers in May make it a good choice to plant beneath a window or by a door. The evergreen leaves are aromatic when crushed. Pruning consists of no more than cutting out any frost-damaged shoots in March.

Cornus (Dogwood): A few species, such as *C. florida* 'Rubra' and *C. mas*, are grown for their flowers; but most are cultivated for their attractive red stems, so conspicuous in winter. *C. alba* is the species usually grown for this purpose, but there are varieties with variegated foliage, which provides interest over a longer period. *C. a.* 'Sibirica Variegata', *C. a.* 'Elegantissima' and *C. a.* 'Spaethii' are all good variegated kinds.

Two other species notable for their winter bark are *C. stolonifera*, the Red Osier Dogwood, and *C. s.* 'Flaviramea', the Yellow-barked Dogwood.

Prune those grown for their coloured bark by cutting back very hard every second March, as this encourages plenty of fresh new growth.

The Cornelian Cherry (*C. mas*) has clusters of small yellow flowers on bare branches in March, and is undemanding to grow.

The Flowering Dogwood (*C. florida* 'Rubra') and *C. kousa* must have an acid soil. But if this can be provided they will both delight with their flowers. The Flowering Dogwood is a choice shrub with conspicuous rosy-red bracts in May. *C. kousa* has creamy-white bracts, and both have good autumn leaf colour. They can form a small tree.

Corylus: The species most of interest to gardeners is *C. avellana* 'Contorta', the Corkscrew Hazel. It is interesting in winter, when the zig-zag pattern of the stems can be seen most clearly. The plant is especially attractive in February when festooned with yellow catkins. As the contorted branches are popular for floral decoration, this usually eliminates the need to prune them.

Cotinus coggyria (Smoke Plant): This shrub, which used to be known as *Rhus cotinus*, is grown for its fluffy flower heads, which give an impression of smoke when viewed from a distance. The leaves turn yellow before falling. (Illustrated on page 30.)

A variety grown for its purple leaves is 'Royal Purple'.

Cotoneaster: The cotoneasters are among our most important shrubs. There are deciduous and evergreen kinds, and many are very diverse in form. They are also very easy to grow, and suit most soils.

The main attraction of cotoneasters lies in their brilliant berries; many also provide autumn colour. Some species are also excellent for ground cover, such as *C. dammeri*, which grows only a few centimetres (inches) high but covers several square metres (yards) in area. Another prostrate kind is *C. conspicuus* 'Decorus', which has long-lasting beautiful red berries. (Illustrated on page 94.)

One of the best deciduous species is the Fish-bone Cotoneaster (*C. horizontalis*), a particularly useful shrub for planting against a north or east wall. It has a lovely herring-bone pattern of growth. The small leaves have good autumn colour, and when they drop there are still the red berries. It is also good for carpeting banks.

Choisya ternata
Mexican Orange Blossom
(see page 101)

Cornus kousa
Dogwood
(see page 101)

Buddleia globosa
Orange Ball Tree
(see page 92)

Rhododendron fortunei
(see page 98)

For an upright specimen shrub, try *C. simonsii*, a semi-evergreen much loved by bees when in flower, and producing a profusion o scarlet berries.

Cytisus (Broom): Gay and spectacular shrubs, easy to grow in mos well-drained soils provided extremely acid or alkaline kinds are avoided, and they are given a position in full sun.

Because Brooms do not like root disturbance it is best to buy container-grown plants.

Pruning needs some care as they will not respond if cut back into old, hardened wood. Cut back the previous summer's growth by up to two-thirds after flowering.

Daboecia: See pages 132 and 134.

Daphne: This is a delightful plant to enhance the garden in February. Its fragrant mauve flowers are borne on bare stems. There is a white form of this shrub. The pink flowers of *D. x burkwoodi* are less spectacular but equally fragrant.

Daphnes, which will grow on a chalky soil, should never be allowed to dry out, and if planted near a wall must have plenty of compost incorporated at planting time.

The scarlet berries are poisonous.

Deutzia: These are pleasant summer-flowering shrubs, useful for a sunny site, although pink-flowered forms have better colour if provided with semi-shade. Shades of pink, red and white are normal, and there are double and single forms. Among the species, *D. x magnifica* is a vigorous shrub with white flowers; there are named varieties, of which 'Longipetala' is one of the best. *D. x rosea* has wide bell-shaped pink or white flowers, depending on variety, on arching branches. This is much more compact than most other types, and forms a shrub of about 90cm (3ft).

Below: *Cotoneaster conspicuus* is a spreading shrub with long-lasting red berries. (See page 93.)

Among the hybrids are 'Magician' (large deep-pink flowers with a mauve-pink edge and a purple stripe on the back of each petal: 'Mont Rose', a rose-pink variety with darker shades, and very free-flowering; and 'Contraste', which has star-shaped lilac-pink flowers with a purple band on the back of each petal.

Elaeagnus pungens 'Maculata': A good, evergreen variegated shrub, each leaf having a bold splash of gold down the centre. Any all-green branches must be cut out. (Illustrated on page 90.)

Erica: See pages 127 to 137.

Escallonia: Although escallonias are often used for hedging, they can look effective when planted as single specimens. This plant is described on pages 156 and 164.

Fatsia japonica: See page 196.

Forsythia: One of the most popular, and one of the easiest shrubs. 'Lynwood' is one of the best forms of *F. x intermedia*, and a justifiably popular variety. The dense yellow flowers smother the branches in early April.

Fuchsia magellanica: See page 157.

Garrya elliptica (Tassel Bush): A nice specimen evergreen, ideal for planting as a wall shrub. It is described on page 119.

Hamamelis mollis (Witch Hazel): An interesting and welcome winter-flowering shrub for moist soil well enriched with peat or leafmould. The sulphur-yellow flowers, borne on leafless branches from December till February, are sweetly fragrant.

Hebe (Veronica): These are nice evergreens, but not fully hardy, and best planted in coastal areas. However, they stand up well to city dust and grime, and it is only long spells of severe weather that are likely to injure the plants.

Among the popular species and varieties are 'Carl Teschner' (an excellent plant; low, spreading habit and spikes of small violet flowers; dainty foliage on wiry dark stems), *H. armstrongii* (unusual cypress-like golden-green foliage, resembling a conifer), 'Margery Fish' (a hardy variety flowering from June to September and beyond; 2·5cm (1in) lavender flower heads fading to white at the base, freely produced). *H. pinguifolia* 'Pagei' is a charming low-growing foliage plant, having small silver-grey leaves and tiny white flowers. It associates well with heathers.

Hedera: See page 115.

Hibiscus: See page 197.

Hippophae rhamnoides: See page 165.

Hydrangea: The climbing hydrangea (*H. petiolaris*) is described on page 116. There are two main types of bushy hydrangea — *H. paniculata*, a hardy white-flowered shrub, and the florist's type (*H. macrophylla*), which is not dependably hardy.

H. paniculata 'Grandiflora' has broad spikes of creamy-white flowers rather like Lilac in shape. Prune all one-year-old wood in early spring to produce large flowers.

The various varieties of *H. macrophylla* are very attractive. Provided they are not in a cold area they will survive with little attention, though they will be much better if provided with plenty of moisture. Flower colour is affected not only by variety but also by soil. In an alkaline soil, the blue varieties will turn pink or mauve, although this can be counteracted by applying a blueing-powder

Forsythia
(see page 104)

Below: *Hypericum patulum* 'Hidcote' bears a profusion of yellow flowers in late summer, and is one of the most popular flowering shrubs. Almost any well-drained soil is suitable for this plant, in sun or semi-shade. (See page 105.)

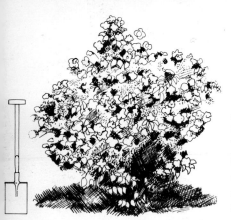

Philadelphus
Mock Orange
(see page 106)

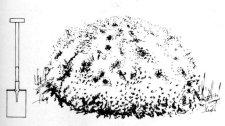

Genista lydia
(see page 104)

Hydrangea paniculata
(see page 105)

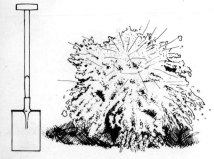

Cytisus x kewensis
(see page 102)

every two weeks throughout the growing season. Leave the dea[d] heads on during the winter as they may afford some protection; i[n] very districts, protection may be required. (Illustrated on page 87[.]

Ilex (Holly): Some good varieties are discussed on page 172. Plan[t] male and female plants to be sure of a good crop of berries.

Jasminum nudiflorum (Winter Jasmine): A good winter-flowerin[g] shrub to grow against a wall, or to scramble up a bank. The yello[w] flowers make a brave display in the worst weather. Prun[e] sideshoots after flowering.

Kalmia latifolia (Calico Bush): A good evergreen for a lime-free soi[l.] A peaty soil in semi-shade will bring out the best in this prett[y] shrub, with its cluster of five-sided pink flowers in June. Littl[e] attention is required beyond removing dead flower heads.

Laurus nobilis (Sweet Bay): See page 172.

Lavandula (Lavender): Although single specimens of this aromati[c] plant can look effective, they are usually grown as a hedge. Se[e] pages 158 and 159.

Ligustrum (Privet): See page 154.

Lonicera: See page 117.

Magnolia: There are many species of this beautiful spring-flowerin[g] shrub or tree. *M. x soulangeana*, with its large tulip-shaped flowers[,] is described on page 172, but another gem, more shrub-like i[n] habit, is *M. stellata*. It grows slowly to 3m (10ft), and the bushes ar[e] covered with white star-shaped blooms in March and April.

Although magnolias are able to tolerate the atmospheric pollu[-] tion of large towns, they must have a deep, rich, and lime-free soi[l] for the best results.

Protect newly-planted specimens from cold winds, and bu[y] balled plants. Mulching will help them to become established.

Mahonia: Useful evergreens, with sprays of yellow flowers in lat[e] winter and early spring. 'Charity' is a hybrid with exquisitel[y] scented flowers smelling rather like Lily-of-the-valley.

Mahonias are useful for shady areas, and good for ground cover[.] The large leaves usually have good autumn colour, and the yello[w] flowers are followed by black berries.

Leafmould and peat added to the soil will improve growth.

Malus (Crab): Can be treated as a shrub or tree; the genus i[s] discussed on pages 173 and 174.

Olearea haastii (Daisy Bush): A good coast shrub, used as [a] specimen or to form a hedge. See page 162.

Osmanthus delavayi (Fragrant Olive): An adaptable shrub that wil[l] grow on most soils, in sun or partial shade. The small tubular whit[e] flowers are fragrant, and contrast well with the deep evergree[n] foliage. (Illustrated on page 99.)

As the shrub is not fully hardy, avoid a cold easterly or northerl[y] aspect.

Osmarea burkwoodii: See page 156.

Philadelphus (Mock Orange): A superb garden plant, undemandin[g] and able to thrive in poor soils, including chalk. See page 158.

Pieris: Nice shrubs for a lime-free soil, associating well wit[h] rhododendrons and Heathers, which have similar requirements.

The colourful red shoots in spring are the main attraction. *P[.]* *formosa* 'Forrestii' and *P. f.* 'Wakehurst' are good varieties, bu[t]

'orest Flame' is hardier. Usually they require a sheltered site where
they will not be subject to rapid thawing from early-morning sun.

Potentilla: These first-rate plants flower from June until the first
frosts. They are easy to grow but perform best on a light, well-
drained soil. They will be satisfactory in partial shade but their
single flowers, in shades of white, yellow or orange-red, are most
prolific in full sun. (Illustrated on page 6.)

Pyracantha (Firethorn): The bright red or orange berries of this plant
are a familiar sight in gardens, and are usually carried well into
winter. They are seen at their best grown up a wall (see page 118).

Pyracanthas are easy to grow, and tolerate most soils, including
chalk. They thrive in sun or partial shade.

To avoid transplanting losses, buy pot or container-grown plants.
Prune to shape in May or June.

Rhododendron: This king of spring flowers must have an acid,
peaty soil. Many species and hybrids grow far too large for the
average garden, but there are types suitable for small gardens –
some are even suitable for a rock garden. Some good species are
listed on page 98.

Rhododendrons must never be allowed to become dry at the
root, but do not water with hard water containing lime. Mulching is
beneficial.

Remove dead flower heads.

Rhus typhina (Stag's Horn Sumach): See page 173.

Ribes (Flowering Currant): This common garden shrub will grow
well in most garden soils. Its pink or red flowers are always a
welcome sight in spring, and they will bloom in sun or shade,
though more prolifically in sun.

Prune out old wood immediately after flowering.

Rosmarinus (Rosemary): See page 159.

Salix (Willow): Not all Willows are large trees. There are shrubby
kinds, such as the Woolly Willow (*S. lanata*), which barely reaches
90cm (3ft). It has silvery-grey felted leaves and golden catkins in
May. *S. hastata* 'Wehrhahnii' is another dwarf species with white
catkins in May, which give the impression of hanging icicles.

Any ordinary soil is suitable, provided it is not too light or dry.
Pruning is seldom necessary for these dwarf species.

Santolina chamaecyparissus (Lavender Cotton): See page 159.

Senecio greyi: A widely-planted and extremely useful grey-leaved
shrub, with a low, spreading habit. It will be happy on most soils,
but prefers full sun.

If the plant becomes too large, cut back quite severely in spring.
It will soon recover.

Besides the grey, felted leaves, the plant is covered with bright
yellow daisy-like flowers in July and August.

Skimmia: A neat evergreen with clusters of tiny scented flowers in
spring. The female plants produce brilliant red berries which
remain through the winter, but plant at least one male to three
females to be sure of a good crop. *Skimmia reevesiana* carries both
sexes on the same plant. (Illustration on page 91.)

A good plant for shade, but avoid alkaline soils.

Spiraea: See page 157.

Symphoricarpos albus (Snowberry): A suckering shrub ideal for the

Deutzia
(see page 103)

Senecio greyi
(see page 108)

Acer palmatum
Japanese Maple
(see page 99)

Spiraea
(see page 108)

97

Rhododendron
(see page 98)

Far right: The Fragrant Olive, *Osmanthus delavayi*, bears a profusion of fragrant, white flowers in April. It grows well on clay, and survives town atmosphere. (See page 96.)
Below: The Glory Tree, *Clerodendron trichotomum*, is a distinctive shrub. The fragrant, white flowers are followed by turquoise berries. (See page 101.)

wilder parts of the garden or to fill waterside banks, but they are also suitable for a large shrub border if kept under control. The rather insignificant summer flowers are followed by shiny white berries, remaining on the plant for many months. Besides the white form there are types with pink or lilac berries.

Syringa vulgaris (Lilac): An excellent shrub for garden decoration or cutting. Lilacs will grow well on most soils, including chalk, but must have full sun for a good display of flowers. Some varieties can be grown as standards.

There are many fine varieties, and the following are only examples of the range available: 'Maud Notcutt' (single, white), 'Souvenir de Louis Spath' (single, purple), 'Charles Joly' (double, purple), 'Katherine Havemeyer' (purple-mauve, very fragrant, double), 'Madame Lemoine' (double, white).

Most pruning can be achieved by cutting flowers for indoor decoration, but any thin, unproductive wood should be cut out immediately after flowering. Also remove any suckers that appear from the base.

Viburnum: See pages 157 and 158.

Weigela: See page 157.

SPECIES RHODODENDRONS

Species	Height	Colour	Flowering Time	Hardy	Description
Rhododendron augustinii	2.4-3.6m (8-12ft)	Pale lilac through to purplish-blue	4-5	★★★★	A tall and willowy shrub with masses of flower trusses.
R. calostrotum	60cm-1.2m (2-4ft)	Rosy-purple or dusky-red	5-6	★★★★	Forms a slow-growing bush with many small flowers.
R. cinnabarinum	1.5-2.4m (5-8ft)	Orange-yellow	5	★★★★	Some forms are darker in colour, and one variety, 'Roylei', is rich plum-red.
R. fargesii	1.5-4.5m (5-15ft)	Rose-pink	3-4	★★★★	A large shrub.
R. forrestii	60cm (2ft)	Waxy-red	4-5	★★★★	Needs a damp position, preferably where the roots can run under a rock.
R. fortunei	2.1-3.6m (7-12ft)	Mauve-pink	4-5	★★★★	Attractive foliage, with flowers which are scented.
R. lacteum	2.1-3.6m (7-12ft)	Creamy-white or yellow	4-5	★★★★	Medium to large trusses of delightful flowers.
R. nerriiflorum	90cm-1.8m (3-6ft)	Brilliant red	4-5	★★★★	The leaves are very attractive, being whitish on the undersides.
R. sinogrande	2.1-3.6m (7-12ft)	Creamy-white with a crimson blotch.	4	★★★★	Very attractive large leaves.
R. thomsonii	2.1-3.6m (7-12ft)	Scarlet to crimson	4-5	★★★★	An excellent rhododendron for the larger garden.
R. williamsianum	60cm (2ft)	Pale pink	4	★★★★	An attractive plant for the small garden or rockery.

GOOD GARDEN SHRUBS

Species and Varieties	Height	Evergreen	Flowering period	Fragrance	Light requirement	Suitable for rock garden	Hardiness	Description
Abelia x grandiflora	1.8m (6ft)		7-10		◯		★★★	A free-flowering semi-evergreen. Pink funnel-shaped flowers with purple-red sepals.
Abeliophyllum distichum	90cm-1.8m (3-6ft)		2-3	✿	◯		★★★	A slow-growing shrub introduced from Korea in 1924. White forsythia-like flowers with orange centres. Grow against a south or west wall.
Acer negundo 'Elegans' Box Elder	9m+ (30ft+)		3-4		⊙		★★★★	Excellent foliage tree that can be grown as a large specimen shrub. Typical Maple leaves are strikingly variegated with bright yellow.
A. n. 'Variegatum' Box Elder	9m+ (30ft+)		3-4		⊙		★★★★	As *A. n.* 'Elegans' except that the variegation is white and green.
A. palmatum Japanese Maple	3-4.5m (10-15ft)				⊙		★★★	Among the elite of foliage shrubs. Some forms have deep purple leaves, others have finely divided foliage.
Arctostaphylos uva-ursi Red Bearberry	90cm-1.2m (3-4ft)	◆	4-7		◯	▲	★★★★	Trailing evergreen with clusters of small pinkish-white flowers.

Species and Varieties	Height	Evergreen	Flowering period	Fragrance	Light requirement	Suitable for rock garden	Hardiness	Description
Artemisia abrotanum Southernwood	90cm (3ft)	●	7-10	🍃	○		★★★★	Feathery grey-green aromatic foliage shrub, popular in old cottage gardens. Prune back to 30cm (1ft) each spring.
Atriplex halimus Tree Purslane	2.4m (8ft)		7		○		★★	An excellent semi-evergreen for seaside planting. Long silvery leaves on arching branches. If damaged by frost it usually recovers.
Aucuba japonica	1.5m (5ft)		3-4		●		★★★★	Useful foliage plant for shade or smoky areas. The type has large green leaves, but there are variegated forms. Female plants have red berries.
Azalea	90cm-1.5m (3-5ft)		4-6					There are both evergreen and deciduous azaleas — see page 91.
Berberis buxifolia 'Nana' Barberry	45cm (18in)	●	5		◐	▲	★★★★	Makes a mound of bottle-green foliage, colouring in winter. The small flowers are amber-yellow. Grows slowly.
B. darwinii Barberry	2.1m (7ft)	●	4-5		◐		★★★★	Brilliant display of small orange-yellow flowers. An outstanding shrub. Berries are bluish-purple.
B. gagnespainii Barberry	1.5m (5ft)	●	5-6		◐		★★★★	Dense growth with narrow crinkled leaves. Will form an impenetrable hedge. Flowers yellow; oval berries black.
Berberis x stenophylla Barberry	3m (10ft)	●	5		◐		★★★★	Cascades of orange-yellow flowers make this a striking shrub. It quickly spreads its branches of spine-tipped leaves.
B. thunbergii Barberry	1.5m (5ft)		5		○		★★★★	A double-value shrub, with pale yellow flowers in spring and bright red fruits and foliage in autumn.
B. wilsonae Barberry	90cm (3ft)		6		○		★★★★	This graceful semi-evergreen is excellent for clothing banks.
Betula nana Birch	60-90cm (2-3ft)				◉	▲	★★★★	A dwarf form of Birch, well suited to a damp spot in the rock garden. Habit is neat.
Buddleia davidii Butterfly Bush	2.1m (7ft)		7-8	✿	○		★★★★	The large panicles, mainly in shades of blue or purple, attract butterflies. Other species are described on page 92.
Buxus sempervirens Box	4.5m (15ft)	●			●		★★★★	A native plant that grows mainly on chalk hills. A fine subject for clipping and topiary work. Small green leaves.
B. s. 'Aurea Maculata'	4.5m (15ft)	●			●		★★★★	Similar to *B. sempervirens* except that the leaves are spotted and blotched with yellow.
B. s 'Elegantissima' Box	90cm (3ft)	●			●		★★★★	Dwarfer than the type. The narrow grey-green leaves are margined light yellow that changes to white. Colour is retained in shade.
Callicarpa bodinieri 'Giraldii'	3m (10ft)		7-9		○		★★	An unusual shrub with an impressive autumn display. Pink flowers are followed by lilac-purple berries. Leaves turn rose-madder.
Calluna (see page 137)								
Camellia japonica	1.5m (5ft)	●	3-4		●		★★★	Beautiful paeony-like flowers, mainly in shades of pink red, and white. Varieties and other species are described on page 92.

Species and Varieties	Height	Evergreen	Flowering period	Fragrance	Light requirement	Suitable for rock garden	Hardiness	Description
Caryopteris x clandonensis Blue Spiraea	1.2m (4ft)		8-10	🍃	○		★★★★	A shrub for massed effect, and one that will grow in almost any soil. Aromatic leaves are grey-green, the small flowers bright blue.
Cassiope lycopodioides	15-45cm (6-18in)	♠	5		◑	▲	★★★★	A prostrate mat forming plant. Flowers are tiny white bells on slender stalks. Rather difficult to grow, requiring cool, moist conditions and lime-free soil.
Ceratostigma willmottianum Plumbago	75cm (2½ft)		7-10		○		★★★★	Blue phlox-shaped flowers. Foliage and seed-heads turn reddish brown. Suitable for shrubbery or herbaceous border.
Chaenomeles speciosa Flowering Quince	1.8m (6ft)		3-6		⊙		★★★★	Lovely shrub trained against a wall — even with a north or east aspect. Flowers mainly red, pink, or white. Fruit edible.
Chamaedaphne calyculata Leather Leaf	60cm (2ft)	♠	4		◑	▲	★★★★	White heather-like flowers on arching branches. Needs a moist, lime-free soil.
Chimonanthus praecox Winter Sweet	2.4m (8ft)		12-1	✿	○		★★★	An excellent wall shrub for winter flower. Yellow cup-shaped flowers are carried on bare twigs. Thrives on chalk.
Choisya ternata Mexican Orange Blossom	1.5m (5ft)	♠	5	✿	◑		★★	Attractive bright green leaves, aromatic when crushed, and clusters of star-like white flowers.
Cistus Rock Rose	60cm-2.4m (2-8ft)	♠	6-7		○		★★	Flowers resemble single roses, and the plants are ideal for hot sunny banks or borders. Attractive white flowers, often blotched.
Clerodendron trichotomum Glory Tree	2.4m (8ft)		8-9	✿	○		★★	A distinctive shrub, its fragrant white flowers being followed by turquoise berries surrounded by crimson calyxes.
Clethra alnifolia 'Paniculata' Sweet Pepper Bush	1.8m (6ft)		8	✿	⊙		★★★★	Long spikes or fragrant creamy-white flowers. Requires a moist, lime-free soil enriched with humus or peat.
Colutea arborescens Bladder Senna	2.4m (8ft)		5-8		○		★★★★	A fast-growing shrub with pinnate leaves and pea-shaped yellow flowers. These are followed by conspicuous inflated pods.
Cornus alba Red-barked Dogwood	2.4m (8ft)		5-6		⊙		★★★★	Like all the Dogwoods, it is easily grown. Produces a thicket of stems that provide crimson colour in winter.
C. a. 'Sibirica Variegata' Westonbirt Dogwood	2.4m (8ft)		5		⊙		★★★★	Winter shoots are brilliant crimson, brighter than the type. Leaves are edged and mottled with white.
C. florida 'Rubra' Flowering Dogwood	3m (10ft)		5		⊙		★★★★	A choice shrub with conspicuous rosy-red bracts at flowering time. It also has good autumn tints and purplish winter twigs.
C. kousa Dogwood	4.5m (15ft)		6		⊙		★★★★	Creamy-white bracts are borne in abundance. Sometimes strawberry-like fruits appear. Like *C. florida* it can form a small tree. Both dislike chalk.
C. mas Cornelian Cherry	4.5m (15ft)		3-4		⊙		★★★★	Masses of small yellow flowers appear on bare branches, followed by red fruit. Has a spreading, open habit.
C. stolonifera Red Osier Dogwood	1.8m (6ft)				⊙		★★★★	A vigorous shrub, sending up many suckers. Dark red shoots in winter.

GOOD GARDEN SHRUBS Continued

Species and Varieties	Height	Evergreen	Flowering period	Fragrance	Light requirement	Suitable for rock garden	Hardiness	Description
C. s. 'Flaviramea' Yellow-barked Dogwood	1.8m (6ft)				◉		★★★★	This yellow-stemmed Dogwood is useful for providing contrast to the red-stemmed kinds in winter.
Corokia cotoneaster Wire-netting Bush	1.8m (6ft)	♠	5		○		★★	The twiggy branches criss-cross to create a tangled effect. Yellow flowers are tiny. Best given protection of a south wall.
Corylopsis spicata	1.8m (6ft)		3-4	✿	◉		★★★	Drooping spikes of fragrant primrose-yellow flowers make this a charming shrub. A sheltered border is best.
Corylus avellana 'Contorta' Corkscrew Hazel	2.4m (8ft)		2		◉		★★★	An interesting plant with its zig-zag stems. Interesting in winter, especially while carrying catkins.
Cotinus coggyria 'Royal Purple' Smoke Plant	3m (10ft)		6-7		◉		★★★★	Fawn-coloured plumes of flowers are produced in profusion. The type has good autumn colour, but this variety has purple leaves
Cotoneaster conspicuous 'Decorus'	30cm (1ft)	♠	5-7		◉	▲	★★★★	Prostrate habit with long whip-like stems. White flowers like miniature Hawthorn, followed by long-lasting red berries.
C. dammeri	7.5cm (1ft)	♠	6		◉	▲	★★★★	In autumn the stems are studded with sealing-wax-red berries
C. franchetii	2.7m (9ft)	♠	6		◉		★★★★	A graceful shrub with arching stems covered with grey-green leaves, and scarlet berries later.
C. horizontalis Fish-bone Cotoneaster	60cm (2ft)		6		◉	▲	★★★★	Ideal for banks or to grow fan-wise against a wall. Branches grow in herring-bone fashion. Small leaves turn orange before falling. Red berries.
C. lactea	3m (10ft)	♠	6		◉		★★★★	Olive green leaves on arching stems. Milky-white flowers. Large clusters of red berries that remain until the New Year.
C. microphyllus	30cm (1ft)	♠	5-6		◉		★★★★	Outstretched branches covered with dark green leaves makes this a good ground cover. Large, bright crimson berries.
C. simonsii	2.7m (9ft)		6-7		◉		★★★★	An erect semi-evergreen, useful as a specimen or for forming a hedge. Bees love the small white flowers. Profusion of scarlet berries.
Cytisus albus White Portugal Broom	2.4m (8ft)		5		○		★★★★	Cascades of white flowers on feathery sprays. Grey-green foliage.
C. x beanii	30cm (1ft)		5-6		○	▲	★★★★	A charming semi-prostrate Broom with golden yellow flowers.
C. x kewensis	30cm (1ft)		5		○	▲	★★★★	Creamy-white or pale sulphur-yellow flowers.
C. scoparius Common Broom	1.8m (6ft)		5		○		★★★★	Widely-grown shrub with pea-like flowers, yellow in the type.
Daboecia (see page 134)								
Danae racemosa Alexandrian Laurel	90cm (3ft)	♠			●		★★★★	Grown for its attractive evergreen foliage.

Above: *Spiraea* x *bumalda* 'Anthony Waterer' is a small but charming shrub that does not look amiss in an herbaceous border. (See page 108.)
Left: The Russian Sage, *Perovskia atriplicifolia*, is a small shrub with attractive sage-scented grey-green leaves. (See page 106.)

GOOD GARDEN SHRUBS Continued

Species and Varieties	Height	Evergreen	Flowering period	Fragrance	Light requirement	Suitable for rock garden	Hardiness	Description
Daphne x *burkwoodii*	90cm (3ft)		5-6	✿	◐		★★★★	A fast-growing semi-evergreen with clusters of fragrant pink flowers.
D. mezereum Mezereon	1.2m (4ft)		2-3	✿	◐		★★★★	A beautiful early flowering shrub with purple-red blooms.
Desfontainea spinosa	1.8m (6ft)	◆	7-9		◐		★	Magnificent plant with trumpet-shaped scarlet and yellow flowers.
Deutzia	1.2-1.8m (4-6ft)		6		☉		★★★★	Easily-grown shrubs of great beauty. Some of the many species and hybrids are described on page 94.
Elaeagnus pungens 'Maculata' Wood Olive	2-4m (8ft)	◆	10-11	✿	☉		★★★★	One of the best variegated shrubs, popular for cutting. Leaves are splashed with a deep yellow.
Enkianthus campanulatus	1.8m (6ft)		5		◐		★★★★	Bell-shaped buff-yellow flowers, veined with red. Leaves turn orange and red in autumn. Needs a lime-free soil.
Erica (see pages 133 to 137)								
Escallonia Chilean Gum Box	2.4m (8ft)	◆	6-7		☉		★★	One of the most attractive flowering evergreens. There are several named varieties with flowers in shades of red and pink.

GOOD GARDEN SHRUBS Continued

Species and Varieties	Height	Evergreen	Flowering period	Fragrance	Light requirement	Suitable for rock garden	Hardiness	Description
Eucryphia glutinosa	4.5m (15ft)		7-8		⊙		★★	A tree-like shrub with rose-like leaves that turn yellow and red in autumn. Large white, saucer-shaped flowers. There is an evergreen species.
Euonymus europaeus Spindle Tree	2.4m (8ft)		5		⊙		★★	A fine berrying shrub. Arched boughs carry large red fruits which open to reveal orange-red seeds. Autumn tints.
E. fortunei	30cm (1ft)	♠			⊙	▲	★★★★	A creeping plant which will grow to 20ft (6m) if trained up the wall of a house.
E. japonicus Evergreen Spindle Tree	1.5m (5ft)	♠			⊙		★★★★	An excellent choice for coastal areas, or for town planting. Forms a dense bush of leathery leaves. There are variegated forms.
Fatsia japonica Fig-leaf Palm	2.1m (7ft)	♠			●		★★	One of the largest-leaved evergreens. Leaves resemble Ivy in shape but are 30cm (1ft) across.
Forsythia x intermedia Golden Bell Bush	2.4m (8ft)		4-5		⊙		★★★★	Justifiably one of the most widely planted spring-flowering shrubs. Clusters of yellow bell-shaped flowers.
Fothergilla monticola	1.5m (5ft)		4-5	✿	⊙		★★★★	The flowers have no petals, just a tuft of stamens. Glorious orange-red autumn tints.
Fuchsia gracilis	1.5m (5ft)		6-10		○		★	Miniature purple and carmine flowers on vigorous upright branches. One of the hardiest fuchsias.
F. magellanica 'Riccartonii'	1.5m (5ft)		7-9		○		★	Forms a twiggy bush and is sometimes used as a hedging plant in mild districts. Small flowers with spreading calyx.
Garrya elliptica Tassel Bush	1.8m (6ft)	♠	2		⊙		★★	A good evergreen wall shrub, although it can be grown as a bush in mild areas. The male plant has long silky catkins.
Gaultheria procumbens	15cm (6in)	♠	7-8		●	▲	★★★★	A fine carpeting plant beneath trees or on humus-rich soil. In spring young leaves are transluscent pink. Red berries
Genista hispanica Spanish Gorse	60cm (2ft)		5-6		○		★★★★	Ideal plant for dry, sunny position. Mass of yellow flowers.
G. lydia	75cm (2½ft)		5-6		○	▲	★★★★	Pendulous shoots become smothered in golden-yellow flowers.
Griselinia littoralis Kupuka Tree	3m (10ft)	♠	5		○		★★	Grown for its leathery, yellowish-green leaves. Flowers green; female plant produces green oblong fruits.
X Halimiocistus sahucii	30cm (1ft)	♠	5-9		○		★★	Profusion of white saucer-shaped flowers about 2.5cm (1in) across.
Halimium lasianthum	60cm (2ft)	♠	5-7		○		★★	Bright yellow flowers like single roses, with a purple blotch at the base of petals. Bushy habit and grey foliage.
Hamamelis mollis Witch Hazel	2.1m (7ft)		12-2	✿	⊙		★★★★	Fascinating yellow flowers carried on bare stems at a most useful time of year. Fragrant.

Species and Varieties	Height	Evergreen	Flowering period	Fragrance	Light requirement	Suitable for rock garden	Hardiness	Description
Hebe	15cm-1.2m (6in-4ft)	●	6-9		◐		★★	Attractive evergreens, especially good in coastal areas. Several species are described on page 95.
Hedera Ivy	—	●			●		★★★★	These climbing plants are described on page 124. They are also useful as a ground cover.
Hedysarum multijugum French Honeysuckle	90cm (3ft)		6-9		○			Rose-purple pea-shaped flowers are borne on a shrub of lax habit.
Helianthemum chamaecistus Sun Rose	30cm (1ft)	●	5-7		○	▲	★★★★	Dainty, crumpled, saucer-shaped flowers. There are several good named varieties.
Helichrysum splendidum	75cm (2½ft)		8-9		○		★★★★	Yellow flowers and grey-felted narrow narrow leaves on a broadly rounded plant.
Hibiscus syriacus Tree Hollyhock	2.4m (8ft)		8-10		○		★★	Large Hollyhock-like flowers in various colours. Will need protection in all but sheltered areas.
Hippophae rhamnoides Sea Buckthorn	3m (10ft)		3-4		○		★★★★	A strong-growing thorny plant, often used as a hedge in coastal areas. Narrow silvery leaves, which fall to reveal orange berries on female plants.
Hydrangea macrophylla	1.8m (6ft)		7-9		◐		★★	The popular florists' hydrangea. Not suitable for limy soil. Description and treatment is given on page 95.
H. paniculata 'Grandiflora'	2.1m (7ft)		7-8		◐		★★★★	Broad spikes of creamy-white flowers, rather like lilac in appearance. An impressive plant.
Hypericum patulum 'Hidcote'	1.5m (5ft)		7-9		◉		★★★★	Large, golden saucer-shaped flowers borne in profusion. Another species, the evergreen H. calycinum, is a useful ground cover.
Hyssopus aristatus Hyssop	60cm (2ft)	●	6-8	🍃	◉		★★★★	Rich green foliage, which smells rather like mint. Usually has a profusion of purple-blue flowers, loved by bees.
Ilex aquifolium 'Aureo-marginata' Holly	4.5m (15ft)	●	5-6		◉		★★★★	The Holly needs no description, but this is one with a yellow margin to the leaves. Will grow taller as a tree.
Jasminum nudiflorum Winter Jasmine	3m (10ft)		11-3		◉		★★★★	A beautiful and useful winter-flowering shrub with small yellow flowers. Grow against a wall (not easterly).
Kalmia latifolia Calico Bush	1.8m (6ft)	●	6		◐		★★★★	An attractive evergreen for a lime-free soil. Clusters of beautiful pink five-sided flowers.
Laurus nobilis Sweet Bay	3m (10ft)	●		🍃	◉		★★	This is the foliage plant frequently seen in tubs outside restaurants. Can be trained to shape.
Lavandula spica 'Hidcote' Lavender	30cm (1ft)	●	7-8	✿	○		★★★★	An old favourite. This variety has deep purple-blue flowers, which contrast well with the silvery foliage.
Ledum groenlandicum Labrador Tea	90cm (3ft)	●	5-6	🍃	◐		★★★★	Clusters of white flowers. Fragrant leaves, which are woolly beneath. Requires a lime-free soil.
Leycesteria formosa Pheasant Berry	1.8m (6ft)		7-8		●		★★★★	Bottle-green stems, attractive in winter. Clusters of pink flowers with claret bracts, followed by reddish-purple berries.

Species and Varieties	Height	Evergreen	Flowering period	Fragrance	Light requirement	Suitable for rock garden	Hardiness	Description
Ligustrum delavayanum Privet	1.8m (6ft)	●	6		●		★★★★	A privet that does not 'rob' the soil. Small leaves. Flowers white with violet anthers, followed by black fruit.
L. ovalifolium 'Aureum' Golden Privet	3m (10ft)	●	7		●		★★★★	Although often seen as a clipped hedge, it makes an attractive free-standing shrub.
Lonicera nitida Shrubby Honeysuckle	1.5m (5ft)	●			◉		★★★★	Used extensively for hedges, but also makes a graceful free-standing shrub.
L. x purpusii	1.8m (6ft)		11-3	✿	○		★★★★	Sweetly-scented, creamy-white flowers, borne at a most useful time. Semi-evergreen.
Lupinus arboreus Yellow Tree Lupin	1.8m (6ft)	●	5-8	✿	○		★★	A short-lived but fast-growing shrub that will flower freely over a long period.
Lycium chinensis Box Thorn	3m (10ft)		5-7		◉		★★★★	A vigorous, rambling shrub, ideally used for poor, dry soil, cliffs and coastal planting. Scarlet berries are very ornamental.
Mahonia aquifolium Holly-leafed Berberis	90cm (3ft)	●	2-4	✿	●		★★★★	A useful ground cover, having large Holly-shaped leaves, which have a purple tinge in autumn. Yellow flowers followed by black berries.
Malus (see page 174)								
Myrica cerifera Candle Berry	6m (20ft)	●	2-4	🍃				Its catkins are of no significance, but it has attractive, fragrant, narrow leaves. Interesting waxy berries.
Olearia x haastii Daisy Bush	1.5m (5ft)	●	7-8	✿	◉		★★	A mound of white daisy-like flowers. Nice bushy habit. Good coastal shrub; may need shelter inland.
Osmanthus delavayi Fragrant Olive	2.1m (7ft)	●	4	✿	●		★★★	Small tubular fragrant white flowers, which contrast with the deep green foliage.
X Osmarea burkwoodii	2.1m (7ft)	●	4	✿	◉		★★★	A first-class evergreen. White tubular, scented flowers. Toothed, pointed glossy leaves.
Pachysandra terminalis Japanese Spurge	15cm (6in)	●	2-3		●		★★★★	Very useful for carpeting beneath trees. Spikes of whitish flowers. A variegated form is available.
Paeonia suffruticosa Tree Paeony	1.5m (5ft)		4-5		◐		★★★	Among the most gorgeously coloured shrubs. Large rose-like flowers in shades of purple, white, crimson, pink, or carmine.
Pernettya mucronata Prickly Heath	90cm (3ft)	●	5-6		●		★★★★	One of the best berried shrubs but male and female plants are required. Varieties are available with red, pink, lilac or white berries.
Perovskia atriplicifolia Russian Sage	1.5m (5ft)		8-9	🍃	○		★★★★	Grey, felted leaves with the fragrance of sage set off feathery spikes of powder-blue flowers.
Philadelphus Mock Orange	1.2-2.4m (4-8ft)		6-7	✿	◉		★★★★	A plant with a heady fragrance, and very easy to grow.
Phlomis fruticosa Jerusalem Sage	90cm (3ft)		6-7		○		★★★★	A semi-evergreen with grey, felted leaves. Spikes of yellow, flowers.

Left: The Japanese Quince, *Chaenomeles speciosa*, sometimes known as Cydonia, is an outstanding shrub for training against a wall. (See pages 92 and 101.)

GOOD GARDEN SHRUBS Continued

Species and Varieties	Height	Evergreen	Flowering period	Fragrance	Light requirement	Suitable for rock garden	Hardiness	Description
Phormium tenax New Zealand Flax	1.8m (6ft)		7-8		◉		★	The sword-shaped leaves that radiate from a central clump make this an exotic-looking 'architectural' plant.
Phyllodoce coerulea	15cm (6in)		6-7		◑	▲	★★★★	Dainty shrub with purple flowers on short stalks. Needs a cool, moist, peaty soil.
Pieris formosa 'Forrestii'	2.1m (7ft)	◆	4	✿	◑		★★★	Grown mainly for the brilliant red colouring of young shoots.
Potentilla fruticosa	30cm-1.2m (1-4ft)		6-9		◉		★★★★	Among the best summer flowering shrubs, blooming over a long period.
Prunus (see page 173 for flowering kinds)								
P. laurocerasus Laurel	6m (20ft)	◆	4		◉		★★★★	A fine evergreen for hedges, with long, dark-green pointed foliage. Will grow very large if left unpruned.
P. lusitanica Portugal Laurel	3m (10ft)	◆	6	✿	◉		★★★★	A useful background evergreen, with a dense and broadly bushy habit. Hawthorn-scented flowers, followed by purple berries.
Pyracantha Firethorn	3m (10ft)	◆	5-6		◉		★★★★	Among the most spectacular berried shrubs.
Rhododendron (see page 98)								
Rhus typhina Stag's Horn Sumach	3m (10ft)		6-7		◉		★★★★	*See pages 173 and 177*
Ribes sanguineum Flowering Currant	2.4m (8ft)		3-4		●		★★★★	Popular spring-flowering shrub. 'King Edward VII' is a good variety.
Romneya trichocalyx Californian Tree Poppy	2.1m (7ft)		7-10	✿	○		★★	Large poppy-like white flowers studded with a mass of yellow stamens in the centre.

Species and Varieties	Height	Evergreen	Flowering period	Fragrance	Light requirement	Suitable for rock garden	Hardiness	Description
Rosa (see pages 148 and 149)								
Rosmarinus officinalis Rosemary	1.8m (6ft)	●	5	leaf	○		★★★★	Aromatic, narrow, grey-green leaves, used as a culinary herb. Blue flowers. Makes a nice hedge on sandy soil.
Rubus cockburnianus	2.4m (8ft)		6		●		★★★★	A relative of the blackberry, and invaluable for winter effect. Stems are covered with a white wax. Purple flowers, black berries.
Ruscus Butcher's Broom	90cm (3ft)	●	5		●		★★★★	A useful foliage plant for dense shade. Small spine-tipped leaves. Female plants have red berries from September onwards.
Salix hastata 'Wehrhahnii'	90cm (3ft)		5		◉	▲	★★★★	A dwarf-growing, shrubby Willow. In spring silvery catkins cover the bush and look like icicles.
S. lanata Woolly Willow	75cm (2½ft)		5		◐	▲	★★★★	A slow-growing shrub, with silvery-grey, felted leaves. Golden catkins in May.
Salvia officinalis Sage	60cm (2ft)	●	6	leaf	○		★★★★	This well-known culinary herb is worth a place in the shrub border, for its grey-green felted leaves. There is a purple form.
Sambucus nigra 'Aurea' Elderberry	4.5m (15ft)		6	flower	◐		★★★★	A golden form of Elder, and one of the brightest yellow-leaved shrubs.
Santolina chamaecyparissus Lavender Cotton	60cm (2ft)	●	7-8	leaf	○	▲	★★★★	Probably the whitest of all shrubs. Leaves covered with a cottony down. Flowers yellow.
Sarcococca humilis Sweet Box	60cm (2ft)	●	2	flower	●	▲	★★★★	Useful for carpeting a shady area. Narrow, bluish-green leaves; white flowers.
Senecio greyi	90cm (3ft)	●	7-8		○		★★★★	An extremely valuable shrub, having a nice bushy habit and attractive white-felted leaves. Gay yellow daisy like flowers.
Skimmia	1.5m (5ft)	●	5	flower	●		★★★★	Neat evergreen foliage, small cream flowers, followed by persistent red berries. Male and female plants may be required. See text.
Spartium junceum Spanish Broom	2.4m (8ft)		6-8	flower	○		★★★★	Sprays of large, yellow pea-like flowers carried on almost leafless stems.
Spiraea x bumalda	90cm (3ft)		7-9		◉		★★★★	A small shrub that would not look amiss in an herbaceous border. Pink or crimson flowers over a long period.
S. x vanhouttei	2.4m (8ft)		5		◉		★★★★	Arching branches covered with sprays of white flowers. Grey-green leaves show autumn colour.
Styrax japonica Snowbell	4.5m (15ft)		6-7		◉		★★★	Abundance of creamy, Lily-of-the-Valley-like flowers. Needs shelter to do well in all but mildest areas.
Symphoricarpos albus Snowberry	1.8m (6ft)		6-9		●		★★★★	Berries the size of marbles persist through the winter. Those of *S. albus* are white, but other species have pink or lilac berries.

Species and Varieties	Height	Evergreen	Flowering period	Fragrance	Light requirement	Suitable for rock garden	Hardiness	Description
Syringa vulgaris Lilac	4.5m (15ft)		5-6		○		★★★★	Although the natural form of *S. vulgaris* is not an outstanding shrub, the named varieties are colourful and spectacular. Some of these are described in the text.
Tamarix pentandra	3m (10ft)		7-8		○		★★★★	Very effective when planted in groups and viewed from a distance. Feathery foliage and a mass of rose-pink flowers.
Thymus serpyllum Thyme	2.5cm (1in)	♠	6-8	🍃	☉	▲	★★★★	A sub-shrub with tiny, fragrant leaves. Creeping habit useful between paving. There is a variegated form.
Ulex europaeus 'Plenus' Double Gorse	1.5m (5ft)	♠	4-5		○		★★★★	A blaze of yellow when in flower. Only suitable for poor soil. An improvement over wild gorse.
Vaccinium vitis-idaea Mountain Cranberry	30cm (1ft)	♠	5-6		◐		★★★★	Grown mainly for red fruits, which are edible. Prefers moist, peaty soil. Some species of vaccinium are deciduous, and a few are tender.
Viburnum davidii	90cm (3ft)	♠	6		☉		★★★★	A compact shrub with leathery oval leaves. Berries are a striking turquoise. Male and female plants are needed.
V. fragrans	2.7m (9ft)		11-2	✿	○		★★★★	One of the most attractive winter-flowering shrubs. Clusters of fragrant white flowers, tinted pink.
V. opulus 'Sterile' Snowball Bush	3m (10ft)		5-6		☉		★★★★	Balls of white flowers borne on a neatly rounded bush. Translucent red berries in the autumn.
V. rhytidophyllum	3m (10ft)	♠	5-6		☉		★★★★	Impressive leaves, about 23cm (9in) long, wrinkled, and with a thick felt beneath. Cream flowers, red berries.
V. tinus Laurustinus	2.4m (8ft)	♠	11-4		○		★★★★	An evergreen with a luxuriant mass of leaves. Useful as an informal hedge or screen. Trusses of white flowers.
Vinca minor Periwinkle	15cm (6in)	♠	4-8		●		★★★★	An excellent carpeting plant, even in shade. It will, however, produce its blue flowers more freely with some sun.
Weigela florida 'Variegata'	2.1m (7ft)		5-6		☉		★★★★	Weigelas are very free flowering, and this variety is especially nice because of its variegated leaves, in addition to pink flowers.
Yucca filamentosa Adam's Needle	75cm (2½ft)	♠	7-8		●		★★	Strap-shaped leaves rise from a central clump, and are very impressive. Spectacular spike of large greenish-white flowers.
Zenobia pulverulenta	1.2m (4ft)		6-7	✿	◐		★★★★	Beautiful, large Lily-of-the-Valley-like fragrant flowers. Needs an acid soil.

Climbers and Wall Shrubs

Even a fairly modest bungalow has about 29sq m (35sq yd) of growing space that is not usually exploited, and a small rear garden on a modern housing estate is likely to have a similar area of close-board or other fencing available for plants. All too often this vertical space is ignored, yet climbers can transform these sites into a beautiful aspect of the garden. And the smaller the garden, the more valuable this space becomes.

Climbers are also invaluable for camouflaging garages, sheds, oil storage tanks and coal bunkers, which often have to be placed in regrettably conspicuous places.

Old trees, particularly gnarled and aged apple trees, can serve as host to a variety of climbers, and such stumps can be transformed into a more attractive sight.

If ready-made sites are not available, it is well worth providing something specially for them. The vertical space such as that provided by a pergola will, in any case, add considerable interest to otherwise flat parts of the garden.

Akebia quinata
(see page 123)

Types of climbers and wall shrubs

Not all climbers will grow unaided up a wall. Those that will are called self-clinging, and include Ivies, Virginia Creepers, and the Climbing Hydrangea. They use aerial roots to cling to walls or other supports. These plants are especially valuable, as they will cover high walls on which it would be impractical to provide climbing aids.

A large number of climbers use naturally twining stems to twist themselves round a branch or other support. These will need a support to climb round, but apart from that will take care of themselves. Clematis and Honeysuckle are examples of plants that climb in this way.

A few plants, such as roses, use spines to secure a hold, but they need to be tied in against walls and fences.

Sweet Peas provide an example of plants that climb with the aid of tendrils, but again they need the benefit of something to which they can cling.

Besides the true climbers, there is another group of plants that can be grown against a wall or fence – the so-called wall shrubs. Some plants, such as choisya, are grown against a wall in cold districts because they benefit from the protection afforded to them, but generally such plants have not been included in this chapter.

Far left: Clematis 'Nelly Moser', with beautiful rosy-mauve flowers bearing carmine bars, is a vigorous variety of considerable merit. (See pages 116 and 121.)

Passiflora caerulea
Passion Flower
(see page 125)

Berberidopsis corallina
Coral Berry
(see page 123)

Jasminum nudiflorum
Winter Jasmine
(see page 124)

CLIMBERS TO GROW UP OR OVER TREES
Actinidia
Celastrus orbiculata (for stumps)
Clematis
Hydrangea petiolaris (for dead stumps)
Vitis coignetiae

CLIMBERS AND WALL SHRUBS FOR SANDY SOIL
Cotoneaster
Indigofera
Lonicera

CLIMBERS THAT HOLD BY TENDRILS OR TWINING
Actinidia chinensis
A. kolomikta
Akebia
Aristolochia
Campsis x tagliabuana
Celastrus orbiculatus 'Haemaphroditus'
Clematis
Jasminum officinale
J. x stephanense
Lonicera x americana
L. henryi
L. japonica
L. periclymenum 'Serotina'
Passiflora caerulea
Polygonum baldschuanicum
Vitis amurensis
V. coignetiae
Wisteria

CLIMBERS AND WALL SHRUBS FOR NORTH WALLS
Hedera
Hydrangea petiolaris
Jasminum
Parthenocissus
Pyracantha

CLIMBERS THAT CAN BE USED FOR CLOTHING BANKS
Hedera colchica
H. helix
Jasminum nudiflorum
Lonicera japonica

CLIMBERS AND WALL SHRUBS FOR COASTAL AREAS
Ceanothus
Cotoneaster horizontalis
Garrya elliptica
Hedera helix
Hydrangea petiolaris
Lonicera x americana
L. periclymenum 'Serotina'
Parthenocissus quinquefolia
P. tricuspidata 'Veitchii'
Polygonum baldschuanicum
Rubus phoenicolasius

CLIMBERS AND WALL SHRUBS FOR CLAY SOIL
Cotoneaster
Osmanthus
Rosa

ANNUAL CLIMBERS
Cobaea
Convolvulus
Cucurbita (Gourds)
Eccremocarpus
Humulus japonicus
Lathyrus (Sweet Pea)
Thunbergia
Tropaeolum (nasturtium)

CLIMBERS AND WALL SHRUBS FOR SHADE
Aristolochia durior (A. sipho)
Berberidopsis corallina
Hedera
Hydrangea petiolaris
Lonicera tellmanniana
Pyracantha

SELF-CLINGING CLIMBERS
Campsis radicans
Hedera
Hydrangea petiolaris
Parthenocisus quinquefolia
P. tricuspidata 'Veitchii'
Schizophragma integrifolia
Vitis henryana

SHRUBS SUITABLE FOR GROWING AGAINST A WALL
Ceanothus
Chaenomeles
Chimonanthus praecox
Cotoneaster horizontalis
Cytisus battandieri
Garrya elliptica
Indigofera gerardiana
Kerria japonica
Osmanthus delavayi
Pyracantha
Rubus phoenicolasius

CLIMBERS AND WALL SHRUBS FOR CHALKY SOIL
Ceanothus
Clematis
Cotoneaster
Lonicera
Polygonum baldschuanicum
Pyracantha

CLIMBERS FOR ACID SOIL
Berberidopsis corallina
Hydrangea petiolaris
Lonicera

On the other hand, there are shrubs such as chaenomeles and pyracantha that are ideally suited to growing against a wall or fence, and these have been included here.

Providing support

If self-clinging climbers are to be grown, or ready-made supports in the form of old trees or stumps are available, the only decisions centre on which plants to grow. But if support has to be provided, the cost and work involved in providing a climbing frame have to be considered.

Garden centres offer a wide range of wooden and plastic trellises suitable for fixing to wooden fences or brick walls, and much is a matter of personal taste – provided the structure is substantial enough for the subject. A thin wooden trellis is perfectly adequate for annual climbers, or perennials without twining woody stems, but after a few years the effect of weather and the thickening of the woody stems of twining climbers, such as Honeysuckles, pressing between the wall and the trellis, can sometimes cause problems.

For plants with relatively few woody branches to train, such as pyracantha, it may be possible to manage with judiciously placed wall nails attached to plastic loops to hold the stem. Another possibility is to stretch strong galvanized or plastic-coated wire between horizontal or vertical vine eyes, with the wires spaced 45cm (18in) apart.

To add height to the back of a border, or in some other suitable spot, it is not difficult to make a wigwam of rustic poles for a climber to scramble over and cover. Making a pergola is a more ambitious piece of garden construction, but if the skills are available it will greatly enhance the garden as a whole.

Before attempting to cover every piece of exposed wall or fence, do consider the maintenance aspect. Ordinary exterior household painting will not pose any problems, for it will do no harm to prune away any stray branches that seem to be encroaching on the brickwork. But if the brickwork needs re-pointing, that should be put right first. Climbers, including the self-clinging type, will do no harm to sound brickwork, but it is pointless to position a plant where the mortar is crumbling.

If the wall is likely to require painting or whitewashing at some time, use a piece of trellis that can be detached and swung clear, and avoid self-clinging climbers.

As many garden fences lack sufficient height for climbers, it is worth considering an extension to the height by adding a trellis.

Self-clinging climbers

Self-clinging plants have a great attraction – they will grow without help, and often to a considerable height. Some of them are also among the best climbers for covering a large area of wall.

At the top of the list must come the Virginia Creeper and Ivies. Both will cover the wall of an average house without difficulty – the Ivy provides attractive evergreen foliage, but the Virginia Creeper excels in brilliant autumn colour.

Kerria japonica
Jew's Mallow
(see page 124)

Lonicera
Honeysuckle
(see page 124)

Indigofera gerardiana
Indigo
(see page 124)

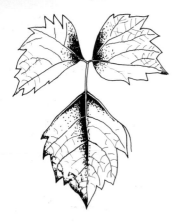

Parthenocissus
(see page 125)

The Virginia Creeper has been at the centre of some most confusing name changes, which need to be appreciated in order to be sure of buying the right plant. Its current name is *Parthenocissus quinquefolia*, but it has also been known as *Vitis quinquefolia* and *V. hederacea*! That's the true Virginia Creeper, but the one most frequently planted and taken as the Virginia Creeper is the Boston Ivy, *Ampelopsis tricuspidata* 'Veitchii', which has been known as *Ampelopsis veitchii* and *Vitis inconstans*.

Even if you end up with the wrong one, you will not be disappointed, for both are excellent plants, readily clothing a wall with lobed leaves (three lobes in the case of Boston Ivy, five in the case of Virginia Creeper) that turn an orange and scarlet of unsurpassed brilliance in autumn.

A close relative of the Virginia Creeper, and even more beautiful in some ways, is *P. henryana*. The two previously mentioned creepers will perform well in sun or semi-shade, but for the most attractive leaf colouring *P. henryana* is best in partial shade, as this brings out the attractive network of white and purple veins on the

Right: The Early Dutch Honeysuckle, *Lonicera periclymenum* 'Belgica', bears a profusion of sweetly-scented flowers. (See pages 117 and 124.)

Below: Ivies are undemanding climbers, suitable for any aspect, and happy in shade. There are variegated kinds, such as *Hedera helix* 'Gold Heart'. (See pages 115 and 124.)

dark green leaves. The warm-red autumn colour is equally attractive.

The Ivy is nothing if not versatile. There can be few plants that will act as a ground cover in dense shade, climb to the top of a tall tree, clothe a wall, and make an attractive houseplant. The Common Ivy (*Hedera helix*) will do all these things, but it is among the various varieties that the most attractive forms are to be found.

Variation in colour is provided by varieties such as 'Buttercup' (also known as 'Golden Cloud' and 'Russell's Gold'), perhaps the best golden Ivy, with small, bright yellow leaves, and not very vigorous habit. 'Discolor' has its small dark green leaves mottled cream and tinted red. (*Hedera helix* 'Gold Heart' is illustrated on page 114, 'Glacier' on page 119.)

Leaf shape is also variable with *Hedera helix*, and among those with unusual leaves are 'Sagittaefolia', which has arrow-head-shaped five-lobed leaves, the central one being especially long. 'Tortuosa' has rather oval leaves that tend to be twisted and curled, more pronouncedly in cold weather. 'Cristata' has pale leaves

Hedera
Ivy
(see page 124)

Left: *Lonicera japonica* 'Aureo-reticulata' is grown for its variegated foliage rather than flowers, the conspicuous golden netting making this an interesting climber to grow against a fence. (See pages 117 and 124.)

Below: Sweet Peas (*Lathyrus*) are traditional cottage garden climbers, and there are now many excellent varieties from which to choose, from dwarf kinds 30cm (1ft) high to climbers of 2.4m (8ft). (See page 124.)

Actinidia chinensis
Chinese Gooseberry
(see page 123)

Hydrangea petiolaris
(see page 124)

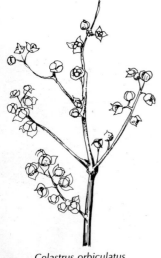

Celastrus orbiculatus
(see page 117)

twisted and crimped at the edges, and 'Deltoidea' has the two basal lobes rounded and overlapping.

There are many more varieties of the Common Ivy that are fun to discover, but there are two other species popular as climbers – H. canariensis (Canary Island Ivy) and H. colchica 'Dentata Variegata' (Persian Ivy). Both have large leaves splashed with gold, but the Persian Ivy is hardier. (Illustrated on page 122.)

One of the most striking flowering self-clinging climbers for a north wall is the Climbing Hydrangea (H. petiolaris). This hardy plant grows to 15m (50ft) or more, and can be most impressive with its heart-shaped green leaves and flattish heads of white flowers, about 13cm (5in) across, like Lacecap hydrangeas. It will need some support until the aerial roots gain a secure hold.

A plant resembling Hydrangea petiolaris, but with more conspicuous flowers, is Schizophragma integrifolia. The heads are about 30cm (1ft) across, with conspicuous cream sepals encircling the insignificant individual flowers.

A more colourful self-clinger can be found in Campsis radicans, one of the Trumpet Vines. Colourful orange and scarlet trumpet-shaped flowers, about 5cm (2in) long, are produced freely in August and September, provided they have a warm sunny wall to ripen the wood and initiate flowers. Other species of campsis will need help with support.

Clematis

Clematis are lovely plants, and whether your taste is for the large and spectacular or the small and dainty, there are species and varieties to please everyone.

The large-flowered hybrids are among the boldest of climbing plants, and colours range from white, through pink and red to blue. Several have attractively striped petals, and some are double-flowered. But perhaps the most wonderful thing about these plants is the way they can be totally covered with bloom. The flowering period spans from May to October, depending on variety. A number of dependable varieties is given on page 121.

Pruning is usually the main difficulty with these plants. Yet there is nothing complicated about the method – it is more a question of when to prune. The table on page 121 gives pruning recommendations, but for varieties not mentioned there, the general rule is to prune hard in early spring those which flower on the current year's growth. Those which flower on growth made in the previous season need only light pruning immediately after flowering. If, however, they have become too bare and woody at the base, they can be pruned hard to rejuvenate them.

The small-flowered species are no less attractive, and what they lack in flower size they make up for in massed effect, and they are generally easier to establish, and grow more quickly.

One of the most widely grown species is C. montana, which has white flowers, but there is a lovely pink form – C. m. 'Tetrarose', which has rather larger flowers.

The Orange Peel Clematis (C. orientalis) is interesting because its thick orange-yellow sepals peel back like the segments of an orange. *C. tangutica* is similar, but bright yellow. Both have attractive silky seed heads.

Clematis require a rich, moist soil containing lime. And like many other climbers, they are happiest with their roots in the shade and heads in the sun. (Clematis 'Nelly Moser' is illustrated on page 110.)

Some other good climbers

The Chinese Gooseberry (*Actinidia chinensis*), is a vigorous twining plant with large heart-shaped leaves and fragrant creamy-white cup-shaped flowers about 4cm (1½in) across, fading to buff-yellow. These are followed by egg-shaped edible fruits, about 4cm (1½in) long and covered with brown hairs.

Celastrus orbiculatus is a fine subject for training up pergolas, old trees, or unsightly objects. Its principal attractions are clear yellow autumn leaves and orange and yellow seed vessels which persist through the winter, and split open to reveal scarlet seeds.

Jasminum officinale and *J.* x *stephanense*, two distinctive Jasmines, are vigorous, easily grown climbers with sweetly fragrant flowers. *J. officinale* is a white-flowered species while *J.* x *stephanense* is pale pink. Both are suitable for growing over pergolas and their fragrant flowers add much to the summer garden.

Honeysuckle (*Lonicera periclymenum*) is another universally popular climber. The red buds open to pale yellow fragrant flowers. There are two main forms, the Early Dutch Honeysuckle, *L. p.* 'Belgica', which opens in May and June, and the Late Dutch Honeysuckle, *L. p.* 'Serotina', flowering from July to October. (*Lonicera periclymenum* 'Belgica' is illustrated on page 114.)

A very different species is the Japanese Honeysuckle, *L. japonica* 'Aureo-reticulata', which is grown for its attractive variegated leaves with a golden-yellow netting effect. (Illustrated on page 115.)

The Russian Vine (*Polygonum baldschuanicum*), is also known as the Mile-a-Minute Vine, which gives some idea of its rampant growth. Once it becomes established it will quickly cover any unsightly object you care to let it scramble over.

From July until the first frost, the plant is covered with a frothy mass of small creamy-white flowers.

Vitis are closely related to the Virginia Creeper in appearance, and the genus contains some magnificent foliage plants. It is difficult to find any climber more spectacular in autumn than *V. coignetiae*, a Japanese species of quite outstanding beauty, with large leaves often 30cm (12in) across which turn brilliant shades of orange and crimson.

All the climbers mentioned so far have their very considerable merits, and are the right plants for many situations, but where space permits, and you can provide a sheltered site on a south- or west-facing wall, it is well worth trying the aristocrat of climbing plants – the wisteria. It may take some years before a wisteria will flower prolifically, but patience is usually well rewarded.

There are two principal species grown – *W. sinensis* and *W. floribunda*. *Wisteria sinensis* has stems that twine anti-clockwise and the other twines clockwise, but the flowers of both

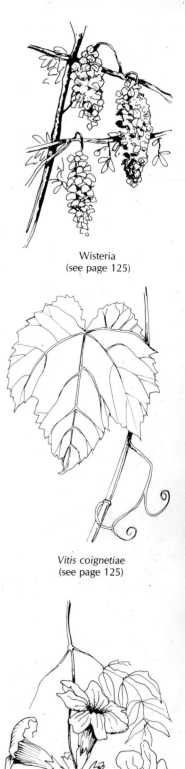

Wisteria
(see page 125)

Vitis coignetiae
(see page 125)

Campsis radicans
(see page 123)

Garrya elliptica
Tassel Bush
(see page 124)

are equally beautiful. In May, huge and fragrant trusses of flower 20cm (8in) long are a delight to behold. Although mauve is the usual colour, there are white forms. Perhaps the most spectacular i *W. f.* 'Macrobotrys' with fragrant lilac racemes up to 90cm (3ft long.

A moist soil is desirable, and container-grown plants are prefer able, as wisterias resent root disturbance.

Annual climbers

Annuals or half-hardy perennials treated as annuals are usually little trouble to grow, and are particularly useful for temporary screens. A list of these can be found on page 112, and some are described or pages 22, 23 and 24.

Wall shrubs

One of the most widely grown and popular wall shrubs is the pyracantha or Firethorn, which is certainly one of the best berried shrubs. Although the white flowers are fairly insignificant, heavy clusters of red, yellow or orange berries are a spectacular sight in autumn. One of the best is 'Orange Glow', an upright plant with masses of orange-red berries carried well into winter.

An early shrub of considerable merit is *Chaenomeles speciosa*,

Right: The Jew's Mallow, *Kerria japonica*, is a useful wall shrub for any aspect, but thrives best in semi-shade. (See page 124.)

Japanese Quince. This used to be known as *Cydonia japonica*, t by whatever name it is known, this is one of the most attractive ll shrubs to flower between March and June. There are some vely varieties, usually in shades of red or pink, but *C. s.* 'Nivalis' is arge white. *C. x superba* is similar, and *C. x s.* 'Knap Hill Scarlet' one of the best. The yellowish-green edible fruits can be used to ake quince jelly. (*Chaenomeles speciosa* is illustrated on page)7.)

Blue-flowered wall shrubs are not plentiful, and one of the finest ceanothus, or the Californian Lilac as it is sometimes called. ere are deciduous kinds, usually grown in the open border, but e evergreen forms are best against a warm wall, where most of em will flower in May and June. The tight clusters of small blue wers are borne so profusely that they almost hide the foliage. By reful choice of varieties, flowers can be spread over a long period *C. dentatus* and *C. impressus* start the season off with flowers in ay and June, 'Autumnal Blue', with its china-blue flowers, takes from July onwards, while *C. x burkwoodii* blooms in the summer d autumn.

Brooms are not usually regarded as wall shrubs, but one of them, *ytissus battandieri*, is excellent for a wall. Its bright yellow ne-shaped clusters of flowers are pleasantly pineapple-scented. It a handsome plant for a warm wall.

For a distinguished wall shrub, it is difficult to improve on *Garrya*

Pyracantha
Firethorn
(see page 125)

Left: Winter Jasmine, *Jasminum nudiflorum*, will grace walls with dainty yellow flowers during the dark days of winter. (See page 124.)

119

Clematis 'Ville de Lyon'
(see page 121)

Cytisus battandieri
(see page 123)

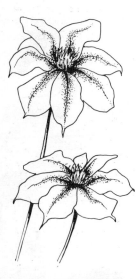

Clematis 'Barbara Jackman'
(see page 121)

elliptica, a glossy-leaved evergreen, with long slender catkins on the male plants in January and February. It is important to buy male plants for the best catkins; and buy container-grown plants.

Planting a climber

There is nothing special about a climber's needs – the same soil preparation that is suitable for non-climbing shrubs will be adequate (see page 89), but proximity to a wall does create its own problems. Often, foundations and rubble may be a problem, and the area at the foot of the wall is often very dry. Overcome both these problems by planting at least 25cm (10in) out from the wall, bridging the gap with a cane, if necessary, until the plant becomes established. And be particularly generous with compost or peat in the planting hole.

Some climbers, notably clematis, prefer to have their roots in shade, and one way of achieving this is to position a small shrub in front. Alternatively, a paving stone placed over the roots may help, provided it does not look out of place.

Dryness can be a major problem, especially during the first year, and it is a good idea to sink an empty plant-pot in the ground by the side of the plant, through which water can be given.

Routine care

During the first year, the best care you can provide will be plenty of water and a liberal mulch. It is only once the plant becomes established that it will start to climb rapidly.

Training is mainly a matter of tying in branches to create an even spread of foliage, and to cut out any that are crossing or growing out at an awkward angle. With established plants it may be necessary to prune vigorous kinds to keep them within bounds and to encourage further flower development. Generally, follow the same pruning principles as for non-climbing shrubs (see page 90).

Once a year, ties should be checked, and replaced as necessary. Other than this, climbers need very little attention.

Pergolas

One way to show climbing plants to the best advantage is to grow them up and along a pergola. The uprights of these structures can be made of either wood or brick, but the horizontal bars at the top are usually constructed of wood. Often, these structures straddle a path, so that anyone viewing the climbing plants from inside the pergola is surrounded by flowers and foliage. There are many climbing plants which look at their best when so planted, not the least being the cascading wisteria, such as *Wisteria floribunda* 'Macrobotrys', with scented lilac-coloured racemes up to 90cm (3ft) long (see page 117).

The spectacularly-coloured vine, *Vitis coignetiae*, one of the Japanese species, is outstanding during the dull autumn days, when it gladdens the garden with large leaves often 30cm (12in) across, and in colours of orange and scarlet.

CLEMATIS FOR THE GARDEN

Species and Varieties	Height	Colour	Flowering Time	Pruning Requirement	Vigour	Fragrance
Small Flowered Clematis						
Clematis alpina	3m (10ft)	Blue or violet-blue	4-5	A	Moderate	
C. chrysochoma	2.4m (8ft)	Pink	5-6	A	Moderate	
C. florida 'Sieboldii'	1.8m (6ft)	White	6-7	B	Moderate	
C. macropetala	4.5m (15ft)	Lavender and blue	4-5	A	Vigorous	
C. m. 'Markham's Pink'	4.5m (15ft)	Reddish-purple and pale lilac	4-5	A	Vigorous	
C. montana	Up to 9m (30ft)	White	5	A	Very vigorous	✿
C. montana rubens	Up to 7.5m (25ft)	Rosy-mauve	5	A	Very vigorous	✿
C. tangutica	4.5m (15ft)	Yellow	6-10	C	Vigorous	
C. viticella	3.5m (12ft)	Violet or blue	7-9	C	Vigorous	
Large Flowered Clematis						
Ascotiensis	3m (10ft)	Azure-blue	7-9	C	Vigorous	
Barbara Jackman	1.8m (6ft)	Bluish-purple with a magenta bar	5-6	B	Moderately vigorous	
Comtesse de Bouchaud	4.5m (15ft)	Pink	6-8	C	Very vigorous	
Gypsy Queen	1.8m (6ft)	Purplish, fading to violet	6-8	C	Vigorous	
Hagley Hybrid	2.4m (8ft)	Rosy-mauve	6-9	C	Moderately vigorous	
Jackmanii Superba	4.5m (15ft)	Reddish-purple	7-9	C	Very vigorous	
Nelly Moser	3.5m (12ft)	Rosy-mauve with a carmine bar	5-6 and 9-10	B	Vigorous	
President	3m (10ft)	Light purple with a silvery-white bar	5-10	B	Vigorous	
Ville de Lyon	3.5m (12ft)	Deep carmine	5-9	B	Vigorous	
Vyvyan Pennell	3m (10ft)	Lavender-blue	5-6	B	Vigorous	

Note: **Pruning requirement**
 A: Immediately after flowering, cut out all shoots that have flowered.
 B: During February and March, cut out all of the dead growth. Also, train and prune back to a pair of strong buds all other shoots.
 C: In February and March, cut all shoots back to a strong pair of buds, 90cm (3ft) or less above the soil level.

Clematis 'Nelly Moser'
(see this page)

Eccremocarpus scaber
Chilean Glory Flower
(see page 124)

Clematis macropetala
(see this page)

Aristolochia durior
Dutchman's Pipe
(see page 123)

Right, above: The Persian Ivy, *Hedera colchica* 'Dentata Variegata', has large leaves with striking variegation, making it a pleasant screening plant. (See pages 116 and 124.)

Right, below: The Passion Flower, *Passiflora caerulea*, is an eye-catching climber for a south or west wall in a sheltered area. (See page 125.)

CLIMBING PLANTS AND WALL SHRUBS

Species and Varieties	Height	Evergreen	Climber/ Wall shrub	Flowering period	Fragrance	Light requirement	Aspect	Hardiness	Description
ctinidia chinensis hinese Gooseberry	7.5m (25ft)		C	6	✿	○	N,S, E,W,	★★★★	Heart-shaped leaves and red hairy stems make this an aristocratic plant for a spacious wall. White flowers are followed by edible fruits.
. kolomikta	3m (10ft)		C	5-6	✿	○	S,W	★★★★	An unusual and attractive vigorous climber, with bold, purplish young foliage maturing to white or pink variegation.
kebia quinata	9m (30ft)		C	5	✿	○	S,E, W	★★★	A vigorous semi-evergreen with deep green oval leaflets. Chocolate-purple fragrant flowers.
ristolochia durior Dutchman's Pipe	9m (30ft)		C	6		◉	N,S, E,W	★★★★	Heart-shaped leaves. Unusual saxaphone-shaped flowers.
Berberidopsis corallina Coral Berry	2.4m (8ft)	♦	C	7		●	N,S, E,W	★	Among the most beautiful evergreen climbers. Dark green leathery leaves. Crimson flowers. Needs shelter and shade.
Bignonia capreolata Cross Vine	9m (30ft)	♦	C	6		○	S	★	A tall climber with clusters of yellow funnel-shaped flowers marked with red. Hardy only in southern counties.
Campsis radicans	9m (30ft)		C	8-9		○	S,W	★★★	Clings with aerial roots. Clusters of tubular, scarlet and orange flowers.
C. x tagliabuana Trumpet Vine	9m (30ft)		C	8-9		○	S	★★★	A handsome climber with brilliant red flowers, but needs plenty of sun to produce a good display.
Ceanothus 'Gloire de Versailles' Californian Lilac	3m (10ft)		WS	5-8		○	S,W	★★★	One of the best ceanothus, having an abundance of powder-blue flowers. Leaves larger than the evergreen kind.
Celastrus orbiculatus	9m (30ft)		C	6		◉	N,S, E,W	★★★★	One of the best climbers for winter effect, its orange-yellow fruit being most striking. Yellow autumn colour.
Chaenomeles speciosa Flowering Quince	1.8m (6ft)		WS	3-6		◉	N,S, E,W	★★★★	Lovely wall shrub. Flowers usually red, pink, or white, followed later in the year by edible fruits.
Chimonanthus praecox Winter Sweet	2.4m (8ft)		WS	12-1	✿	○	S,W	★★★	An excellent wall shrub for winter bloom. Yellow, fragrant flowers are carried on bare twigs.
Clematis (see page 121)									
Cobaea scandens (see page 26)									
Convolvulus (see page 26)									
Cotoneaster horizontalis Fish-bone Cotoneaster	2.4m (8ft)		WS	6		◉	N,S, E,W	★★★★	Branches grow in herring-bone fashion. Small leaves turn orange before falling. Red berries last well.
Cucurbita Gourds	1.8m (6ft)		C(A)			○	S,W	★	A fascinating climber to grow up a trellis or netting. The decorative fruits can be dried and varnished.
Cytisus battandieri	3m (10ft)		WS	7	✿	○	S,W	★★	Grey, laburnum-like leaves and pineapple-scented yellow flowers. Useful for a high wall.

Species and Varieties	Height	Evergreen	Climber/ Wall shrub	Flowering period	Fragrance	Light requirement	Aspect	Hardiness	Description
Eccremocarpus scaber Chilean Glory Flower	4.5m (15ft)		C	6-8		○	S,W	★	A half-hardy semi-woody tendril climber. Tubular orange-scarlet flowers freely produced.
Garrya elliptica Tassel Bush	3m (10ft)	●	WS	2		◉	N,S, E,W	★★	A good evergreen wall shrub, with impressive long, silky catkins.
Hedera colchica Persian Ivy	3m (10ft)	●	C	9-10		●	N,S, E,W	★★★★	Bold, heart-shaped leaves, forming a very effective screen. There is also a form with yellow variegation.
H. helix Common Ivy	4.5m (15ft)	●	C	9-10		●	N,S, E,W	★★★★	Ivies are invaluable plants for covering walls. There are many leaf shapes and variegations.
Humulus japonicus (see page 24)									
Hydrangea petiolaris	15m (50ft)		C	6		◉	N,S, W	★★★★	A tall-growing, self-clinging climber with heart-shaped dark green leaves and large heads of white flowers.
Indigofera gerardiana Indigo	2.4m (8ft)		WS	7-9		○	S	★★★	Elegant mimosa-like foliage and rose-purple, pea-shaped flowers.
Ipomoea Morning Glory	3m (10ft)		C(A)	7-8		○	S,W	★	Effective half-hardy flowering climbers for temporary or decorative screens. Several varieties are available.
Jasminum nudiflorum Winter Jasmine	3m (10ft)		WS	11-3		◉	N,S, W	★★★★	A beautiful and useful winter-flowering shrub with small yellow flowers.
J. officinale Jasmine	9m (30ft)		C	6-10	✿	○	S,E, W	★★★	A well-known, vigorous twining climber. White, sweetly scented flowers.
J. x stephanense	4.5m (15ft)		C	6-7	✿	○	S,E, W	★★★	An extremely beautiful climber — similar to J. officinale but with pale pink flowers.
Kerria japonica Jew's Mallow	1.8m (6ft)		WS	4-5		◐	N,S, E,W	★★★★	Slender green branches with pale green lanceolate leaves, which act as a foil for the yellow flowers.
Lathyrus (see page 28)									
Lonicera x americana	9m (30ft)		C	6-7	✿	◐	N,E, W	★★★★	A magnificent honeysuckle, having fragrant purple-rose flowers. Produces a spectacular display.
L. henryi	4.5m (15ft)	●	C	7		◐	N,S, E,W	★★★★	Glossy dark green foliage. Small flowers are followed by purple-black berries.
L. japonica 'Aureoreticulata'	4.5m (15ft)	●	C	6-8	✿	◐	S,E, W	★★★★	Small evergreen leaves, mottled with gold. A pleasant, strong-growing variegated climber.
L. periclymenum 'Serotina' Late Dutch Honeysuckle	4.5m (15ft)		C	8-9	✿	◐	N,E, W	★★★★	Strongly scented purple and yellow flowers. Vigorous growth.
L. x tellmanniana	9m (30ft)		C	6-7		●	N,W	★★★★	Beautiful golden-yellow flowers about 5cm (2in) long, carried in large clusters.
Osmanthus delavayi Fragrant Olive	2.1m (7ft)	●	WS	4	✿	◉	S,W	★★★	Small tubular, fragrant white flowers. Pleasant, pointed and toothed green leaves.

CLIMBING PLANTS AND WALL SHRUBS

Species and Varieties	Height	Evergreen	Climber/Wall shrub	Flowering period	Fragrance	Light requirement	Aspect	Hardiness	Description
Parthenocissus henryana	7.5m+ (25ft+)		C			◑	N,S, W	★★★★	A beautiful creeper, whose leaves have an attractive network of purple and white variegation, although a shady wall is required for the best colour. Red in autumn.
P. quinquefolia Virginia Creeper	7.5m+ (25ft+)		C			☉	N,S, E,W	★★★★	This popular creeper has deeply cut, five-lobed bright green leaves, which turn orange and scarlet in autumn.
P. tricuspidata 'Veitchii' Boston Ivy	7.5m+ (25ft+)		C			☉	N,S, E,W	★★★★	The autumn colour of this self-clinging climber is unsurpassed in brilliance.
Passiflora caerulea Passion Flower	6m (20ft)		C	6-9	✿	○	S,W	★	In favoured districts this can be a vigorous and beautiful climber. The interesting flowers, 7.5-10cm (3-4in) across, are creamy white.
Polygonum baldschuanicum Russian Vine	6m (20ft)		C	7-10		○	N,S, E,W	★★★★	An extremely rampant climber, useful for hiding sheds, garages, etc. Masses of small white flowers, tinged pink.
Pyracantha Firethorn	4.5m (15ft)	♠	WS	6		☉	N,S, E,W	★★★★	Magnificent berrying shrub for a wall. Most species and varieties are suitable, giving a choice of red or orange berries.
Rosa (see page 140)									
Rubus phoenicolasius Japanese Wineberry	2.4m (8ft)		WS	6		☉	S,E, W	★★★★	An attractive wall shrub with a bonus of bright orange-red edible berries. Rambling red-berried stems can be trained on wires or up pergolas or poles.
Schizophragma integrifolia	3m (10ft)		C	7		☉	S,W	★★★★	A vigorous hydrangea-like climbing shrub with cream-coloured flower heads up to 30cm (1ft) across. Self-clinging and suitable for high walls, tree trunks or pergolas.
Thunbergia alata Black-eyed Susan	1.5m (5ft)		C(A)	7-8		○	S	★	Only suitable for planting out in a warm sunny position from June onwards. Useful for porches and balconies. White, buff or orange flowers with black centres.
Tropaeolum canariensis Canary Creeper	3m (10ft)		C(A)	7-8		●	N,S, E,W	★	Easily grown, and attractive with its canary-yellow nasturtium-like flowers. Raise indoors and plant out in late May. Suitable varieties of ordinary nasturtiums can also be used.
Vitis amurensis	9m+ (30ft+)		C			☉	N,S, E,W	★★★★	The large, shield-shaped leaves turn ruby colour in autumn. An ornamental vine of merit.
V. coignetiae	9m+ (30ft+)		C			☉	N,S, E,W	★★★★	A vigorous ornamental vine with leaves sometimes 30cm (1ft) across.
Wisteria sinensis	9m (30ft)		C	5-6	✿	○	S,W	★★★	The aristocrat of the climbers. Magnificent cascading trusses of mauve flowers.

WS: Wall shrub   C: Climber   C(A): Annual climber   N: North;   S: South;   E: East;   W: West

Heathers For Year-round Colour

Gardeners are becoming increasingly aware of the wonderful opportunity Heathers provide for an almost maintenance-free garden, with colour practically the whole year round. One variety or another can be had in bloom every month of the year, in addition to which some have attractively coloured foliage.

As with dwarf conifers, the value of these plants in gardens of all sizes is now well appreciated, and these two groups of plants associate well together. A few strategically placed dwarf conifers can provide height and contrast of colour and form in a bed of Heathers.

The possibility of planting a few heathers in the rock garden should not be overlooked. True alpines are usually a riot of colour in spring, but tend to leave the rock garden bare for the rest of the year. Heathers do not look amiss in such a setting, and will certainly bring some patches of colour to the scene in what would otherwise be 'off' times. Obviously, there is no point in planting spring-flowering varieties, but for summer, autumn and winter flowers the choice is open. Even in the rock garden it is best to plant three of a variety together to make a bold splash of colour, rather than dotting them about. Keep to dwarf varieties, and do not attempt to use the Tree Heaths in this situation.

A less obvious use for Heathers is to form an edging or small hedge. The use of Heathers for hedges is described on page 159, but many of the dwarf varieties should be considered for a neat and colourful edging. Bear in mind that those plants with the most attractively coloured foliage are usually rather shy when it comes to flowering, so it's a matter of preference.

Heathers are often bought for their ground-covering ability. The drawback as a ground cover is that mostly they will not thrive in shade, and it is often within the shade of trees that ground cover is required. One of the most commonly planted varieties for ground cover, *Erica carnea*, will, however, tolerate partial shade. 'Springwood White' is a variety often used in this situation.

Never plant less than three of a variety together, and where space is available seven would not be too many for a really spectacular bed. It is in the boldness of the massed planting and contrasting blocks of colour that much of the beauty of the Heathers lies when viewed from a distance.

Silver Birches make an effective background, and so do pines and rhododendrons. The ideal aspect is a south or south-west facing slope exposed to the sun.

Erica cinerea
Bell Heather
(see page 135)

Far left: *Erica carnea* varieties will tolerate some lime in the soil, and also stand up well to atmospheric pollution and salt spray. The variety illustrated is *E. c.* 'Vivellii'. (See page 133.)

Erica vagans
Cornish Heath
(see page 134)

Once established, these accommodating plants are extremely easy to maintain. They will only need an annual clipping and a topdressing.

It is convenient to think of the Heather year as starting at the beginning of June, for that is when the first of our native Bell and Cross-leaved Heathers come into flower (*Erica cinerea* and *E. tetralix*). In early autumn the Cornish Heaths (*Erica vagans*) bloom, followed by the Lings (*Calluna vulgaris*), which take us through to the winter-flowering Mountain Heaths (*Erica carnea*). The gap between then and summer is filled with the spring-flowering Irish Ericas, *E. mediterranea*.

The foliage of most varieties is green, but there are some with gold, orange-reddish or bronze foliage. One variety, *Calluna vulgaris* 'Multicolor' has foliage with red, orange, yellow and bronze tints at different times of the year.

Soil for heathers

Far too frequently, gardeners are deterred from trying Heathers and their relatives because of common misapprehensions. Peat is not necessary (they will grow in sand), and some varieties *can* be grown in an alkaline soil.

As a family there is no doubt that they are acid-lovers, and the majority of Heaths and Heathers will be at their best in such soils. But if your garden is alkaline, these plants can still be enjoyed – either by creating a bed raised above the normal soil level, or by growing suitable species. As the purpose of this book is to help in the selection of plants that will thrive without going to such extremes as creating special beds, the latter course is recommended.

It is possible to divide the Heaths and Heathers into two broad groups – those that will tolerate lime and those that must have acid soil. If your soil is limy, choose from the following: *Erica arborea, E. australis* (Tree Heaths), *E. mediterranea* (Irish Erica), *E. carnea* (Mountain Heath), *E. lusitanica, E. terminalis*, and *E. x veitchii*.

The Cornish Heath (*Erica vagans*) is a borderline case, as it will tolerate only a small amount of lime.

The other major group consists of those species only suitable for acid soils. These include: *Calluna vulgaris* (Ling), *Daboecia cantabrica* (Irish Heath), *Erica canaliculata, E. ciliaris* (Dorset Heath), *E. cinerea* (Bell Heather), *E. tetralix, E. x watsonii*, and *E. x williamsii*.

An acid soil does not necessarily mean a peaty one, as many sandy soils are acid. Heathers will grow perfectly satisfactorily in such soils; the only problem is that they tend to dry out, so it is wise

incorporate as much humus as possible, though it needn't be
at; good compost will be adequate provided it does not contain
he.

There is no doubt, however, that a few good handfuls of peat
ded to the planting hole will be beneficial. Sedge peat is better
an sphagnum peat, as it retains moisture better and does not break
wn so quickly.

Clay soil can present a problem as the roots are rather delicate
d suffer from deep planting in heavy soil. In this situation
corporate plenty of organic matter such as peat or compost, and
not plant too deeply.

Although a moist soil is appreciated, it should be well-drained,
d only a few Heaths, such as *Erica tetralix* and *Daboecia
ntabrica*, will tolerate very wet conditions. *Erica ciliaris* is also
orth trying.

Heaths and Heathers are excellent ground-cover plants, and will
once established – suppress weeds admirably. For the first season
two weeding is necessary, and there is no substitute for starting
th soil relatively clear of perennial weeds. New weeds will
rminate, but at that stage they are easy to deal with. Before
anting it is best to cultivate the bed deeply, removing the roots of
rennial weeds, and incorporating garden compost or peat. If the
nount of peat available is small, save it for the planting holes or to
e as a topdressing; the value of a small amount may be lost in the
alk of soil.

A rich soil is not required; if overfed, lush growth will be made at
e expense of flowers, and the compact form lost. Sappy growth is
sceptible to damage in severe weather.

Heathers prefer a sunny position, where they flower most freely
nd the foliage kinds have the most intense colour. Partial shade is
cceptable to some species, but full shade should be avoided.

Coastal areas present no problems for many species, but most
lerant of salt spray are *Calluna vulgaris*, *Erica mediterranea* and
carnea.

Daboecia cantabrica
Irish Heath
(see page 134)

ultivation

ery little routine maintenance is needed, which is one reason for
he popularity of these plants. The main requirement is an annual
im after the flowers have died, although in the case of *E. ciliaris*
nd *E. tetralix* this is perhaps best done in early spring so that the
lants have a little extra protection during winter.

Erica carnea does not even need this degree of attention, and a
im every two or three years, in March or April, is sufficient.

Occasionally, a dead branch will need to be pruned out, and
ome of the Tree Heathers sometimes have branches damaged by
how or animals, and these will need to be removed.

More severe pruning may be indicated if the plants produce
nany small spikes or clusters instead of fewer but larger spikes.
lard pruning should improve this, but callunas will not sprout from
eally old wood, so do not cut into anything more than a couple of
ears old. *Erica mediterranea*, however, can be cut right back into
ld wood and it will sprout afresh.

Secateurs are best used on small beds, but for larger areas there
no practical alternative to shears.

Apart from pruning, mulching is the only other treatment nece
sary. Sedge or moss peat, or leafmould, can be used. Apart from t
usual benefits of a mulch, and keeping the soil acid, it will al
encourage surface rooting and natural layering, which will help
secure rapid ground cover.

Feeding with inorganic fertilizers is not normally necessary, bu
light dressing of a general fertilizer every couple of years will n
come amiss.

There is little point in attempting to grow acid-loving Heathe
on alkaline soil and then trying to combat the effect with t
chemical Sequestrene. The problem is not a lack of iron inta
alone, but the fact that certain beneficial fungi that the Heathe
need for health do not thrive in alkaline soils.

Heath and Heather types

Calluna vulgaris (Scottish Heather or Ling): This is the most plentif
of the British Heaths, and it differs from ericas mainly by the fa

Right: *Erica* x *darleyensis* 'Arthur Johnson', one of the erica hybrids, will tolerate
lime, but should not be planted on shallow, chalk soil.
Below: The native Scottish Heather or Ling
is *Calluna vulgaris*. There are many
varieties, but 'Robert Chapman' is especially valuable because of its attractive
foliage, which is gold in spring changing
through orange to red.

that it is the calyx and not the corolla (petals) that is the colourful part of the flower. Some varieties tolerate clay quite well, particularly 'H. E. Beale', and they will even survive rough treatment – being walked upon and eaten by sheep and cattle in the wild.

The varieties are very varied in habit, from carpeters of only 5cm (2in), such as 'Golden Carpet', to tall kinds like 'Alportii' at 90cm (3ft). Although most have olive-green foliage, some varieties are golden, bronze or silver. Flower colours range from white to pinks, purples and crimson. Although they are mainly singles, some have double flowers. (Illustrated on page 130, 134 and 135.)

Erica arborea (Tree Heath): In their native habitat these plants will grow to 6m (20ft), but happily they are content with more modest proportions in our gardens. They will, however, still reach about 1·8m (6ft). They grow naturally on alkaline soils, and are not dependably hardy in cold districts.

The white flowers are Hawthorn-scented, but not spectacular.

Erica australis (Southern Tree Heath): One of the most beautiful of the tall-growing kinds, with bright pink tubular flowers. It is easily damaged by wind and snow, and is not dependably hardy.

Erica canaliculata (Channelled Heath): This is one Tree Heath that

Below: Heather gardens are becoming increasingly popular for year-round interest. Here, *Erica carnea* 'Aurea' contrasts well with *Calluna* 'J. H. Hamilton'.

will not tolerate lime. It is not hardy enough to be planted outdoors except in mild districts. The flowers are white if grown in a greenhouse, but become a delicate pink if planted outdoors.

Erica carnea (Mountain Heath): This erica, one of our most widely-grown plants, is now considered by botanists to be better named as *E. herbacea*. As it is not commonly known by this name, and most catalogues list it under *E. carnea*, the longer-established name has been used in this book. The varieties of Mountain Heath are surely among the most useful in the Heather garden. They will grow in limy soil, withstand atmospheric pollution that would harm other species, tolerate considerable salt spray, and flower through snow and ice. The species does not have such a good colour range as in some other kinds, most being pink, but there are many shades and the fact that they bloom during the bleakest months of the year makes them invaluable. (Illustrated on pages 10, 126 and 131.)

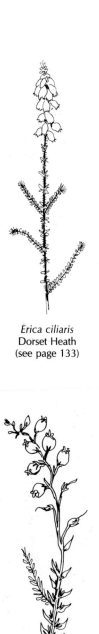

Erica ciliaris
Dorset Heath
(see page 133)

Erica ciliaris (Dorset Heath): This is perhaps the most beautiful of our native species. The rich pink, white or red flowers are pitcher-shaped, almost 12mm (½in) long, and produced three in a row, all facing one way, at intervals up the spike. Neither lime nor atmospheric pollution are tolerated.

Erica cinerea (Bell Heather): A plant for a warm sunny position; it will tolerate dry conditions better than callunas, but waterlogged ground is very detrimental. The soil must be acid.

Heights vary from 15cm (6in) to 60cm (2ft). There is a good colour range, including red, pink, lilac, mauve, lavender, purple and white.

Erica lusitanica (Portuguese Heath): A tall-growing tree form with white, slightly fragrant flowers from December to April.

Erica mediterranea (Irish Erica): This has been another victim of name-changing, *E. erigna* now being considered correct. For the sake of simplicity *E. mediterranea* has been used in this book.

As this plant actually gets washed by very high tides in some of its natural habitats, it will withstand salt spray from the sea. On the other hand, it is not completely hardy, and its brittle branches are easily damaged by snow. Pink, white and red shades are the principal colours.

Erica terminalis (Corsican Heath): Useful as a tall summer-flowering kind, growing to about 90cm (3ft), or slightly more. It bears pink flowers.

Erica tetralix (Cross-leaved Heath): An acid soil is absolutely essential, and a wet, peaty position is ideal. Most of the varieties have grey foliage, and flowers are the usual white, pink or red shades.

Erica vagans (Cornish Heath): A neutral or slightly alkaline soil will satisfy this plant, but do not attempt to grow it on very limy soils. The flowering period is July to October. Growth is quite strong, and as with the Dorset Heath the lower flowers turn brown before those at the tips have expanded.

Daboecia cantabrica (Irish Heath): This is not an easy plant to grow in the garden, as it is not hardy in severe winters, and will not tolerate dry conditions. It is another lime-hater. The plant forms a strong bush of about 60cm (2ft) high, and bears its rosy-purple white, pink or purple flowers from May to October.

Daboecia cantabrica
Irish Heath
(see page 134)

DORSET HEATH

Species and Varieties	Height	Flowering Period	Flower Colour	Description
Erica ciliaris 'Aurea'	23cm (9in)	7-8	Pink	Excellent for masses of golden foliage the year-round.
E. c. 'Corfe Castle'	30cm (1ft)	7-9	Salmon-pink	A Dorset Heath to attract everyone.
E. c. 'David McClintock'	45cm (1½ft)	7-10	Whitish-pink	Good garden plant
E. c. 'Rotundiflora'	30cm (1ft)	7-10	Pink	Distinctive large and rounded flowers.
E. c. 'Stoborough'	45cm (1½ft)	7-10	White	Vigorous plants with light green foliage.

Note: The Dorset Heath dislikes lime in the soil and atmospheric pollution. In severe winters it is often damaged and should be posiponed in a sheltered comer in full sun.

MOUNTAIN HEATHS

Species and Varieties	Height	Flowering Period	Flower Colour	Description
Erica carnea 'Adrienne Duncan'	15cm (6in)	1-3	Carmine-red	Has attractive bronzy shoots with coppery tips.
E. c. 'Aurea'	15cm (6in)	12-4	Vivid pink	Bushy plant with greenish-golden foliage.
E. c. 'December Red'	15cm (6in)	1-3	Deep pink	Good garden variety, which spreads.
E. c. 'Eileen Porter'	15cm (6in)	10-4	Carmine-pink	Slow-growing variety.
E. c. 'Foxhollow Fairy'	15cm (6in)	1-3	Creamy-pink	Vigorous and spreading.
E. c. 'Gracilis'	15cm (6in)	12-3	Pink	Small and neat plants, ideal for providing winter colour.
E. c. 'King George'	23cm (9in)	1-4	Rich pink	Well-known garden variety, verwith very bright flowers.
E. c. 'Loughrigg'	15cm (6in)	2-3	Reddish-purple	Vigorous, with dark green foliage.
E. c. 'Pink Spangles'	23cm (9in)	1-4	Pink	A strong plant, with very pretty flowers.
E. c. 'Ruby Glow'	15cm (6in)	3-4	Carmine	Attractive green foliage.
E. c. 'Springwood Pink'	15cm (6in)	2-4	Pink	Exceptionally vigorous plant that tends to smother weeds.
E. c. 'Vivellii'	15cm (6in)	2-4	Carmine-red	Plant with bronze foliage.
E. c. 'White Glow'	30cm (1ft)	2-4	White	A good bushy plant.
E. c. 'Winter Beauty'	15cm (6in)	1-3	Bright Pinkpink	Excellent for winter garden colour.

Note: These Mountain Heaths will withstand salt-laden sea spray and atmospheric pollution. They tolerate lime in the soil and will grow in sun or partial shade. They are easy to grow, and have the advantage of smothering weeds.

Erica carnea
Mountain Heath
(see this page)

Erica tetralix
Cross-leaved Heath
(see page 134)

CROSS-LEAVED HEATHS

Species and Varieties	Height	Flowering Period	Flower Colour	Description
Erica tetralix 'Alba Mollis'	23cm (9in)	6-10	White	An attractive plant with numerous flowers and silvery-grey foliage.
E. t. 'Con Underwood'	23cm (9in)	6-10	Crimson	Vivid flowers, superbly contrasting silver-grey foliage.
E. t. 'Melbury White'	23cm (9in)	6-10	White	Attractive silvery foliage and large flowers.
E. t. 'Pink Glow'	23cm (9in)	7-8	Pink	Many small flowers, and silvery foliage.
E. t. 'Rubra'	15cm (6in)	7-10	Red	Grey-green foliage.
E. t. 'Tina'	23cm (9in)	7-9	Pale pink	Unusual foliage which is slightly woolly.

Note: This distinctive species is the Cross-leaved Heath, with bell-like flowers and silvery-grey foliage. Fully hardy in the British Isles, but must have a lime-free soil. Needs plenty of peat around its roots and a position in full sun.

Below: *Calluna vulgaris* 'Peter Sparkes' bears double pink flowers on long spikes, making it a useful variety for cutting. (See pages 130 and 137.)

THE IRISH HEATHS

Species and Variety	Height	Flowering Period	Flower Colour	Description
Daboecia cantabrica 'Alba'	60cm (2ft)	6-10	White	Variety for long flowering. Large flowers.
D. c. 'Atropurpurea'	60cm (2ft)	5-10	Rich purple	Attractively dark foliage.
D. c. 'Bicolor'	60cm (2ft)	6-10	White and purple	Flowers which may be white, purple or bi-coloured.
D. c. 'Praegerae'	45cm (1½ft)	6-10	Salmon-pink	Superbly coloured large bells.

Note: Plants of Irish Heath are often damaged by very severe winters. They need sun or partial sun and a lime-free soil.

CORNISH HEATHS

Species and Varieties	Height	Flowering Period	Flower Colour	Description
Erica vagans 'Kevernensis Alba'	30cm (1ft)	8-10	White	A distinctive variety with dark green foliage.
E. v. 'Lyonese'	45cm (1½ft)	8-10	White	Flowers on long spikes amid bright green foliage.
E. v. 'Mrs. D.F. Maxwell'	45cm (1½ft)	8-10	Deep cerise	Variety, famed for its glorious flowers and dark foliage.
E. v. 'St. Keverne'	45cm (1½ft)	8-10	Salmon-pink	Eye-catching pastel-coloured variety.
E. v. 'Valerie Proudley'	45cm (1½ft)	8-9	White	One of the best Cornish Heaths for coloured foliage — golden the year-round.

Note: Many of the varieties will form spreading bushes, displaying masses of attractive flower spikes. The Cornish Heath is fully hardy and grows well in heavy soil where peat has been added. It will tolerate soils with only small amounts of lime.

SCOTTISH ERICA (BELL HEATHER)

Species and Varieties	Height	Flowering Period	Flower Colour	Description
Erica cinerea 'Alba'	23cm (9in)	6-8	White	Attractive, with long and free-flowering spikes.
E. c. 'Atrorubens'	15cm (6in)	6-10	Ruby-red	Handsome flowers in long and attractive sprays
E. c. 'Duncan Fraser'	30cm (1ft)	7-8	White, tinged with pink	A vigorous plant.
E. c. 'Eden Valley'	15cm (6in)	6-9	Lilac	Large flowers.
E. c. 'Glencairn'	23cm (9in)	6-8	Deep pink	Coloured foliage, with bright red tips in the winter.
E. c. 'Golden Sport'	30cm (1ft)	7-8	Mauve	The yellow foliage turns to orange.
E. c. 'Knap Hill Pink'	30cm (1ft)	6-10	Rose-pink	A robust and vigorous plant.
E. c. 'Lavender Lady'	30cm (1ft)	7-9	Lavender	A good garden plant.
E. c. 'Pentreath'	23cm (9in)	7-9	Rich purple	Dark green foliage on a bushy plant.
E. c. 'Plummer's Seedling'	30cm (1ft)	7-8	Rich red	Attractively long flower spikes.

Note: This heather needs a well-drained lime-free soil in full sun.

Below: *Calluna vulgaris* 'Elsie Purnell' is a distinctive variety with its silvery-pink flower spikes. (See pages 130 and 137.)

Erica arborea
Tree Heath
(see this page)

Erica terminalis
Tree Heath
(see this page)

TREE HEATHS

Species and Variety	Height	Flowering Period	Flower Colour	Description
Erica arborea 'Alpina'	1.5m (5ft)	3-5	White	Distinctive erica with many scented flowers.
E. a. 'Estrella Gold'	1.8m (6ft)	3-5	White	Covered with golden foliage the year-round.
E. a. 'Gold Tips'	1.6m (5½ft)	3-5	White	Tips of foliage are golden during the spring months.
E. australis	1.6m (5½ft)	4-6	Bright pink	Good garden plant with showy flowers.
E. a. 'Riverslea'	1.8m (6ft)	4-6	Purplish-pink	Has very large flowers.
E. canaliculata	2.4m (8ft)	1-5	Whitish-pink	Best in sheltered gardens totally free of lime.
E. lusitanica	1.6m (5½ft)	12-4	White	Delightful feathery foliage.
E. terminalis	1m (3½ft)	6-10	Pink	An excellent variety for a summer-flowering hedge.
E. x veitchii	1.6m (5½ft)	12-5	White	Scented flowers, on vigorous plant.

Note: Tree Heaths are all hardy, but they can be seriously damaged by heavy falls of snow, which tend to break branches and to flatten them. Will tolerate a little lime in the soil.

ERICA HYBRIDS

Species and Varieties	Height	Flowering Period	Flower Colour	Description
Winter-flowering (E. x darleyensis hybrids)				
'Arthur Johnson'	60cm (2ft)	11-4	Rosy-pink	A superb variety with long flower spikes.
'Darley Dale'	45cm (1½ft)	11-5	Pale pink	A hardy, winter-flowering plant.
'George Rendall'	30cm (1ft)	12-5	Deep pink	Attractive foliage in spring.
'Jack H. Brummage'	30cm (1ft)	1-4	Pink	A variety that is superb during the spring.
'Silberschmelze'	45cm (1½ft)	11-5	White	Attractive flower spikes.

Note: These are crosses between Erica mediteranea and Erica carnea. Lime tolerant, and flower over a long period.

Summer-flowering				
Erica x praegeri 'Irish Lemon'	23cm (9in)	6-10	Clear pink	Lemon-tipped foliage in the spring.
Erica x watsonii 'Dawn'	23cm (9in)	6-11	Rosy pink	Superb for ground cover as it will smother weeds. Vivid red foliage tips in spring.
Erica x williamsii 'Gwavas'	30cm (1ft)	6-9	Pale pink	Golden shoots in spring.
Erica x williamsii 'P.D. Williams'	30cm (1ft)	6-9	Pale pink	Carries many small flowers.

Note: These are crosses between Erica tetralix and other species. These heathers dislike lime in the soil and prefer a sunny position. Flower over a long period.

SCOTTISH HEATHER (Ling)

Species and Varieties	Height	Flowering Period	Flower Colour	Description
Calluna vulgaris 'Alba Plena'	54cm (1¾ft)	9-10	White	Double flowers on a plant that is ideal for smothering weeds.
C. v. 'Cupraea'	30cm (1ft)	8-9	Purple	Attractive coppery foliage the year round.
C. v. 'Darkness'	30cm (1ft)	8-9	Crimson-purple	Freely flowering heather.
C. v. 'Elsie Purnell'	75cm (2½ft)	9-10	Silvery-pink	Double flowers amid grey-green foliage.
C. v. 'Finale'	45cm (1½ft)	10-12	Rich purple	Late-flowering variety.
C. v. 'Fred J. Chapple'	45cm (1½ft)	8-9	Purple	Double flowers amid foliage with year-round appeal.
C. v. 'Gold Haze'	60cm (2ft)	8-9	White	Long flower sprays surrounded by bright gold foliage.
C. v. 'H.E. Beale'	60cm (2ft)	9-11	Soft pink	Double flowers on long spikes.
C. v. 'Hibernica'	15cm (6in)	10-11	Bright pink	Good autumn and early winter variety.
C. v. 'Joan Sparkes'	23cm (9in)	8-9	Mauve	Attractive double flowers.
C. v. 'Orange Queen'	60cm (2ft)	8-9	Pink	Golden foliage that turns orange.
C. v. 'Peter Sparkes'	45cm (1½ft)	8-10	Deep pink	Double flowers on long spikes.
C. v. 'Ruth Sparkes'	23cm (9in)	8-9	White	Double flowers and golden foliage.
C. v. 'Summer Orange'	45cm (1½ft)	8-9	Pink	Orange-colour foliage.

Note: These *Calluna vulgaris* varieties are tolerant of salt-laden sea spray and will even survive moderate atmospheric pollution. Plant them in a sunny situation which has lime-free soil.

Calluna vulgaris
Scottish Heather
(see this page)

IRISH ERICA

Species and Varieties	Height	Flowering Period	Flower Colour	Description
Erica mediterranea 'Alba Compacta'	45cm (1½ft)	3-5	White	A compact and shapely bush, covered in delicate flowers.
E. m. 'Brightness'	75cm (2½ft)	3-5	Reddish-purple	Deep coloured flowers and glaucous foliage.
E. m. 'Nana Alba'	45cm (1½ft)	3-5	Pale pink	Excellent for forming neat and compact bushes.
E. m. 'Superba'	1.4m (4½ft)	3-5	Silvery-pink	Delightfully scented, with many large flowers.
E. m. 'W. T. Rackliff'	60cm (2ft)	3-5	White	Pure white flowers on a rounded bush.

Note: This native of Ireland is tolerant of lime in the soil. Also it survives sea spray and is almost completely hardy.

Erica australis
Tree Heath
(see page 136)

Roses

Roses have been appreciated for many hundreds of years, but it is only since the end of the eighteenth century that modern garden roses, the result of hybridization, have been grown. Botanists and plant breeders have produced what is, perhaps, the world's most popular flower.

The most widely planted roses are the hybrid-teas, but useful though these are, many other types are likely to enhance the garden in equal measure. Not only are there many types, including some delightful species, but the use of roses in the garden stretches far beyond setting them in rigid arrangements in formal beds.

Climbers and ramblers are usually trained up walls, where they look delightful in bloom, but they can be used equally effectively to cover old tree stumps or to clamber through the branches of an otherwise uninteresting old tree. The shrub border is an ideal place for shrub roses. Also, several types make practical and beautiful hedges.

Rosa rugosa
(see page 144)

Soil and site

Roses will grow well on a wide variety of soils, and the old belief that heavy clay is necessary for vigorous growth is no more than a myth. Roses will grow well in clay soils, but they can be grown just as successfully in other types. Evidence of this is the National Rose Society's show ground at St. Albans, which is gravelly.

Modern rootstocks can also have an influence on the type of soil best suited to roses. Although *Rosa canina*, the native Briar, enjoys a heavy soil, *R. rugosa* prefers a light, sandy one — but is intolerant of chalk. Another rootstock, known as Simplex, succeeds on shallow, sandy soils. This will continue to grow in prolonged dry weather after *R. canina* would have stopped.

Most bush roses are likely to have been grafted or budded on to *R. canina*, although *R. rugosa* is usually used for standards and half-standards and some climbers.

The chances are that unless there is something extreme about the soil structure, roses will grow perfectly satisfactorily. However, if the soil is very heavy, drainage should be improved by digging in plenty of organic material. Deep digging is also important. On sandy soils, however, deep digging is not advisable, although the humus content must be increased as much as possible to increase fertility and moisture-retaining capacity.

Far left: *Rosa* 'Ballerina', a Hybrid Musk rose, adds grace to any garden, displaying apple-blossom flowers in large clusters. (See pages 144 and 146.)

Ena Harkness
(see page 147)

Rosa gallica
(see page 144)

Orange Sensation
(see page 148)

ROSES SUITABLE FOR EXHIBITION
Ena Harkness
Fragrant Cloud
Grandpa Dickson
Montezuma
Peace
Perfecta
Silver Lining
Wendy Cussons

CLIMBING ROSES
Casino
Danse de Feu
Golden Showers
Parade
Royal Gold

RAMBLER ROSES
Alberic Barbier
Albertine

POLYANTHA POMPONS
Cameo
Golden Polyantha
Margot Costa
Yesterday
Yvonne Rabier

SHRUB ROSE — REPEAT FLOWERING
Bonn
Chinatown
Felicia
Joseph's Coat
Nevada
Prosperity

ROSES FOR BEGINNERS
Buccaneer
Ena Harkness
Fragrant Cloud
Frau Karl Druschki
Grandmere Jenny
Grandpa Dickson
Lady Sylvia
Montezuma
Peace
Piccadilly
Spek's Yellow
Super Star
Sutter's Gold
Wendy Cussons

HYBRID TEA ROSES RESISTANT TO RAIN DAMAGE
April Silk
Brandenberg
Ena Harkness
Grandmere Jenny
Grandpa Dickson
Lady Sylvia
Mrs. Sam McGredy
Peace
Silver Lining
Spek's Yellow
Super Star
Sutter's Gold
Wendy Cussons

ROSES FOR HEDGES
Ballerina
Bonn
Cornelia
Dorothy Wheatcroft
Felicia
Frau Dagmar Hastrup
Heidelberg
Lady Sonia
Nevada
Peace
Penelope
Prosperity
Queen Elizabeth
Vanity
Zephirine Drouhin

FRAGRANT ROSES
Albertine
Climbing Ena Harkness
Climbing Etoile de Hollande
Elizabeth of Glamis
Ena Harkness
Fragrant Cloud
Josephine Bruce
Lady Sylvia
Orange Sensation
Silver Lining
Super Star
Sutter's Gold
Wendy Cussons
Zephirine Drouhin

ROSES WITH ATTRACTIVE HIPS
Frau Dagmar Hastrup
Rosa x cantabrigiensis
R. hugonis
R. moyesii
R. primula
R. rubrifolia
R. xanthina 'Canary Bird'

SHRUB ROSES — SUMMER FLOWERING
Rosa x cantabrigiensis
R. gallica 'Versicolor'
R. 'Highdownensis'
R. hugonis
R. moyesii
R. rubrifolia
R. xanthina 'Canary Bird'

ROSES FOR WALLS
Danse de Feu
Ena Harkness, Climbing
Etoile de Hollande, Climbing
Masquerade, Climbing
Mermaid
Mrs. Sam McGredy, Climbing
Parkdirektor Riggers
Paul's Lemon Pillar
Royal Gold
Spek's Yellow, Climbing
Zephirine Drouhin

Far more critical than the structure of the soil can be the alkalinity. Roses prefer a slightly acid soil, in the pH range 6·0 to 6·5. They will grow at figures above this, but on very chalky soils they are unlikely to thrive as well as they would on a more acid soil.

A sunny site is required. If full sun is not possible then choose a position where they will receive sun for more than half the day.

Types of rose

The work of hybridists has produced some lovely roses, but it makes many of them difficult to classify. Many shrub roses are hybrids between species and roses of garden origin. The floribunda 'Queen Elizabeth' has large flowers more like a hybrid tea than a floribunda, and its vigour puts it in a class of its own, being twice as high as many floribundas. This has led some people to give it a status of its own, and in the United States it is known as a Grandiflora. In Britain the trend has been to adopt the name of 'floribunda hybrid-tea type'. The ability of the rose to 'sport' or unexpectedly produce a variant, leads not only to many colour versions of the same plant, but to climbing hybrid-teas.

The division between hybrid-teas and floribundas used to be reasonably clear-cut, but they have been crossed with each other, and there is now an increasing number of floribundas with large double flowers like the hybrid-teas, and hybrid-teas with more flowers to the stem, such as 'Fragrant Cloud' and 'Pink Favourite'. These blurrings of definition should be borne in mind when reading the following descriptions. The naming and re-naming of plants is a continuing process, and roses have not escaped this treatment. The names used here are common in many current nursery catalogues, but recent changes have altered the classification of many groups.

Hybrid-tea roses produce large, double flowers, singly or in twos or threes. They have a long flowering period, but the peak is in June, with a secondary flush in late summer, though they will flower intermittently in between, and continue in bloom until severe weather arrives. (Illustrated on page 142.)

Floribunda roses usually have single or semi-double flowers, smaller in size than the hybrid-teas, but in many-flowered clusters. They are more effective than hybrid teas for massed effect, and the flowering appears more continuous because as some flowers in a head fade, others open – and usually by the time one truss has finished, another is just starting. As a group they lack fragrance compared with hybrid-teas. (Illustrated on page 143.)

Standards are usually hybrid tea or floribunda roses budded on 1·2m (4ft) stems. Weeping standards are usually produced by budding rambler varieties on the stem.

Polyantha-pompons were the forerunners of the modern floribundas. They are much smaller than the floribundas, 30–38cm (12–15in) being usual, but the clusters of dainty flowers are attractive, and a few varieties are useful today, particularly to plant in the foreground of a mixed border or to make a low hedge or edge to a path or drive.

Miniatures have flowers less than 12mm (½in) in diameter, and the rest of the plant is in proportion. Heights vary from 13 to 45cm

Frau Dagmar Hastrup
(see page 147)

Super Star
(see page 149)

Parkdirektor Riggers
(see page 148)

(5–18in). Although they are traditionally used in sink and roc
gardens and window-boxes, they also make a good edging
borders. If they are used in window-boxes or the rock garden, it
important to ensure they have at least 25cm (10in) of soil depth,
their roots require a deep, cool root run.

A fascinating way to use these plants is in a miniature ro:
garden, with beds laid out and gravel or small paving stone path
There are even miniature climbers that can be used as a backclotl
although these will grow to 1·2m (4ft), and also miniature standar
add more interest.

Climbers have larger flowers than ramblers, and they are not alway
borne in clusters. They are likely to flower intermittently over th
season, rather than in one flush like the ramblers, and they bloor
well on old wood. New shoots often arise from the main cane:
rather than from the base of the plant.

Although we call them climbers they are not able to clim
unaided. In nature they use their thorns to hook themselves a
anchorage, but in the garden they normally have to be tied in.

Climbers are of two main sorts — those derived from *Ros*
gigantea and other natural species, and sports of hybrid-teas c
floribunda bush roses. It is worth bearing in mind that the climbin
forms of hybrid-teas and floribundas seldom flower as prolifically a
the bush forms.

Ramblers have clusters of small flowers, usually produced in on
flush in midsummer, and these are borne on the strong new cane
that arise from the base of the plant each year.

Many of the ramblers are hybrids of *R. wichuraiana*, an

Below: The world-famous rose 'Peace' is a Hybrid-tea with a spectacular display of yellow flowers that turn to a coarse-pink, then a soft pink. (See pages 141 and 148.)

enerally they have the characteristic of flowering only once in the
ason. Many of them are susceptible to mildew, and for that
ason are best grown away from walls, where the air circulation is
etter. For scrambling up pergolas or trees they are ideal. If planting
ne against a tree, position it on the windward side, so it is blown
gainst the tree and not away from it.

pecies and shrub roses are the bushy, less formal roses, sometimes
ferred to as 'old fashioned' roses. It is an unfortunate term, for
ost of them have a place in the modern garden. If viewed as
rdinary flowering shrubs, rather than comparing individual
looms with show-bench hybrid-teas, the rose species are marvel-
us plants by any standards.

hrub roses

Modern Shrub Roses: This group includes a miscellany of hybrids
f mixed parentage, and which cannot be classified as 'old
ashioned' roses. Most of these shrub roses grow fairly large — up to
·5m (5ft) or a little more — but generally they have the considerable
dvantage over some of the other species and older shrub roses in
aving a long flowering period: they tend to bloom profusely
hroughout the summer.

An example of this group is the variety 'Nevada', which has
reamy-white semi-double blooms about 10cm (4in) across, with
right yellow stamens. The reddish-brown stems are smothered
vith flowers early in the season. Flowers continue intermittently for
he rest of the season, although they may be smaller.

Elizabeth of Glamis
(see page 146)

Left: 'Chinatown' is one of the vigorous
floribundas, with a spreading habit and
dark green foliage. (See pages 141 and
146.)

143

Rosa moyesii
(see page 149)

Nevada
(see page 148)

Hybrid Musks: These excellent shrubs bloom continuously throughout summer, bearing large trusses of floribunda-like flowers. They are, in fact, only distantly related to the proper Musk rose, but it is almost certainly from this ancestor that they derive their vigour and sweet fragrance. (Illustrated on pages 138 and 147.)

'Vanity' is a good example from this group, having huge open trusses of large, single, deep pink flowers with Sweet Pea fragrance. It makes a large, open plant of arching habit, and is useful for planting at the back of a wide border. 'Prosperity' has large trusses of ivory-white semi-double flowers flushed with lemon towards the centre. It is delightfully scented. 'Ballerina' is smaller, growing to about 1·2m by 1·2m (4ft by 4ft), but is not particularly fragrant. It has hydrangea-like heads of small, single, pink flowers. There are other varieties in the usual rose colours.

China Roses: Although the flowers are small they bloom steadily throughout the season, and their twiggy habit makes them suitable for a place in the front of a shrub border. Pruning is best restricted to removing old and weak wood.

Japanese or Rugosa Roses: Distinctive roses with large open flowers, and usually a rich scent. They are particularly good for hedges, being prickly shrubs that will grow under poor conditions. Their long display also makes them useful in the shrub border. The foliage is usually luxuriant, deeply veined and resistant to disease.

Representative of the Rugosas is 'Frau Dagmar Hastrup', which has delicately veined flesh-pink single flowers, with cream-coloured stamens. Towards the end of the season, hips from the first flowers appear at the same time as new flowers are opening.

Some 'old-fashioned' roses

Many of these varieties have been around for hundreds of years, but there is every reason to grow them in today's gardens. Their only disadvantage is that with the exception of the Bourbons they only flower once a year — but that is the case with most shrubs, and they are charming plants and most have a strong fragrance.

Gallica Roses: These are among the oldest garden roses, and there are some fine examples, with beautiful flower formation and a magnificent mixture of colours. And like all old roses, the fragrance is heady.

Alba Roses: An old type, dating back to the Middle Ages. The flowers have a delicate appearance, but are very hardy. The colours are shades of pink or white, set off by greyish foliage.

Damask Roses: These are noted for their wonderful fragrance. The flowers are held in open bunches.

Centifolia Roses: Popularly known as 'cabbage' roses, being large and globular. The weight of petals sometimes causes them to hang down, but this can look quite pleasing. They are very fragrant, and the shrub has a lax, open habit. It has rather coarse leaves and many thorns.

Rosa rubrifolia: A pleasant almost thornless shrub with coppery-mauve foliage and clear pink, single flowers paling to white in the centres, though the foliage is the main attraction. Dark red hips are a further attraction.

sa xanthina 'Canary Bird' has bright yellow single flowers about
m (2in) across all along 1·8m (6ft) arching canes of attractive and
licate ferny foliage.

uning and feeding

ning is always a contentious subject among rose-growers. Much
bate centres on when to prune rather than how. Some people
your pruning hybrid-teas and floribundas in autumn, others prefer
ring. Devotees of both methods achieve good results, and a
mpromise between the two is to reduce any heavy top growth on
gorous plants in the autumn, to prevent wind-rock damage, then
complete the pruning in spring before new growth starts. The best
ne is just as the sap is beginning to rise, which will vary by as
uch as a month from one part of the country to another.

Ramblers should be pruned in late summer after the flowers fade,
en the new shoots are tied in.

Newly planted hybrid teas and floribundas should be cut back to
e third or fourth outward-growing bud from the base. This will
sure that plenty of new shoots are formed and a well-balanced
ape is established.

In subsequent years, most modern hybrid-teas should only be
uned moderately, cutting back the previous year's growth by half.
this allows the bush to become too tall, hard pruning to three or
ur buds from the ground every third year is advised. Floribundas
subsequent years should have basal growth from the previous
ar just tipped back, and the last year's laterals cut back by half.
lder wood should be pruned to within two or three buds from the
se.

Wichuraiana ramblers such as 'Dorothy Perkins', with long and
iable canes, should have all flowered canes cut out after flower-
g, and new ones tied in to replace them.

Wichuraiana climbers, which have stiffer growth than the ramb-
rs, and have a good portion of the new growth emanating laterally
om old stems and not from the base, should have new growth
tained, and as much old wood as can be spared cut out.

Repeat-flowering climbers, usually used on pillars, and includ-
g varieties such as 'Golden Showers', need little pruning other
an to control overcrowding of the branches, and to cut back old
terals to within two or three eyes from the main stem.

Climbing sports of floribunda and hybrid-tea varieties should not
e pruned the first spring after planting, and it should be done
paringly in subsequent years. Just remove dead or diseased wood
nd shorten lateral growths on old canes to two or three eyes from
he main stem.

Shrub roses need no pruning for the first few years, and then it is
onfined to cutting away twiggy growth and dead or diseased
rowth, and removing a proportion of old wood.

Miniature roses are pruned with nail scissors. Only remove
iseased or dead wood, trimming just to shape the bush.

Roses are rank feeders and will benefit from a proprietary rose
ertilizer, of which there are several. A thick mulch will also help
uring the summer.

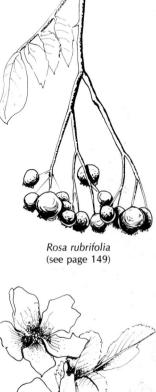

Rosa rubrifolia
(see page 149)

Rosa xanthina 'Canary Bird'
(see page 149)

145

GOOD GARDEN ROSES

Varieties	Height	Type of rose	Colour	Flowering Time	Fragrance	Hardiness	Description
Albéric Barbier	2.1-3.6m (7-12ft)	Wich. Cl.	Canary-yellow	7		★★★★	A vigorously growing rose.
Albertine	2.4-3.6m (8-12ft)	Wich. Cl.	Coppery-pink	7	✿	★★★★	This is one of the best ramblers, with dark foliage.
April Silk	105cm (3½ft)	H.T.	Rich apricot	6-10	✿	★★★★	Attractive foliage. Fairly vigorous plant.
Ballerina	1.8-2.4m (6-8ft)	Hybrid Musk	Apple-blossom pink	6-7	✿	★★★★	Flowers displayed in large clusters.
Bonn	1.8-2.4m (6-8ft)	Shrub	Orange-scarlet	6-7	✿	★★★★	Semi-double flowers on a free-flowering large bush.
Brandenberg	90cm (3ft)	H.T.	Salmon	6-10	✿	★★★★	Attractive foliage.
Buccaneer	90cm (3ft)	H.T.	Buttercup yellow	6-10		★★★★	A tall variety, ideal for the back of a border
Cameo	45cm (1½ft)	Poly. pompon	Pink	6-7		★★★★	Double flowers in attractively shaped clusters.
Cornelia	1.8m (6ft)	Hybrid Musk	Apricot-pink	6-7	✿	★★★★	A vigorous, fragrant, variety with dark green foliage.
Casino	3.0-3.6m (10-12ft)	Cl. H.T.	Yellow	6-10	✿	★★★★	A vigorous rose, ideal for covering fences and pergolas
Chicago Peace	105cm (3½ft)	H.T.	Pink, yellow and copper	6-10	✿	★★★★	The blooms are an attractive mixture of colours.
Chinatown	1.5m (5ft)	Flor.	Golden-yellow	6-10	✿	★★★★	A vigorous and spreading bush, with dark green foliage
Danse de Feu	1.8-3m (6-10ft)	Cl.	Orange-scarlet	6-8		★★★★	Ideal for a north or east facing wall. Vigorous.
Dorothy Wheatcroft	90cm (3ft)	Flor.	Orange-red	6-10		★★★★	Semi-double flowers in large trusses on a vigorous bush.
Elizabeth of Glamis	90cm (3ft)	Flor.	Soft salmon	6-10	✿	★★★★	A free-flowering rose with vigorous growth.

Right: One of the charms of *Rosa moyesii* is its beautifully coloured and attractively shaped hips. The flowers are blood-red in colour. (See page 149.)

Far right: *Rosa* 'Mermaid' is a vigorous climber, ideal for a south or west facing wall. (See page 148.)

Extreme right: 'Penelope', a Hybrid Musk shrub rose, has a strong musk fragrance and is ideal for hedges. (See page 144.)

GOOD GARDEN ROSES Continued

Varieties	Height	Type of rose	Colour	Flowering Time	Fragrance	Hardiness	Description
...na Harkness	75cm (2½ft)	H.T.	Crimson-scarlet	6-10	✿	★★★★	Excellent flowers, but often the stems are weak.
...na Harkness, Climbing	1.8-3m (6-10ft)	Cl. H.T.	Crimson-scarlet	6-9	✿	★★★	A climber for a south or west facing wall. A vigorous rose.
...toile de Hollande, Climbing	3m (10ft)	Cl. H.T.	Velvety-crimson	6-10	✿	★★★	A climber for a south or west facing wall. A vigorous rose.
...elicia	1.5m (5ft)	Hybrid Musk	Salmon to yellow	6-7	✿	★★★★	Very fragrant. Strong, bushy growth.
...ragrant Cloud	90cm (3ft)	H.T.	Coral-scarlet	6-10	✿	★★★★	Exceptionally strong growth, and very attractive flowers.
...rau Dagmar Hastrup	1.5m (5ft)	Rugosa shrub	Rose-pink	6-7		★★★★	Large, single flowers produced throughout the summer.
...rau Karl Druschki	105cm (3½ft)	H.T.	White	6-10		★★★★	A vigorous variety which is susceptible to mildew.
...Golden Polyantha	45cm (1½ft)	Poly. pompon	Golden-yellow	6-7		★★★★	Small, semi-double flowers on a bushy plant.
...Golden Showers	1.8m (6ft)	Cl.	Golden-yellow	6-10		★★★★	A variety that may require protection from black spot.
...Grandmere Jenny	105cm (3½ft)	H.T.	Yellow	6-10		★★★★	An attractive upright habit.
Grandpa Dickson	105cm (3½ft)	H.T.	Lemon-yellow	6-10		★★★★	An early-flowering variety, which produces further flushes of flowers.
Iceberg	1.2m (4ft)	Flor.	White	6-10	✿	★★★★	Abundant medium-green foliage.
Ideal Home	90cm (3ft)	H.T.	Carmine-pink	6-10	✿	★★★★	Vigorous upright growth, with globular flowers.
Jiminy Cricket	75cm (2½ft)	Flor.	Orange-vermilion	6-10	✿	★★★★	A free-flowering rose with a bushy habit.

Varieties	Height	Type of rose	Colour	Flowering Time	Fragrance	Hardiness	Description
Lady Sylvia	90cm (3ft)	H.T.	Light pink	6-10	✿	★★★★	A variety that flowers well into the autumn.
Lady Sonia	90cm (3ft)	H.T.	Golden-yellow	6-10		★★★★	Large flowers borne freely.
Margot Costa	45cm (1½ft)	Poly pompon	Salmon-pink	6-7		★★★★	An attractive rose for edging a border.
Masquerade	75cm (2½ft)	Flor.	Salmon-pink	6-7		★★★★	The buds are a rich yellow, eventually becoming a deep scarlet.
Masquerade, Climbing	1.8-3.6m (6-12ft)	Cl. Flor.	Pink	6-10		★★★★	A vigorous rose, well suited to a north or east facing wall.
Mermaid	1.8-3.6m (6-12ft)	Cl.	Primrose-yellow	6-7		★★★	A very vigorous rose for a south or west facing wall.
Montezuma	90cm (3ft)	H.T.	Salmon-red	6-10		★★★★	Tall and vigorous upright growth.
Mrs. Sam McGredy	75cm (2½ft)	H.T.	Coppery-scarlet	6-10		★★★★	A variety that may require treatment against black spot.
Mrs. Sam McGredy, Climbing	1.8-3.6m (6-12ft)	Cl.	Coppery-red	6-9		★★★	A vigorous rose for a south or west facing wall.
Nevada	1.8-3m (6-10ft)	Shrub	Creamy-white	6 and 8		★★★★	A vigorous rose, which will produce two flushes of flowers in the summer.
Opera	75cm (2½ft)	H.T.	Orange-scarlet	6-10	✿	★★★★	A variety that may need protection against black spot and rust.
Orange Sensation	75cm (2½ft)	Flor.	Bright orange	6-10	✿	★★★★	Very attractive dark green foliage.
Parade	1.8-3.6m (6-12ft)	Cl.	Carmine-red	6-8		★★★★	Vigorous and abundant glossy-green foliage.
Parkdirektor Riggers	1.8-3m (6-10ft)	Cl.	Blood-red	6-7		★★★★	A vigorous rose for a north or east facing wall.
Paul's Lemon Pillar	1.8-3.6m (6-12ft)	Cl.	Pale yellow	6-7	✿	★★★★	A vigorous rose for a north or east facing wall.
Peace	90cm (3ft)	H.T.	Yellow	6-10		★★★★	The large and full flowers open as yellow, but slowly turn to a cerise-pink, then a soft pink.
Penelope	1.8m (6ft)	Hybrid Musk	Pink	6-7	✿	★★★★	Strong musk fragrance. Good for hedges.
Perfecta	90cm (3ft)	H.T.	Cream and rose	6-10		★★★★	Well-formed blooms, but they can be damaged by rain.
Piccadilly	90cm (3ft)	H.T.	Scarlet flushed gold	6-10	✿	★★★★	A vigorous and upright bush.
Prosperity	1.5-1.8m (5-6ft)	Hybrid Musk	White, tinged pink	6-9	✿	★★★★	Hybrid Musk rose. Attractive pompon-like flowers borne in clusters.
Queen Elizabeth	1.8m (6ft)	Flor.	Pink	6-10		★★★★	Hybrid-tea-like blooms on vigorous stems. Large, glossy leaves.
Rosa x cantabrigiensis	1.8m (6ft)		Yellow	5-6		★★★★	Semi-double early flowers, followed by small, orange-red hips. Graceful fern-like foliage.

GOOD GARDEN ROSES Continued

Varieties	Height	Type of rose	Colour	Flowering Time	Fragrance	Hardiness	Description
R. gallica 'Versicolor'	0.9-1.2m (3-4ft)		Red	6		★★★★	Semi-double flowers, red, striped with white.
R. 'Highdownensis'	1.5-1.8m (5-6ft)		Rose-red	6-7		★★★★	Single flowers, followed by bottle-shaped scarlet fruits.
R. hugonis	1.8m (6ft)		Pale yellow	5		★★★★	Single flowers, followed by maroon-coloured hips. A graceful rose with fern-like foliage.
R. moyesii	3m (10ft)		Blood-red	6		★★★★	Single flowers borne in clusters, followed by bottle-shaped hips.
R. primula	1.8m (6ft)		Primrose-yellow	5		★★★★	Single flowers followed by small, reddish hips. The leaves have an aromatic fragrance.
R. rubrifolia	1.8m (6ft)		Clear pink	6		★★★★	Single flowers followed by brownish-red hips. Decorative foliage.
R. xanthina 'Canary Bird'	1.5-1.8m (5-6ft)		Deep canary-yellow	5		★★★★	Single flowers in May, followed by dark maroon hips. Fern-like foliage.
Royal Gold	1.8-3.6m (6-12ft)	Cl.	Deep yellow	6-8	✿	★★★	A moderately vigorous rose for a south or west facing wall.
Silver Lining	75cm (2½ft)	H.T.	Silver	6-10	✿	★★★★	A variety which is ideal for bedding purposes, but has rather small foliage..
Spek's Yellow	90cm (3ft)	H.T.	Deep golden-yellow	6-10		★★★★	A very free-flowering variety.
Spek's Yellow, Climbing	1.8-3.6m (6-12ft)	Cl.	Rich golden-yellow	6-7		★★★	A vigorous rose for a south or west facing wall.
Sterling Silver	75cm (2½ft)	H.T.	Silvery lilac	6-10	✿	★★★★	A variety that may require protection from black spot.
Super Star	90cm (3ft)	H.T.	Vermilion	6-10	✿	★★★★	Vigorous growth, and masses of flowers.
Sutter's Gold	90cm (3ft).	H.T.	Orange-yellow	6-10	✿	★★★★	Tall but often spindly growth.
Teenager	90cm (3ft)	H.T.	Rose-pink	6-10	✿	★★★★	Tall and upright, and very vigorous.
Vanity	1.8-2.4m (6-8ft)	Hybrid Musk	Deep rose-pink	6-9	✿	★★★★	Hybrid Musk Rose. Large flowers on strong growths.
Wendy Cussons	90cm (3ft)	H.T.	Rosy-red	6-10	✿	★★★★	A reliable rose with a rich damask fragrance.
Woburn Abbey	75cm (2½ft)	Flor.	Orange-yellow	6-10	✿	★★★★	A vigorous rose with shiny dark green foliage.
Yesterday	90cm (3ft)	Poly.pompon	Lilac-pink	6-7	✿	★★★★	Graceful sprays of flowers.
Yvonne Rabier	1.2m (4ft)	Poly. pompon	White	6-7	✿	★★★★	Sprays and clusters of double flowers.
Zephirine Drouhin	1.8-3.6m (6-12ft)	Bourbon cl.	Bright carmine-pink	6-7	✿	★★★★	A vigorous rose for a north or east facing wall.

Cl. Climbing rose; Cl. Flor. Climbing floribunda; Cl. H.T. Climbing hybrid tea; Flor. Floribunda; H.T. Hybrid Tea; Poly. pompon Polyantha pompon; Wich. Cl. R. wichuraiana climber

Hedges

Hedges are vital to a garden; affording protection to some plants and screening off parts of the garden, so that not all of it is seen at once – adding an air of mystery which is so essential to a garden. And if all hedges are removed from a garden, not only will the landscape be depleted, but the whole range of plants which could have been grown is affected. In fact, the entire ecology of the garden is altered.

Hedges are more than mere boundary markers. They should be as much an integral part of garden design as any other aspect. The plants should be chosen with as much thought and consideration as those for a shrub border. In many ways even more care should be taken, for a hedge is a long-term feature of the garden – many are there for the life of the garden. And the expense of taking one up to replant with another choice, not to mention the often long wait for newly planted hedge to become established, deter all but the most enthusiastic from indulging in the exercise.

It is essential to be absolutely clear about the functions a hedge is expected to perform – most commonly it is to mark a boundary and to deter animals and people from wandering over the garden. But a fence or wall would do that just as effectively, and there are obviously many other reasons for choosing a living boundary – foremost of which is the fact that it looks nice.

Although most hedges are inevitably destined to become boundary markers, they are invaluable as windbreaks and noise filters. Their use within the garden to screen an unsightly aspect, or as a backing to set off a border, or to divide the garden into separate vistas, should never be overlooked. Increasingly, perhaps as a result of modern housing estate design, hedges are being appreciated as decorative features in their own right. Lavender, Lavender Cotton (*Santolina chamaecyparissus*), and various Barberries (*Berberis* spp), are examples of plants often used to edge a front lawn where it bounds the roadside, yet they could hardly be considered impenetrable hedges. But they look attractive and become an essential feature in the overall concept. They are grown because of their appearance, not because they are particularly functional.

Occasionally, requirements dictate the other extreme; where a shelter belt or impenetrable barrier is more important than appearance, plants like the Field Maple (*Acer campestre*) or Hawthorn (*Crataegus oxyacantha*) are the practical answer.

Whether a formal or an informal hedge is chosen is largely a matter of personal preference – to many the neatly trimmed outline

Escallonia
Chilean Gum Box (1.2–1.5m/4–5ft)
(see page 164)

Far left: The Bridal Wreath Spiraea, *Spiraea* x *arguta*, forms a hedge 1.2–1.8m (4–6ft) high with cascades of white flowers in spring. (See pages 157 and 164.)

151

Fagus sylvatica
Beech (1.8–2.4m/6–8ft)
(see page 165)

Berberis x stenophylla
Barberry (2.1–3m/7–10ft)
(see page 165)

HEDGES FOR CHALKY SOIL	HEDGES FOR DRY, SANDY SOIL
Acer campestre	*Berberis*
Berberis	*Buxus*
Buxus	*Carpinus*
Cotoneaster	*Cotoneaster*
Crataegus	*Crataegus*
Cupressus	*Escallonia*
Escallonia	*Fagus*
Euonymus japonicus	*Fuchsia*
Fagus	*Griselina*
Forsythia	*Hebe*
Fuchsia	*Hippophae*
Greselinia	*Ilex*
Hebe	*Lavandula*
Hippophae	*Ligustrum*
Ilex	*Lonicera*
Lavandula	*Olearia*
Ligustrum	*Osmarea*
Lonicera	*Pittosporum*
Olearia	*Potentilla*
Philadelphus	*Prunus*
Pittosporum	*Pyracantha*
Potentilla	*Rosmarinus*
Prunus	*Santolina*
Pyracantha	*Spiraea*
Rosa	*Symphoricarpos*
Rosmarinus	*Tamarix*
Santolina	*Ulex*
Spiraea	*Viburnum*
Symphoricarpos	
Tamarix	**CONIFER HEDGES**
Taxus	*Chamaecyparis lawsoniana*
Ulex	X *Cupressocyparis leylandii*
Viburnum	*Cupressus macrocarpa*
Weigela	*Taxus baccata*

of Yew, Chinese Honeysuckle (*Lonicera nitida*), or the dwarf Box edging represents all that is desirable in a hedge. To others there is nothing to excel the spectacular sight of a forsythia hedge in full bloom, even though it may be rather uninspiring for the rest of the year.

The question of formal or informal hedging is linked with pruning and trimming. Some formal hedges, such as the ubiquitous Privet and Chinese Honeysuckle, require frequent trimming if they are not to look neglected, whereas many of the subjects suitable for informal hedges will perform admirably with a once-a-year pruning. The difficulty with some of these lax-growing kinds comes when boundary hedges border a public right of way. Roses and other plants with spines or thorns must not be allowed to become a nuisance to passers-by.

The position of the hedge will also affect choice. A sunny, open but not draughty position will suit most hedges, but very exposed sites will call for a tough shrub, while one of the most difficult places to position a hedge is in the shady and usually very draughty area between two houses. Holly, Hornbeam, and Hawthorn are of the right stature for the job, and the often despised Privet will also tolerate these very difficult conditions. The same position at the seaside is frequently aggravated by gales and salt spray, but there are plants that will stand up to it all – *Hippophae rhamnoides*, *Euonymus japonicus*, and Tamarisk (tamarix).

HEDGES WITH ATTRACTIVE FLOWERS	HEDGING PLANTS FOR INDUSTRIAL AREAS AND CITIES
Berberis	Berberis
Erica	Buxus
Escallonia	Cotoneaster simonsii
Forsythia	Euonymus japonicus
Fuchsia	Fagus
Hebe	Forsythia
Lavandula	Ilex
X Osmarea burkwoodii	Ligustrum
Philadelphus	Lonicera nitida
Potentilla	Olearia
Rhododendron	X Osmarea
Rosa	Prunus lusitanica
Rosmarimus	Pyracantha
Santolina	Rhododendron
Spiraea	
Tamarix	**HEDGES FOR DAMP SITES**
Ulex	Hippophae
Viburnum	Rhododendron
Weigela	Spiraea
FIELD HEDGES	Viburnum opulus
Acer campestre	
Carpinus betulus	**COASTAL HEDGES**
Crataegus oxycantha	X Cupressocyparis leyandii
Fagus sylvatica	Cupressus macrocarpa
Ilex aquifolium	Escallonia
Prunus cerasifera	Euonymus japonicus
	Griselinia
FRAGRANT HEDGES	Hebe
Lavandula	Hippophae
Olearia x haastii	Lonicera nitida
X Osmarea burkwoodii	Olearia x haastii
Philadelphus	Prunus cerasifera
Romarinus	Tamarix
Rosa	Taxus
Santolina	Ulex

Ligustrum ovalifolium
Privet (1.2–1.8m/4–6ft)
(see page 164)

What makes a good hedge

The range of plants that can be used for hedging is surprisingly large – from small, herb-like plants such as Lavender Cotton (*Santolina chamaecyparissus*) and true Lavender to trees such as Beech and Hornbeam. What they have in common is a tolerance of close planting, clipping and shaping, and they are well furnished with branches and foliage to ground level.

The Beech is a prime example of a hedging plant that will grow into a majestic specimen tree if given the room and opportunity to develop, often reaching 24m (80ft), yet by planting 45cm (1½ft) apart and pruning to shape once a year, and removing the leading shoots once the required height is reached, it makes an excellent hedge.

Because many of the shrubs and trees mentioned in this chapter can be kept within bounds by suitable pruning, the heights given in the charts on pages 161 to 165 can only be a guide, and often they will grow taller unless trimmed to size. An example of this is the common Privet, which is best as a hedge 1·2–1·8m (4–6ft) high, but it is sometimes seen forming a nice hedge twice this size; more often, however, once Privet reaches this size it is usually through neglect, and the regular trimming becomes a difficult chore.

The tables on pages 161 to 165 will enable you to narrow the choice within various height groupings, and some of the choice subjects are described in the following pages.

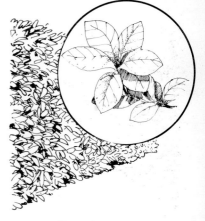

Prunus laurocerasus
Common Laurel (2.4–3m/8–10ft)
(see page 155)

Some good evergreens

Any list of good evergreen hedges must start with that most traditional of formal hedges – the Box (*Buxus sempervirens* 'Suffruticosa'), which was so popular in the past for edgings to formal gardens. Few modern gardens have the space to go in for beds of this kind, but it is still worth considering this neat, compact, small-leaved plant as a low 'demarcation hedge' in what would otherwise be an open-style garden.

Plant names are often confusing, yet seemingly minor variations can make large differences, and the Box is a good example. *B. s.* 'Handsworthensis', for instance, will make a hedge over 1·8m (6ft) high.

A plant often confused with Box, because of its small, oval leaves, is the Chinese Honeysuckle (*Lonicera nitida*). This plant has become very popular for hedging, and has tended to vie with Privet for planting in towns. It makes a neat hedge, but lacks the strength of Privet, and tends to look singed and brown after a hard winter. There is golden-leaved form, *L. n.* 'Baggessen's Gold'. (*Lonicera nitida* is illustrated on page 162.)

The Privet needs no introduction – many gardeners who have the job of clipping it regularly throughout the summer feel they know it only too well. Yet this adaptable plant should not be dismissed, for it will thrive in poor soils, tolerate lime, and put up with atmospheric pollution. The best green-leaved form is *Ligustrum ovalifolium*,

Below: The Hornbeam, *Carpinus betulus*, forms a hedge resembling Beech. The leading shoots should not be pruned until the required height has been reached. (See pages 157 and 165.)

but the golden-leaved form, *L. o.* 'Aureo-variegatum', makes a more interesting hedge. The bright yellow colour of the Golden Privet makes it a cheerful hedge, but you will need to prune out any branches that start to revert to the more normal green colouring. A nice hedge can be formed of green and golden Privet planted as a mixed-hedge – but allow two of the golden variety to one green, to compensate for the stronger growth of the green form. (*Ligustrum ovalifolium* 'Aurea-variegatum' is illustrated on page 159.)

Laurels were popular in Victorian plantings, the Common Laurel (*Prunus laurocerasus*) being used to form substantial hedges. It is a first-class windbreak, and a useful screen, but where a more refined hedge is required, and especially on chalk soil, a better choice is the Portugal Laurel (*P. lusitanica*). This handsome evergreen, with bay-like leaves, makes dense growth and forms a hedge of 1·5– 1·8m (5–6ft). When grown informally it has long 'candles' of small white flowers in June, followed by purple berries.

Holly is a good choice for an evergreen armed with a prickly defence – but fallen leaves can make hand weeding in adjacent borders a rather hazardous occupation. It makes one of the most impeneterable hedges, and if well cared for will be clothed with leaves down to the ground. It also succeeds well in town gardens. *Ilex aquifolium* is an excellent variety to grow for hedging, but consider one of the variegated ones, such as *I. a.* 'Aurea Marginata' (narrow yellow margin).

Below: X *Cupressocyparis leylandii* is a fast-growing conifer with few equals as a hedge or screen, and it is ideal for coastal areas. (See pages 157 and 161.)

Hollies are unlikely to produce many berries if treated as a clipped hedge, but will fruit if grown informally. For a good crop of berries it is necessary to plant male and female plants. Most variegated varieties are male, but 'Golden King' is female! This apparent nonsense in naming arose because it was named before it had flowered.

Less familiar as a hedging plant, but a first-class evergreen, is X Osmarea burkwoodii. Its dark green box-like foliage is enhanced by fragrant white flowers in April or May. There are not many hedging plants that can offer flowers and fragrance and to year-round foliage.

Although lacking fragrance, escallonias must rank high on any list of evergreen flowering hedges. The small, toothed, oval leaves set off the small bell-shaped pink to crimson flowers beautifully. The plants make fine windbreaks, and because they will tolerate salt spray are justifiably popular for hedges in coastal areas.

There are several good varieties of escallonia, 'C. F. Ball' being a vigorous form with large crimson flowers, and one that can be encouraged to give a second flush of flowers if pruned immediately after flowering. Do not plant too close together.

The Barberries are an invaluable group of plants, and provide both evergreen and deciduous shrubs suitable for hedges. Berberis darwinii is one of the finest evergreen Barberries, having, small, shiny, dark green leaves with small spines, and masses of deep golden-yellow flowers in April or May. These are followed by plum-purple berries in autumn. It makes a most attractive informal hedge, 1·2–1·8m (4–6ft) high.

For a larger Barberry hedge, B. x stenophylla, with its long, arching sprays of yellow flowers in April or May, will make an impenetrable hedge of 2·1–3m (7–10ft). B. verruculosa is suitable for a smaller hedge of 1–1·2m (3–4ft); this has small, glossy green leaves that are white on the undersides and turn reddish in autumn.

Some of the most magnificent evergreens can be found among the conifers, and these include some fine screening plants.

The Yew is known to most gardeners, but is usually confined to churchyards or large gardens. Indeed Yew will make a large hedge if time is allowed, 3–4·5m (10–15ft) being feasible for a hedge and up to 6m (20ft) for a screen; but there is no difficulty in maintaining a height of 1·5–1·8m (5–6ft). Although Yew (Taxus baccata) will grow slowly once a certain size has been reached, it is not as slow in the early years as is often believed. Once established it can put on 30–45cm (1–1½ft) of growth in a year. (Illustrated on page 158.)

There is nothing sombre about conifers, and what they lack in brilliant colour they make up for in subtle shades and textures. The Lawson Cypress (Chamaecyparis lawsoniana) is one of the most popular coniferous hedges, and is first-rate for hedging or as a screen or windbreak. There are varieties with blue-green, grey-green, and gold foliage, as well as bright green. Most of them will make a hedge or screen 3m (10ft) or more high, but some varieties are suitable for smaller hedges. C. l. 'Allumii', which has glaucous blue-green foliage, will make an attractive hedge if beheaded at 2·4m (8ft), while C. l. 'Fletcheri', with blue-grey feathery foliage, makes a fine hedge of 1·2–1·8m (4–6ft).

Viburnum opulus 'Compactum'
Guelder Rose (60–90cm/2–3ft)
(see page 162)

Buxus sempervirens 'Suffruticosa'
Box (30cm/1ft)
(see page 161)

For a fast-growing screen or windbreak, the Leyland Cypress (X *Cupressocyparis leylandii*) is difficult to improve upon – indeed it is the fastest-growing evergreen apart from a couple of species of eucalyptus. X *Cupressocyparis leylandii* is illustrated on page 155.)

The Monterey Cypress (*Cupressus macrocarpa*) was once popular for tall hedges or screens, and it is still worth planting in mild, coastal districts, but inland it can succumb to severe weather.

Although not evergreen in the usual sense, both Beech (*Fagus sylvatica*) and Hornbeam (*Carpinus betulus*) hold their browned leaves through the winter, and therefore retain an attraction throughout the darkest months. Hornbeam is best for chalk or heavy soils, which Beech detest. (*Carpinus betulus* is illustrated on page 154.)

Flowering hedges

Sometimes it is worth sacrificing an evergreen for a comparatively short-lived but spectacular display of flowers. Occasionally, of course, it is possible to have the best of both worlds, as with X *Osmarea*, escallonia, or some of the evergreen Barberries, all of which have been described. In addition to the evergreen Barberries, there are some notable deciduous species – *Berberis thunbergii* being especially desirable. Apart from the small red and yellow flowers there is a bonus of red berries and brilliant autumn foliage.

One of the most spectacular flowering hedges must be forsythia, which is a dazzling splash of yellow in April. For good results, careful pruning is essential, and must be done immediately after flowering. The widely planted *F. x intermedia* 'Lynwood' lends itself to this treatment, and so does the more bushy *F. ovata*, although it is important not to prune the latter too severely. Forsythias will grow on most soils, but do not like shade.

Weigela is another attractive flowering shrub for an informal hedge, usually flowering in May and June. Several good varieties are available, including the free-flowering, ruby-red 'Bristol Ruby', and rose-pink 'Abel Carriere'. To add leaf interest, *W. florida* 'Foliis Purpureis' has purple foliage and pink flowers; *W. f.* 'Variegata' has cream-edged leaves and clear pink flowers.

For sheer length of display, the shrubby potentillas take some beating. They bloom from about May to October, yellow or white Buttercup-shaped flowers covering the low bushes. They are useful for an informal hedge 1–1·2m (3–4ft) high.

Fuchsias are attractive flowers by any standard, but unfortunately few of them are hardy. There is one kind, however, that can be used to form an outdoor hedge in mild districts, especially coastal areas – *F. magellanica*. The flowers are small, but they make up for that with numbers. The result is a very pleasing informal hedge.

Another useful group of plants for informal hedges can be found among the spiraeas. Bridal Wreath (*S. x arguta*) is festooned with arching sprays of small white flowers in April. Somewhat similar in appearance, with umbels of pure white flowers in May, and rather fern-like foliage, *S. x vanhouttei* makes a good hedge. (*Spiraea x arguta* is illustrated on page 150, and *Spiraea x vanhouttei* is illustrated on page 163.)

Chamaecyparis lawsoniana
Lawson Cypress (3m+/10ft+)
(see page 161)

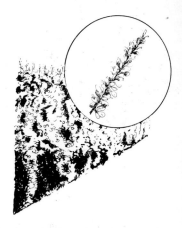

Berberis thunbergii 'Atropurpurea Nana'
Barberry (45–60cm/1½–2ft)
(see page 161)

Another white-flowered shrub sometimes used for hedging is th Guelder Rose (*Viburnum opulus*). The flattish heads of whi flowers in June are followed by bright red berries. The ordinary typ grows large, but there is a good variety for a hedge of about 90c (3ft) – *V. o.* 'Compactum'.

For white flowers and a heady fragrance, Mock Orange must b considered the best candidate. The pineapple scent is one of th joys of warm June and July evenings. It forms a pleasant inform hedge or summer screen, but cut back to within 30–60cm (1–2ft) ground level after planting, to induce bushy growth. There ar several good Mock Oranges, *Philadelphus* 'Manteau d'Hermin being one of them; it's a bushy grower, forming a hedge of abou 90cm (3ft), bearing fragrant, double white flowers.

Roses are almost universally admired, and there is no reaso why they can't be enjoyed as a hedge too. A number of specie make good hedges, and floribundas can also be pressed into servic in this capacity. In addition to fragrance and colour, there is often bonus of colourful hips – and the thorns make for a function hedge as well as a decorative one. Suitable varieties are suggeste on page 140.

Dwarf and internal hedges

Hedges do not have to be impenetrable boundary markers – there every reason to use dwarf or informal hedges to divide one part the garden from another, or to edge a path. Some of the flowerin plants already mentioned can be used for this purpose, includin philadelphus, potentilla and *Viburnum opulus* 'Compactum', and of course, the edging Box (*Buxus sempervirens* 'Suffruticosa') traditionally used to create a formal edge to flower beds an vegetable or herb gardens.

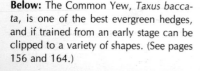
Below: The Common Yew, *Taxus baccata*, is one of the best evergreen hedges, and if trained from an early stage can be clipped to a variety of shapes. (See pages 156 and 164.)

Some herbs have found popularity as low hedges, the most familiar being Lavender and Rosemary, both of which have the merit of aromatic foliage. Lavender is ideal for a low hedge, as an edging to paths or lawns, or to grow on top of a low wall. There are varieties suitable for hedges from 30cm–1·2m (1–4ft), and a few of these are listed on pages 161 and 162. Lavender is very suitable for a light soil, but it will need to be kept neatly trimmed, as a neglected hedge can look very tatty.

Rosemary (*Rosmarinus officinalis*) will make a hedge up to 1·2m (4ft), with spikes of small blue-mauve flowers from mid-April to mid-May. It is important not to cut back into old wood when pruning.

Santolina chamaecyparissus (Lavender Cotton) is probably the whitest of all hardy shrubs, and the white-felted leaves are agreeably aromatic. It makes a useful little hedge of 45–60cm (1½–2ft). Button-like yellow flower heads are produced in July and August, and these should be trimmed off with shears when they have faded.

Suitable Heathers can make an attractive dwarf hedge, forming an integral part of the flower garden. *Erica mediterranea* will make a hedge of about 90cm (3ft), and this species will tolerate lime better than most.

How to plant a hedge

Hedges are usually intended to be permanent, so they should be afforded care and attention at planting time. No amount of adding fertilizers later will compensate for poorly prepared ground.

Wise planting starts with the order for plants to the nursery. There is always the temptation to buy large plants in the hope of having an established and reasonably respectable hedge that much more quickly, but small plants will almost certainly become established more quickly and grow away to overtake the larger ones, which transplant less well. And, of course, you will save money with the smaller plants. As a general rule, plants less than 60cm (2ft) should transplant well.

Planting distances are indicated in the tables on pages 161 to 165. Sometimes, it is useful to set the plants in a staggered row, which forms a thicker hedge. Staggering a double row is especially useful where conifers are used as a screen. Where space permits, an effective way to reduce road noise is to plant one hedge about 1·5m (5ft) in from the other. But with any hedge, the practicalities of trimming or pruning must be borne in mind.

Preparing the ground for a hedge is hard work, and it is prudent to make a start well in advance of the plants' arrival – to avoid the temptation to skimp on the job. Just as much effort should go into soil preparation as preparing a trench for Runner Beans or exhibition Sweet Peas. The ground should be double dug for an area of 45–60cm (1½–2ft) either side of the planting line, as the roots will spread outwards as well as downwards. Add as much compost or manure as you can to the bottom of the trench, and if the area is established grass, skim this off and bury it, roots up, on top of the forked bottom spit. Once the ground has been prepared in this way, and allowed to settle for some weeks, a garden line should be used

Below: The Golden Privet, *Ligustrum ovalifolium* 'Aureo-variegatum', makes a bright hedge the year round. (See pages 155 and 164.)

to mark out the planting trench, which will need to be about 30 (1ft) wide and deep. If the plants arrive before the trench is rea they can be 'heeled in' a temporary trench on a spare piece ground.

Whether the plants have been heeled-in or arrived straight fr the nursery, it does no harm to soak the roots in a bucket of wa for twenty-four hours before planting. The bottom of the tren should be forked over again, as planting proceeds, and the s returned and firmed around the roots with the foot. Spread out t roots of bare-root plants, but take care to keep the root-ball balled conifers or container grown plants intact.

To finish the job, a dressing of 135g per sq m (4oz per sq yd) o general fertilizer, lightly forked in round the plants, will get them to a good start. If a liberal quantity of moist peat can be worked in the same time, so much the better.

When to plant

Evergreens can be planted in September or October, or in Mar and April. Deciduous subjects can be planted whenever the grou is workable between early November and March. Container-grov plants can, of course, be planted at any time, provided the grou is not frozen or waterlogged.

The first year

Deciduous hedges are usually best pruned after planting (or March or April if planted during autumn or winter), as this w promote bushy growth. Beech and Hornbeam, however, are be left at this stage. Evergreens can be lightly tipped back, althou conifers should not be touched.

A newly-planted hedge is most vulnerable during long dry spe in the first summer, and liberal watering is advisable. Mulches moist peat or compost will also help. Evergreens, especial conifers, can be sprayed overhead with clear water in the evening

Pruning

Pruning details are given for specific species in the tables on pag 161 to 165, but there are a few general rules. Garden shears a excellent for small-leaved plants, but they can ruin the appearanc of broad-leaved kinds such as Portugal Laurel, as the slashed leav look unsightly.

Young hedges should not be allowed to become too large befo they are pruned – and it is best to start training to shape as soon possible. It is wise to shape the hedge so that it has sloping side with the base wider than the top, as this prevents snow causin damage, and allows a little more light to the base of the plant and the garden.

If electric shears are used, do be sure they are properly earthe and if in doubt have a qualified electrician look at them. Even the it is essential to work methodically with the wire kept well clear the cutters – and of your feet.

For added safety, have a qualified electrician service the shea every year, and store them during the winter in a damp-proof place

HOW TO USE THE TABLES

he tables below and on the following pages are divided into height ranges. This will enable a shortlist of suitable
andidates to be viewed at a glance. Other priority considerations are whether an evergreen is required, or whether
lowers are more important (occasionally both can be found on the same plant). The colour of both flowers and
oliage are given in the key below.

olours:
, blue; B-P, blue-purple; G, green; G-B, blue-green; GY, grey or silver; L, lavender; M, mauve; P, purple; PK, pink; R,
ed; W, white; Y, yellow; Y-G, yellowish-green; Y-R, yellow-red.

runing: A: trim during winter. B: prune and shape in spring. C: trim in spring and summer. D: prune after
lowering. E: remove dead flower heads after flowering, and trim in April. F: prune or trim annually in August.
: trim in June and again in August. H: trim as necessary throughout the growing season.

TALL HEDGES AND SCREENS

Species and Varieties	Height	Evergreen	Foliage Colour	Flower Colour	Flowering Period	Planting Distance	Pruning	Hardiness	Description
Chamaecyparis lawsoniana 'Green Hedger' Lawson Cypress	3m+ (10ft+)	●	G			90cm (3ft)	B	★★★★	A dense pyramid of rich, bright green foliage.
C. l. 'Stewartii'	3m+ (10ft+)	●	Y			60cm (2ft)	B	★★★★	A golden version of Lawson Cypress
X Cupressocyparis leylandii	4.5m+ (15ft+)	●	G-GY			60cm (2ft)	B	★★★★	A fast-growing conifer, useful for forming a screen quickly. Unsurpassed for providing a tall screen quickly.
Cupressus macrocarpa Monterey Cypress	3m+ (10ft+)	●	G			60cm (2ft)	B	★★	Bright green foliage. Quick-growing. Useful for coastal areas, but young plants can be damaged in cold areas inland.
Populus nigra 'Italica' Lombardy Poplar	15m+ (50ft+)		G			1.8m (6ft)		★★★★	A popular upright tree, rapidly forming a tall screen. Plant only as a screen, not as a hedge.

All the trees listed above can be grown as tall screens, in which case they should be planted about 1.8m (6ft) apart; they can be
thinned later if necessary. Trees such as the Poplar can be pollarded when they reach the required height.

HEDGES UP TO 60cm (2ft) HIGH

Species and Varieties	Height	Evergreen	Foliage Colour	Flower Colour	Flowering Period	Planting Distance	Pruning	Hardiness	Description
Berberis thunbergii 'Atropurpurea Nana' Barberry	45-60cm (1½-2ft)		P	Y-R	5	38cm (15in)	A	★★★★	Thornless. Compact. Rounded habit. Red berries.
Buxus sempervirens 'Suffruticosa' Box	30cm (1ft)	●	G	Y-G	4	30cm (12in)	C	★★★★	Makes a neat edging to borders. Good dwarf formal hedge.
Hebe anomala Veronica	60cm (2ft)	●	G	W	7-9	45cm (1½ft)	B	★★★	Erect and compact. Pleasing in Winter.
Lavandula 'Hidcote' Lavender	30-60cm (1-2ft)	●	GY	B-P	7-8	30cm (1ft)	E	★★★★	Compact version of a very popular aromatic plant.
Santolina chamaecyparissus Lavender Cotton	45-60cm (1½-2ft)	●	GY	Y	6-8	23cm (9in)	E	★★★★	Makes a nice silver-grey edging.

HEDGES 60cm-1.2m (2-4ft) HIGH

Species and Varieties	Height	Evergreen	Foliage Colour	Flower Colour	Flowering Period	Planting Distance	Pruning	Hardiness	Description
Berberis verruculosa	90cm-1.2m (3-4ft)	●	G (A)	Y	5-6	60cm (2ft)	B	★★★★	Leaves silvery beneath. Red tints in autumn.
Erica mediterranea 'Superba'	90cm-1.2m (3-4ft)	●	G	PK	5-6	45cm (1½ft)	D	★★★★	Deep pink heather flowers. Does well on lime or chalk.
E. m. 'W. T. Rackliff'	60-90cm (2-3ft)	●	G	W	1-3	45cm (1½ft)	D	★★★★	Makes an excellent dwarf hedge. White bell-shaped flowers.
Lavandula spica Lavender	90cm-1.2m (3-4ft)	●	G	L	7-8	45cm (1½ft)	E	★★★★	Will become leggy unless trimmed. Do not cut back into old wood.
L. vera Dutch Lavender	60-90cm (2-3ft)	●	G	B	7-8	38cm (15in)	E	★★★★	A Lavender with soft blue flowers, and dense, spreading habit.
Olearia x *haastii* Daisy Bush	1.2m (4ft)	●	G	W	7-8	90cm (3ft)	D	★★	Daisy-like flowers. Does well in coastal areas.
Philadelphus 'Manteau d''Hermine'	90cm-1.2m (3-4ft)		G	W	6	60cm (2ft)	D	★★★★	Fragrant double white flowers.
Potentilla 'Jackman's Variety'	90cm-1.2m (3-4ft)		G	Y	5-10	60cm (2ft)	B	★★★★	Bright yellow flowers. Bushy, upright habit. Continuous display of flowers.
Viburnum opulus 'Compactum' Guelder Rose	60-90cm (2-3ft)		G	W	5-6	30cm (1ft)	A	★★★★	Bright red berries are borne in profusion.

Far right: *Spiraea* x *vanhouttei* forms a most attractive hedge with its graceful arching sprays of white flowers on vigorous stems. (See pages 157 and 164.)

Right: Yew or Privet is usually used for topiary, but the Chinese Honeysuckle, *Lonicera nitida*, can also be used. (See pages 154 and 164.)

HEDGES 1.2-1.8m (4-6ft) HIGH

Species and Varieties	Height	Evergreen	Foliage Colour	Flower Colour	Flowering Period	Planting Distance	Pruning	Hardiness	Description
Berberis darwinii Darwin's Barberry	1.2-1.8m (4-6ft)		G	Y	4-5	60cm (2ft)	D	★★★★	Has bluish-purple berries. Can become thin at the base on poor soil.
B. thunbergii Barberry	1.2-1.8m (4-6ft)		G (A)	Y-R	5	60cm (2ft)	A	★★★★	Lovely autumn colour. Bushy habit.
B. t. 'Atropurpurea'	1.5-1.8m (5-6ft)		P	Y-R	5	60cm (2ft)	A	★★★★	Reddish-purple foliage. Spreading habit.
Chamaecyparis lawsoniana 'Fletcheri' Lawson Cypress	1.2-1.8m (4-6ft)		G-B			60cm (2ft)	B	★★★★	A conifer with feathery foliage. Can be trimmed closely.
Cotoneaster simonsii	1.5-1.8m (5-6ft)		G	W	6-7	45cm (1½ft)	A	★★★★	Profusion of scarlet berries, persisting for most of winter.

Species and Varieties	Height	Evergreen	Foliage Colour	Flower Colour	Flowering Period	Planting Distance	Pruning	Hardiness	Description
Escallonia 'C. F. Ball' Chilean Gum Box	1.2-1.5m (4-5ft)	●	G	R	6-7	75cm (2½ft)	D	★★	Very attractive flowers and pretty evergreen leaves.
Forsythia ovata Golden Bell Bush	1.2-1.5m (4-5ft)		G	Y	4	45cm (1½ft)	D	★★★★	*F. x intermedia* 'Lynwood' also makes a nice hedge. Both are spectacular in flower.
Fuchsia magellanica 'Riccartonii'	1.2-1.5m (4-5ft)		G	R+P	7-9	45cm (1½ft)	B	★	Needs a protected site, but does well by the sea in favourable areas.
Ilex aquifolium Holly	1.5m (5ft)	●	G			45cm (1½ft)	F	★★★★	Too well known to need detailed description. There are variegated forms.
Ligustrum ovalifolium Privet	1.2-1.8m (4-6ft)	●	G			30cm (1ft)	H	★★★★	Probably the most popular hedging plant. Best cut wedge-shaped rather than flat-topped.
L. o. 'Aureo-variegatum' Golden Privet	1.2-1.8m (4-6ft)	●	Y			30cm (1ft)	H	★★★★	Makes a bright hedge.
Lonicera nitida Chinese Honeysuckle	1.2-1.8m (4-6ft)	●	G			30cm (1ft)	H	★★★	Box-like foliage. Makes a neat hedge but does not have the strength of Privet.
Prunus x cistena Crimson Dwarf	1.2m (4ft)		R	PK		60cm (2ft)	D	★★★★	Deep crimson foliage.
P. lusitanica Portugal Laurel	1.5-1.8m (5-6ft)	●	G	W	6	60cm (2ft)	B	★★★★	Bay-like leaves; dense growth. Purple fruits.
Pyracantha watereri Firethorn	1.2-1.8m (4-6ft)	●	G	W	5-6	60cm (2ft)	C	★★★★	Masses of red berries in autumn.
Rosmarinus officinalis Rosemary	1.2m (4ft)	●	G	B	5	60cm (2ft)	B	★★★★	An aromatic hedge. Avoid cutting back into old wood.
Spiraea x arguta Bridal Wreath	1.2-1.8m (4-6ft)		G	W	4	60cm (2ft)	D	★★★★	Cascades of white flowers in spring.
S. x vanhouttei	1.5-1.8m (5-6ft)		G-GY	W	5	90cm (3ft)	D	★★★★	Elongated heads of white flowers on arching stems.
Symphoricarpos 'White Hedger' Snowberry	1.2-1.5m (4-5ft)		G			60cm (2ft)	B	★★★★	An excellent hedging plant. White berries in autumn.
Tamarix pentandra Tamarisk	1.2-1.5m (4-5ft)		G	PK	7-8	60cm (2ft)	B	★★★★	A nice informal hedge for coastal areas.
Taxus baccata Yew	1.5-1.8m (5-6ft)	●	G			60cm (2ft)	F	★★★★	One of the finest evergreen hedges. Is not as slow-growing as often thought.
Ulex europaeus 'Plenus' Double-flowered Gorse	1.2-1.5m (4-5ft)	●	G	Y	4-5	60cm (2ft)	D	★★★★	Makes a broad hedge. Very bright in flower. Best suited to poor soil.
Weigela florida 'Variegata'	1.2-1.8m (4-6ft)		G+W	PK	5-6	60cm (2ft)	D	★★★★	Other good varieties, not variegated, include 'Bristol Ruby' and 'Newport Ruby' (both red).

HEDGES OVER 1.8m (6ft) HIGH

Species and Varieties	Height	Evergreen	Foliage Colour	Flower Colour	Flowering Period	Planting Distance	Pruning	Hardiness	Description
Acer campestre Field Maple	1.8-3m (6-10ft)		G (A)			45cm (1½ft)	A	★★★★	Nice autumn tints, but only suitable for boundary hedges in large gardens.
Berberis x *stenophylla* Barberry	2.1-3m (7-10ft)	●	G	Y	5-6	60cm (2ft)	D	★★★★	Dense arching habit. Red berries if left untrimmed.
Buxus sempervirens 'Handsworthensis' Box	1.8-2.4m (6-8ft)	●	G	Y-G	4	60cm (2ft)	C	★★★★	A compact, upright form of the smaller Box edging.
Carpinus betulus Hornbeam	1.8-2.4m (6-8ft)		G			45cm (1½ft)	F	★★★★	Forms a hedge like Beech.
Chamaecyparis lawsoniana 'Allumii' Lawson Cypress	2.4m (8ft)	●	G-B			90cm (3ft)	B	★★★★	A conifer that will make an attractive hedge if beheaded at 2.4m (8ft).
Cornus mas Dogwood	1.8-2.4m (6-8ft)		G (A)	Y	3	90cm (3ft)	D	★★★★	The yellow flowers are borne on bare branches.
Cotoneaster lacteus	2.4-3m (8-10ft)	●	G	W	6	90cm (3ft)	D	★★★★	Clusters of long-lasting red berries.
Crataegus oxyacantha Hawthorn	1.8-2.1m (6-7ft)		G	W	5	30cm (1ft)	H	★★★★	Widely planted as a farm hedge, but can also be used effectively in the garden.
Euonymus japonicus Spindle	1.5-2.4m (5-8ft)	●	G			45cm (1½ft)	B	★★	Good hedge for coastal areas in the South. There are variegated forms.
Fagus sylvatica Beech	1.8-2.4m (6-8ft)		G			45cm (1½ft)	F	★★★★	Brown leaves persist through the winter.
F. s. 'Cuprea' Copper Beech	1.8-2.4m (6-8ft)		P			45cm (1½ft)	F	★★★★	Coppery-purple leaves, otherwise like ordinary Beech.
Griselinia littoralis Kupuka Tree	1.8-2.1m (6-7ft)	●	G	G	5	60cm (2ft)	B	★★	An excellent hedge for suitable coastal locations. Leathery yellowish-green leaves.
Hippophae rhamnoides Sea Buckthorn	1.8-2.1m (6-7ft)		G	GY		75cm (2½ft)	B	★★★★	Suitable only for coastal planting, where its coarse growth and spines make it a good barrier. Orange berries.
X *Osmarea burkwoodii*	1.8-2.4m (6-8ft)	●	G	W	4	60cm (2ft)	D	★★★	Fragrant flowers. A first-class evergreen.
Pittosporum tenuifolium	1.8-2.4m (6-8ft)	●	G			45cm (1½ft)	H	★	A good hedging plant for mild areas, especially by the sea. Not suitable elsewhere.
Prunus cerasifera Myrobalan Plum	1.8-2.7m (6-9ft)		G	W	3	30cm (1ft)	G	★★★★	Fast grower. Cut back a newly planted hedge to 30cm (1ft) in March.
P. c. 'Nigra'	1.8-2.7m (6-9ft)		R	PK	3	60cm (2ft)	G	★★★★	Ruby-red leaves. Make a nice background hedge.
Rhododendron ponticum Common Rhododendron	1.8-3m (6-10ft)	●	G	M	5-6	90cm (3ft)	D	★★★★	Leaves attractive at any time of the year. Avoid wet, heavy soil.

Rosa
(see page 140)

Trees

Trees are traditionally planted for future generations, and in most great English gardens splendid examples of this forethought can be seen and enjoyed. Recently, gardeners and tree enthusiasts have been encouraged to take over where the great landscapers of the past left off, with the 'Plant a Tree Year' scheme highlighting the great benefits of planting more trees. The problem is that most modern gardens are small, and ambitious plantings of large trees are out of the question.

The answer, perhaps, is to donate a large tree for planting on the village green or local playing field. There, you can watch its progress with satisfaction, and the chances are that future generations will be able to admire its full glory. Unless the garden is large, confine tree planting to species of reasonable proportions.

Fortunately, it is among the smaller species that some of the most beautiful flowering trees can be found – including laburnum, Flowering Cherries, Flowering Crabs, and some of the magnolias. There are also many trees with attractive foliage that will beautify and enhance a small garden – gleditschia, robinia, eucalyptus and some of the variegated forms of *Acer negundo* are examples.

If space is limited, do not try to cram in more trees than the garden will effectively take. It would be better to settle for one specimen tree – perhaps a Flowering Cherry or one of the weeping trees – set in a lawn, where its full beauty can be admired. If the choice is limited by space, the Crabs must also be considered for specimen planting. Apart from pleasant flowers, there is usually a heavy crop of very attractive fruits, often retained well into winter. There are very few gardens unable to support at least one tree – it is just a question of selection.

Some trees, such as *Acer negundo*, the Flowering Cherries and the Crabs, are mentioned in the shrub chapter, and these plants highlight the dificulty of deciding whether a plant is a tree or shrub – for in these cases it all depends how it is grown.

A simple definition is that a tree has a single main stem or trunk, while a shrub has several stems from a low level. The examples just mentioned can be trained to branch at an early stage, or may have all the side-shoots removed to create a clean stem or trunk. This treatment also affects the ultimate height of the same plant – one trained as a tree will grow taller than a bush form.

Most deciduous trees, such as Crabs and Flowering Cherries, are supplied as standards, on a clear stem of about 1·5m (5ft), but half-standards are available, with a stem of about 75cm (2½ft).

Betula pendula 'Youngii'
Young's Weeping Birch (4.5m/15ft)
(see page 175)

Far left: For attractive autumn foliage few trees surpass the spectacular Sweet Gum, *Liquidambar styraciflua*, with its vivid hues from crimson to gold. (See page 176.)

TREES WITH ATTRACTIVE FRUIT OR BERRIES
Arbutus unedo
Catalpa bignonioides
Crataegus
Ilex
Koelreuteria
Malus (see page 174)
Sorbus

TREES FOR COASTAL AREAS
Arbutus unedo
Crataegus
Fraxinus
Salix alba
Ulmus minor sarniensis

TREES FOR HEDGES
Carpinus betulus
Fagus sylvatica
F. s. 'Cuprea'
Laurus nobilis (see page 105)

WEEPING TREES
Betula pendula 'Youngii'
Cotoneaster hybridus 'Pendulus'
Crataegus monogyna 'Pendula'
Fraxinus excelsior 'Pendula'
Prunus (see page 173)
Pyrus salicifolia 'Pendula'
Salix alba 'Tristis'
S. caprea 'Pendula'
Tilia petiolaris
Ulmus glabra 'Pendula'

TREES WITH ATTRACTIVE FLOWERS
Aesculus
Amelanchier canadensis
Catalpa bignonioides
Cercis siliquastrum
Laburnum
Liriodendron
Magnolia
Malus (see page 174)
Prunus (see page 173)

TREES WITH ATTRACTIVE FOLIAGE
Acer ginnala*
A. negundo 'Elegans'
A. n. 'Variegatum'
A. rubrum*
Ailanthus
Alnus incana 'Aurea'
Amelanchier canadensis*
Eucalyptus gunnii
Fagus*
Fraxinus oxycarpa 'Raywood'*
Gleditschia triacanthos 'Elegantissima'
G. t. 'Sunburst'
Ilex
Koelreuteria*
Laurus nobilis
Liquidambar*
Liriodendron tulipifera*
Malus tschonoskii*
Nyssa*
Parrotia*
Robinia pseudoacacia
Sorbus aria
*: good autumn colour

SMALL SPECIMEN TREES FOR LAWNS
Acer ginnala
A. hersii
A. negundo 'Elegans'
A. n. 'Variegatum'
A. nikoense
Gleditschia
Magnolia
Malus (see page 174)
Prunus (see page 173)
Robinia
Sorbus americana 'Decora'

(see also weeping trees)

TREES FOR MOIST SOILS
Fraxinus
Nyssa
Populus
Salix

GOOD TOWN TREES
Acer (not A. negundo or A. palmatum)
Aesculus
Ailanthus altissima
Amelanchier canadensis
Betula pendula
Cercis siliquastrum
Crataegus lavallei
C. oxyacantha
Gleditschia triacanthos
Laburnum
Malus (see page 174)
Populus
Prunus (see page 173)
Rhus typhina
Robinia

GOOD FASTIGIATE (UPRIGHT) TREES
Betula pendula 'Fastigiata'
Carpinus betulus 'Pyramidalis'
Crataegus monogyna 'Stricta'
Fagus sylvatica 'Fastigiata'
Populus nigra 'Italica'
Prunus serrulata 'Erecta'
Quercus robur 'Fastigiata'
Robinia pseudoacacia 'Fastigiata'
Ulmus carpinifolia sarnensis

TREES FOR ACID SOIL
Amelanchier
Arbutus
Betula
Ilex
Liquidambar
Magnolia
Parrotia

TREES FOR CHALKY SOIL
Acer (not Japanese varieties or A. rubrum)

Arbutus unedo	Ilex
Betula	Laburnum
Carpinus	Magnolia kobus
Cercis	Malus
Crataegus	Populus
Fagus	Prunus
Fraxinus	Sorbus aria

Acer negundo 'Variegatum'
(9m/30ft)
(see page 175)

Salix alba 'Tristis'
Golden Weeping Willow (6m+/20ft+)
(see page 177)

Weeping trees

Trees with pendulous branches, or weeping trees as they are usually known, can make charming specimens set in a lawn. Some, such as *Salix alba* Tristis' and *Tilia petiolaris*, are naturally pendulous, but most have occurred as 'sports' or freaks among ordinary kinds. Many of them are really prostrate in growth, but to give them a weeping appearance they are grafted on a tall stock.

Some weeping trees are grown solely for their attractive shape, such as the Willows (salix) and Elm (ulmus), but those which bloom profusely can be truly beautiful – and include *Crataegus monogyna* 'Pendula' (Hawthorn), and various *Prunus*.

Planting

The smaller the tree, the easier it will transplant to a fresh position. Large trees can be moved, but it usually requires special equipment and skills, as well as expense, and is not an acceptable proposition for amateurs. If instant effect is really important, it may be possible to buy deciduous trees with stems up to 4·5m (15ft) high, from good nurseries, which will probably survive transplanting if the roots are not allowed to become dry – but a tree only half that size would probably overtake it within a few years.

Trees grown in containers naturally receive less of a set-back than bare-root plants. The treatment and method of planting trees is the same as that described for shrubs, on page 89.

The best time to transplant deciduous trees is between October and March, provided the weather is not too severe and the ground not frozen or waterlogged. Drying winds are harmful, although these are sometimes difficult to avoid.

Evergreens continue to lose water through their leaves during winter, so it is important to move them when the damaged feeding roots can quickly be replaced by actively growing new roots. In effect that means autumn or spring.

Container-grown trees can, of course, be planted at almost any time, provided the soil is in a suitable condition.

The principal difference between planting a shrub and a tree is that the tree will probably need some form of support until it becomes established, particularly if the position is exposed. A stake should be driven into the soil close to the stem, but on the windward side, so the tree is not blown against it. The stake itself should be a little stouter than the stem, but unless the tree is particularly slender, it need only come half way up the stem.

It is always best to insert the stake at planting time, when it can be positioned between the roots safely before the soil is returned to the hole. Unless you are adept at tying knots that will prevent the tying material biting into the stem, it is best to use proprietary tree-ties. These cause less damage to the tree and can usually be adjusted as the tree grows.

Pruning

Trees are much simpler to prune than shrubs. With shrubs, much of the pruning is aimed at improving the quality or quantity of flower,

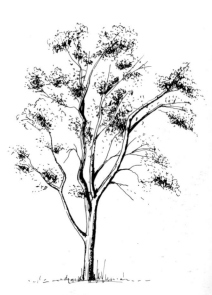

Eucalyptus gunnii
Cedar Gum (7.5m/25ft)
(see page 176)

Amelanchier canadensis
Snowy Mespilus (5.4m/18ft)
(see page 175)

which involves decisions on flowering time and whether they bloom on new or old wood. Pruning trees is largely a matter of maintaining a good shape.

In practical terms it involves keeping the main stem or trunk clear, by removing any branches that appear too low down, cutting out shoots or suckers that appear from low down or around the base of the tree (these may in any case be different stock if the tree has been grafted or budded), and maintaining an attractively shaped head.

It is most important that the leading shoot at the centre of the tree is not pruned out, and that any tendency for the main stem or leading shoot to branch into two is corrected at once.

Any other pruning is confined to removing overlapping and crossing branches and shortening side-shoots if they become too aggressive.

Some good garden trees

Acer ginnala: This small tree or large bushy shrub is one of the best acers for autumn colour, the leaves turning a beautiful fiery red before falling. The small, creamy-white flowers borne in May are very fragrant, and followed by red 'keys' about 2·5cm (1in) long.

Acer hersii (Snake-bark Maple): Although this will make a broad, round-headed tree of medium size in time, it is well worth planting wherever space permits. It is attractive at all times of the year, with its bark beautifully striated with whitish lines, and in autumn the leaves turn brilliant red.

Acer negundo (Box Elder): There are two beautiful variegated forms – A. n. 'Elegans', with striking yellow variegation, and A. n. 'Variegatum', which has white variegation. These large shrubs or small trees are among the most beautiful of variegated trees.

Acer nikoense (Nikko Maple): A beautiful and slow-growing Maple with rich red autumn colour.

Amelanchier canadensis (Snowy Mespilus): For a short period, often only a week or ten days, this broad tree is a foaming mass of pure white flowers. The fact that the flowers are short-lived and often blown off the tree is compensated for by soft red autumn colour.

Arbutus unedo (Strawberry Tree): An interesting evergreen, bearing the previous year's strawberry-like fruits, 18mm (¾in) across, at the same time as the current flowers.

Betula pendula 'Fastigiata': Despite the apparent contradiction in name, this Birch makes a slender pyramid, resembling a Lombardy Poplar in form.

Betula pendula 'Youngii' (Young's Weeping Birch): One of the finest weeping trees. It is slow-growing and forms a dome-shaped tree with branches to the ground.

Cercis siliquastrum (Judas Tree): A delightful sight in May; when the whole tree seems covered with bright pink pea-shaped flowers, which look all the more conspicuous because they open before most of the leaves. It makes a rounded, low-forking tree. Full sun is essential for a good display of flowers. (Illustrated on page 174.)

Crataegus lavallei: Most of the Hawthorns make attractive trees,

Below: Spring-flowering trees are always a cheerful sight, and the Flowering Cherries are among the most popular. This example shows how charming these small trees can be. (See page 173.)

some having pink or red flowers in May. They have the added attraction of berries, and one of those notable in this respect is *C. lavallei*, which used to be known as *C. carrierei*. The orange-red berries, about 18mm (¾in) in diameter, remain well into winter.

Crataegus monogyna 'Pendula' (Weeping Thorn): This is a weeping version of the common hedgerow plant. It has graceful arching branches and white flowers.

Crataegus monogyna 'Stricta': A useful plant for a limited space, as its growth is upright rather than spreading. The flowers are white.

Crataegus oxyacantha (Hawthorn): Outwardly, this is very similar to *C. monogyna*. And like the Common Hawthorn it makes a neat, round-headed tree. There are single and double forms, in white, pink and red. One of the most popular is *C. o.* 'Coccinea Plena', perhaps better known as 'Paul's Scarlet'.

Eucalyptus gunnii (Cedar Gum): Although this tree will grow quite tall in favoured localities, there is always the risk of it being short lived; but they are easily raised from seed.

As suggested, these trees are not completely hardy, but will survive all but very worst winters in the South.

The beauty of this evergreen lies in its aromatic foliage – round, penny-shaped and silvery-blue with a waxy bloom when young, narrow, pointed and grey-green once the juvenile stage is passed.

The peeling bark is also an attractive feature.

Gleditschia triacanthos (Honey Locust): This pleasant tree is grown for its foliage, which is almost fern-like with its leaflets arranged either side of long stems. It is armed with strong spines. *G. t.* 'Elegantissima' is a small elegant tree, and a good lawn specimen, thriving even in a smoke-polluted atmosphere. 'Sunburst' has almost golden leaves, and a wide-spreading, rather larger habit.

Ilex (Holly): There can be few gardeners who are not familiar with

Below, left: The Stag's-horn Sumach, *Rhus typhina*, comes into its glory in autumn, when its large, pinnate leaves colour before falling. The flowers and conical clusters of crimson fruits are also an attraction on female plants. (See pages 172 and 177.)

Below: The Tupelo, *Nyssa sylvatica*, is grown primarily for its brilliant scarlet foliage in autumn. It makes a dense-headed tree of medium size. (See page 177.)

the common green Holly (*Ilex aquifolium*), which is usually grown in its shrub form. It can be trained to form a tree, however, and some of the variegated types can be particularly impressive. With time they can form a dense, pyramidal tree of some size, well clothed to the ground. Some of the attractive forms of Holly are described on page 102.

Laburnum (Golden Rain): The laburnums must rank among the most beautiful of all hardy trees, and they are small enough to find a home in almost any garden. They are quick growing and rarely exceed 6m (20ft).

The best garden form is *L.* x *vossii*, which has long, bright yellow drooping pendulous tassels of pea-like flowers in May and June. It makes a sturdy, upward-branching tree, and this species sets little seed, which is reassuring to anyone with children, as the seeds are poisonous.

Laurus nobilis (Sweet Bay): This is another example of a tree that is sometimes grown as a shrub (see page 105).

Magnolia soulangeana: Perhaps the most widely planted magnolia, and a forking tree of great beauty. It is often grown as a shrub. The large, white cup-shaped flowers, tinged purple on the outside, are borne on leafless stems in April.

Malus (Flowering Crab): Another group of plants sometimes treated as trees, and at other times as shrubs. In whatever form they are grown, they are a valuable addition to any garden. They are beautiful in flower in spring, and a wonderful spectacle in autumn and early winter when they are usually laden with bright fruit. There are numerous species and varieties from which to select, and a few of them are listed on page 174.

To some extent, the ultimate size of these trees depends on the rootstock used, the moderately vigorous Malling II and Malling Merton 111 being the most commonly utilized. Strong staking is normally necessary until the trees are well established.

Parrotia persica: One of the best trees for autumn colour – the leaves turning pink, gold, crimson and orange. It will reach 6m (20ft) or more eventually, but should be grown if space permits. A lime-free soil and a sunny position suit it best.

Prunus: These are undoubtedly some of the finest garden trees, for the genus includes Flowering Cherries and Almonds. They flower between March and May and are usually available as trees or as shrubs. The colours range from white to deep pink. They represent blossom trees at their best, and there are many excellent varieties from which to choose. A selection of them is given below.

Although nearly all the species flower in spring, *P. subhirtella* 'Autumnalis' produces its single or semi-double white flowers intermittently from November to March. (Illustrated on page 170.)

Pyrus salicifolius 'Pendula' (Weeping Willow-leaf Pear): This graceful tree makes a beautiful specimen for planting in a lawn or by water. It makes a dense head of arching branches that cascade to the ground, bearing silvery-grey narrow willow-like leaves.

Rhus typhina (Stag's Horn Sumach): A tree with rather open shrub-like growth. Long, pinnate leaves hang dramatically in their autumn tints of yellow-orange to red. During the summer the densely-packed cone-shaped flowers, about 15cm (6in) long, are

Laburnum x *vossii*
Golden Rain (6m/20ft)
(see page 176)

Robinia pseudoacacia
False Acacia (7.5m/25ft)
(see page 177)

rne on female plants, and these turn into conspicuous crimson
ads. (Illustrated on page 171.)

The variety 'Laciniata' has more finely cut and divided leaflets.

binia pseudoacacia (False Acacia): This is a rapid grower with
liage like acacia. The normal type is too vigorous and large for a
nall garden, but there is a narrow, upright form even narrower in
oportions than the Lombardy Poplar, and because it takes up little
orizontal room is suitable for small gardens. There is also a variety
alled 'Frisia', which has golden foliage and is smaller in growth.

Robinias grow well on poor or sandy soils, and tolerate the
mosphere of industrial areas, but are notoriously susceptible to
ind damage. Branches often break off in strong gales.

A similar tree in appearance is *Gleditschia triacanthos*.

alix caprea 'Pendula' (Kilmarnock Willow): This is a weeping form
f the native Goat Willow, popular for its yellow catkins, produced
n naked branches in March and April.

orbus americana 'Decora' (American Mountain Ash): This is a
nrubby tree of rather stiff habit. It has the usual pinnate leaves of
ne Mountain Ash, and large, sealing-wax-red berries.

Prunus sargentii
(see page 172)

FLOWERING CHERRIES AND ALMONDS

Species and Varieties	Height	Colour	Flowering time	Description
Prunus 'Accolade'	(See note below)	Pink	4	Has a spreading, graceful habit with masses of pink buds.
P. cerasifera 'Pissardii'	(See note below)	White	3	Foliage is a rich ruby red in spring, later darkening to purple. Flowers are single and not very significant.
P. padus 'Grandiflora'	(See note below)	White	5	One of the bird cherries, with many pendulous white flowers. Excellent tree for larger gardens, being quite vigorous.
P. persica 'Pink Charming'	(See note below)	Bright pink	4	A flowering peach tree bearing semi-double rosette-like flowers. Has upright appearance.
P. serrulata 'Erecta' ('Ama-noGawa')	(See note below)	Pale pink	4-5	This is the popular 'Lombardy Poplar Cherry', with clusters of semi-double scented flowers.
P. subhirtella	(See note below)	Pink	3	Tree with deep rose-pink buds, opening to pink. Has a dense and rounded head.
P.s. 'Autumnalis'	(See note below)	White	Late autumn and into winter	Single or semi-double flowers are produced on this tree with a spreading habit.
P.s. 'Pendula'	(See note below)	Pale pink	4	A tree with weeping branches.

Note: These prunus species and varieties are usually available as trees or bushes. As
trees they may ultimately develop to 6.0-7.5m (20-25ft) high, and as bushes
3.0-4.5m (10-15ft) high.

Sorbus
Mountain Ash (4.5m/15ft)
(see page 177)

FLOWERING CRAB TREES

Species and Varieties	Height	Colour	Flowering time	Description
Malus x atrosanguinea	3.6-4.5m (12-15ft)	Deep red buds turning to deep pink	Mid-season	A small tree with a pendulous habit.
M. x eleyi	4.5-6.3m (15-21ft)	Deep wine red.	Early	A beautiful tree, with a rounded head and purplish-red fruits in autumn.
M. floribunda	3.6-4.5m (12-15ft)	Deep red in bud, turning to white.	Early	A variety with very decorative purplish-red fruits in autumn. It is often called the 'Japanese Flowering Crab'.
M. 'John Downie'	4.5-6.3m (15-21ft)	White	Late	One of the best fruiting 'Crab' trees. The fruits are bright scarlet and conical in shape.
M. x lemoinei	4.5-6.3m (15-21ft)	Dark crimson	Mid-season	This tree has a spreading habit, with reddish-purple fruits in the autumn.
M. sargentii	2.4-3.0m (8-10ft)	White	Late	One of the smallest malus trees, being ideal for a small garden.
M. tschonoskii	2.4-3.0m (8-10ft)	White	Late	Excellent small garden tree, with magnificent autumn coloured leaves.

Note: All of the Flowering Crabs are tolerant of lime in the soil. These magnificent trees flower from April and May, but the exact dates depend on the climate of the area. Therefore, these trees are classified as early, mid-season or late.

Below, right: The Judas Tree, *Cercis siliquastrum*, produces spectacular clusters of bright purple-rose pea-like flowers on slender stalks before the leaves appear in late spring. It requires full sun and good drainage. (See pages 170 and 175.)

Below: The Tulip Trees, *Liriodendron tulipifera*, bears unusually-shaped leaves that turn bright yellow in the autumn. The greenish-yellow Tulip-shaped flowers appear on mature trees in June and July. (See page 176.)

GOOD GARDEN TREES

...ecies and Varieties	Height	Evergreen	Flowering period	Fragrance	Autumn colour	Suitable for small garden	Hardiness	Description
...cer ginnala	4.5m (15ft)		5	●	●	●	★★★★	One of the best Maples for autumn colour. Makes a small tree or large shrub of bushy habit.
. hersii ...nake-bark Maple	6m+ (20ft+)		5		●		★★★★	A tree of considerable merit, possessing brilliant autumn colour and useful winter bark colour. Young wood is red, and the older has whitish stripes.
... negundo 'Elegans'	9m+ (30ft+)		3-4			●	★★★★	Excellent foliage tree, sometimes grown as a large shrub. Maple leaves strikingly variegated with bright yellow.
... n. 'Variegatum'	9m+ (30ft+)		3-4				★★★★	As A. n. 'Elegans' except that the variegation is white and green.
... nikoense	6m (20ft)		4		●	●	★★★★	A slow-growing Acer, with soft, rich red autumn leaf colour. A beautiful tree.
... rubrum Canadian Red Maple	7.5m+ (25ft+)		3-4		●		★★★★	Beautiful scarlet and yellow foliage and red fruit make this a very striking tree in the autumn.
Aesculus x carnea 'Briottii' Pink Horse Chestnut	6m+ (20ft+)		5				★★★★	A pink form of the well-known Horse Chestnut. A smaller tree than the white-white-flowered kind, but not a small garden tree.
Ailanthus altissima Tree of Heaven	10.5m+ (35ft+)		6-7				★★★★	Very large ash-like leaves, and smooth bark. Fast-growing, becoming a tall tree with a rounded head.
Amelanchier canadensis Snowy Mespilus	5.4m (18ft)		4		●	●	★★★★	A foaming mass of white flowers before the leaves have fully developed. Maroon-purple fruits in June. Autumn tints.
Arbutus unedo Strawberry tree	4.5m (15ft)	●	10			●	★★★★	A beautiful evergreen tree, forking and carrying red pitcher-shaped flowers and strawberry-like fruits simultaneously.
Betula pendula Silver Birch	7.5m+ (25ft+)		3-4				★★★★	A graceful tree, with attractive silver bark, which peels. Semi-pendulous habit.
B. p. 'Fastigiata'	4.5m+ (15ft+)		3-4			●	★★★★	Despite the apparent conflict in name, this is a slender, upright tree. Dark green leaves and a silver bark on old specimens.
B. p. 'Youngii' Young's Weeping Birch	4.5m (15ft)		3-4			●	★★★★	A weeping Birch with a most attractive weeping habit.
Carpinus betulus Hornbeam	6m+ (20ft+)		3				★★★★	Useful as a hedging plant on heavy soil, but also makes a specimen tree. Hop-like catkins.
C. b. 'Pyramidalis'	6m+ (20ft+)		3				★★★★	An upright form, although it does spread with age.
Catalpa bignonioides Indian Bean Tree	4.5m+ (15ft+)		7-8				★★★	A distinctive specimen tree, with white, foxglove-like flowers flecked yellow and purple. Fruit like runner beans.
Cercis siliquastrum Judas Tree	4.5m (15ft)		4-5			●	★★★★	Clusters of bright purple-rose flowers on slender stalks before the leaves.
Cotoneaster x hybridus 'Pendulus'	2.4m (8ft)	●	6			●	★★★★	Is ideal as a small, weeping specimen tree. Large red berries in autumn.

175

GOOD GARDEN TREES Continued

Species and Varieties	Height	Evergreen	Flowering period	Fragrance	Autumn colour	Suitable for small garden	Hardiness	Description
Crataegus lavallei	4.5m (15ft)		5			● (tree)	★★★★	Sturdy, upright habit and large glossy leaves. Flat clusters of white flowers; orange-red berries.
C. monogyna 'Pendula' Weeping Thorn	4.5m (15ft)		5			● (tree)	★★★★	A Hawthorn with graceful, arching branches. White flowers.
c.m. 'Stricta'	4.5m (15ft)		5			● (tree)	★★★★	A vigorous, upright, form of thorn. White flowers
C. oxycantha 'Coccinea Plena'	4.5m (15ft)		5			● (tree)		A double, scarlet form of Hawthorn.
Eucalyptus gunnii Cedar Gum	7.5m (25ft)	●	—	(fragrance)			★★	The hardiest of the Australian Gums. Blue-grey foliage with a waxy bloom. Grows rapidly.
Fagus sylvatica Beech	6m+ (20ft+)	—					★★★★	One of our most beautiful native trees.
F. s. 'Cuprea' Copper Beech	6m+ (20ft+)	—					★★★★	Impressive purple-red-leaved version of the Beech. A beautiful tree but only suitable for the largest gardens.
F. s. 'Fastigiata' Dawyck Beech	6m+ (20ft+)	—					★★★★	A narrow, upright Beech — useful as a specimen tree for a large garden.
Fraxinus excelsior 'Pendula' Weeping Ash	6m+ (20ft+)		4				★★★★	An outstanding umbrella-shaped tree, given space to develop.
F. oxycarpa 'Raywood'	9m+ (30ft+)		4		(autumn leaf)		★★★★	An excellent specimen tree. Bluish-green fern-like foliage. Leaves turn a smoky plum-purple before falling. Upright habit.
Gleditschia triacanthos 'Elegantissima' Honey Locust	4.5m (15ft)		6			● (tree)	★★★★	A tree of spreading habit, with branches of beautiful pinnate foliage. A good specimen tree in a lawn.
G. t. 'Sunburst'	4.5m (15ft)		6			● (tree)	★★★★	Similar to the type, but with brighter yellow leaves.
Ilex Holly	3.6m (12ft)	●				● (tree)	★★★★	Too well known to need description. Can eventually form a large tree, but is slow growing, and usually grown as a shrub.
Koelreuteria paniculata	6m+ (20ft+)		7-8		(autumn leaf)		★★★★	A late-flowering tree with spikes of small yellow blooms. Bladder-like seed pods. Attractive foliage, bright yellow in autumn.
Laburnum x vossii Golden Rain	6m (20ft)		5-6			● (tree)	★★★★	Long racemes of yellow flowers, in profusion. Does not set much seed.
Laurus nobilis Sweet Bay	3m (10ft)	●		(fragrance)		● (tree)	★★★★	Usually grown as a shaped shrub or small tree, well-known for its aromatic leaves.
Liquidambar styraciflua Sweet Gum	6m+ (20ft+)		5		(autumn leaf)		★★★★	A handsome straight-trunked tree with a pyramidal head. One of the best trees for autumn tints.
Liriodendron tulipifera Tulip Tree	7.5m+ (25ft+)		5-6		(autumn leaf)		★★★★	Unusually shaped leaves, which turn yellow in autumn. Greenish-yellow cup-shaped flowers.
Magnolia kobus	7.5m+ (25ft+)		4				★★★★	Although the tree does not usually flower until it is some years old, it then bears its lovely creamy-white flowers in profusion.

GOOD GARDEN TREES Continued

Species and Varieties	Height	Evergreen	Flowering period	Fragrance	Autumn colour	Suitable for small garden	Hardiness	Description
M. x soulangeana	6m (20ft)		4-5			🌳	★★★★	A forking tree of great beauty. Large white flowers tinged with purple, borne on leafless branches at first.
Malus (see page 174)								
Nyssa sylvatica Tupelo	9m+ (30ft+)		6		🍂		★★★★	Grown primarily for its autumn colour, which is brilliant scarlet.
Parrotia persica	3m (10ft)		1-3		🍂	🌳	★★★★	Small red flowers during late winter, but its main attraction is the autumn colour — orange, red, and gold.
Populus nigra 'Italica' Lombardy Poplar	15m+ (50ft+)		3-4				★★★★	An excellent screen or windbreak, but only suitable for a large garden. Do not plant near drains or buildings.
Prunus (see page 173)								
Pyrus salicifolius 'Pendula' Weeping Willow Leaf Pear	4.5m+ (15ft+)		4			🌳	★★★★	A nice specimen tree, forming a dense head of arching branches with silver-grey willow-like leaves.
Quercus robur 'Fastigiata' Cypress Oak	4.5m+ (15ft+)		5				★★★★	The answer for anyone who wants an Oak that will not take up too much space. Columnar in habit.
Rhus typhina Stag's Horn Sumach	6m+ (20ft+)		—			🌳	★★★★	Can be grown as a tree or shrub.
Robinia pseudoacacia False Acacia	7.5m (25ft)		5-6	🌸			★★★★	Grown for its attractive pinnate foliage, which resembles acacia.
R. p. 'Fastigiata'	7.5m (25ft)		5-6			🌳	★★★★	An upright form of R. pseudoacacia.
Salix alba White Willow	4.5m+ (15ft+)		5				★★★★	One of our most beautiful native trees. Shoots and leaves have a grey silky down.
S. a. 'Tristis' Golden Weeping Willow	6m+ (20ft+)		5				★★★★	Considered by many to be our most beautiful weeping tree. Bright yellow branches in winter. Typical willow leaves in summer.
S. caprea 'Pendula' Kilmarnock Willow	2.4m (8ft)		3			🌳	★★★★	A pendulous willow grown for its attractive catkins in early spring.
Sorbus americana 'Decora' American Mountain Ash	4.5m (15ft)		6			🌳	★★★★	A shrubby tree with attractive pinnate leaves and large sealing-wax red berries.
S. aria Whitebeam	4.5m+ (15ft+)		5	🌸			★★★★	Leaves are green on the upper surface, surface, felty white beneath. Very effective in a slight breeze. Red berries.
Tilia petiolaris Weeping Silver Lime	9m+ (30ft+)		7	🌸			★★★★	A weeping version of the Lime of our parklands and roadsides. Undersides of the leaves are white.
Ulmus minor sarniensis Wheatley Elm	7.5m+ (25ft+)		3				★★★★	Narrowly pyramidal in outline. Useful for coastal planting.
U. glabra 'Pendula' Weeping Elm	7.5m+ (25ft+)		3				★★★★	Broad, dark green leaves carried on an umbrella-like framework. Yellowish seed bracts in April.

Heights are those likely to be attained about 20 years from planting, although the actual height may vary significantly, depending on conditions and climate. A + sign indicates the species will continue to grow beyond that height — sometimes exceeding it by two or three times. Large trees are well worth planting for future generations, where space is available, but for small gardens it is best to keep to those trees indicated as suitable.

Conifers

onifers are becoming very fashionable, with more and more
rdeners recognizing the very considerable virtues of these plants.
iis is due in no small measure to the increasing awareness of the
varf and slow-growing species, which are ideally suited to the
odern, smaller garden.

The vast majority of conifers are evergreen, and have a very
stinctive form of growth, giving an attractive outline at any time of
e year. For that reason they have an invaluable architectural use
the garden, forming an excellent focal point. On the large scale,
ll-sized trees can be used, but conifers are available in such a
nge of sizes that suitable species and varieties can be found for
rtually any size of garden. There are even varieties suitable for a
indow-box (see pages 192 and 195).

Some of our most majestic and beautiful trees are large conifers —
e lovely pyramidal Swamp Cypress (*Taxodium distichum*), with its
elicate and feathery green foliage turning warm russet in autumn,
nd the picturesque layered effect of the Cedar of Lebanon (*Cedrus
pani*), are examples.

Such trees are the preserve of the very large garden, but even
me of the tall-growing types have a use in gardens of average
ze, as centre-pieces or as hedges and screens.

A number of conifers make excellent hedges and screens,
articularly varieties of *Chamaecyparis lawsoniana* and X *Cupres-
ocyparis leylandii*; these and other suitable hedging or screening
ees are mentioned on page 152.

all-growing conifers

ne of the least conifer-like conifers in appearance is the Monkey
uzzle (*Araucaria araucana*), and this strange tree never fails to
tract attention. It will ultimately grow into a tall tree, but one sees
em planted in quite small front gardens, and although they totally
ominate the scene the tree is of such a shape and habit that it isn't
verpowering. However, in no way are small gardens able to do
istice to this conifer.

Practically everything about the Monkey Puzzle is strange — even
s arrival in Britain. In the early 1790s, Archibald Menzies was on a
irvey ship that visited Chile, and he pocketed some of the nuts
erved as a dessert, which he then planted on board ship. When he
rrived in England several years later he had five thriving plants —
nd one of them survived at the Botanic Gardens at Kew until 1892.

Pinus sylvestris 'Beauvronensis'
(1.2m/4ft)
(see page 185)

Far left: The Himalayan Deodora, *Cedrus
deodora*, is a tall conifer rising to more
than 6m (20ft), with a graceful, pendulous
shape, and excellent for planting as a lawn
specimen. (See page 187.)

179

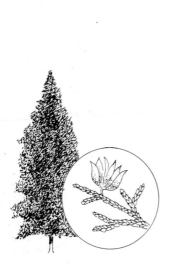

Thuja occidentalis
American Arbor-vitae (6m+/10ft+)
(see page 189)

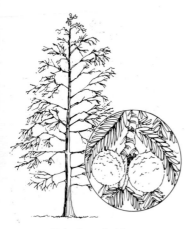

Taxodium distichum
Swamp Cypress (10.5m+/35ft+)
(see page 189)

CONIFERS FOR DAMP SITUATIONS Abies Cryptomeria Metasequoia Picea sitchensis Thuja Taxodium distichum* *: Suitable for swampy ground	**CONIFERS SUITABLE FOR PROVIDING A WINDBREAK OR COASTAL SHELTER BELT** X Cupressocyparis leylandii Cupressus matrocarpa Pinus nigra 'Austriaca' P. contorta 'Latifolia' P. pinaster P. radiata
CONIFERS FOR AUTUMN COLOUR Cryptomeria japonica 'Elegans' Ginkgo biloba Metasequoia Taxodium distichum	**CONIFERS FOR CLAY SOIL** Cedrus deodara Chamaecyparis Cryptomeria japonica Juniperus communis 'Hibernica' Picea abies P. pungens 'Glauca' Taxus baccata Thuja occidentalis
SOME PENDULOUS CONIFERS Cedrus atlantica 'Glauca Pendula' Chamaecyparis lawsoniana 'Glauca Pendula' C. l. 'Pendula' C. nootkatensis 'Pendula' Ginkgo biloba 'Pendula' Larix leptolepsis 'Pendula' Taxus baccata 'Dovastonii'	
CONIFERS FOR SANDY SOIL Cedrus atlantica 'Glauca' Chamaecyparis lawsoniana X Cupressocyparis leylandii Juniperus Larix Pinus pinaster Thuja occidentalis	**CONIFERS FOR CHALKY SOIL** Cedrus Cupressus Juniperus Larix Pinus (not radiata or certain other species) Taxus Thuja

The other common name for this tree is Chile Pine, but Monke Puzzle fits its unique branch formation better. The branches star out from the main straight trunk horizontally, in regular tiers of fi to seven, and the dark, shining stalkless leaves on the branches a arranged spirally, overlapping at the base. As many as twenty-fo of these overlapping evergreen leaves can be packed into 2·5c (1in) of stem. Altogether it is an intriguing tree; but it needs to l planted as an isolated specimen as it does not blend in well wi other plant combinations. It is a conifer that is able to withstar severe winds.

Although Cedars are also large trees, where room is availab there are few more beautiful conifers to plant in a lawn. And it w take about twenty years to reach 7·5m (25ft). There are sever excellent types, Cedrus atlantica 'Glauca' being one of the be This tree is always admired, with its lovely glaucous-blue foliage arching and semi-pendant branches. It is pyramidal in outline whe young, although it ultimately becomes flat-topped. There is also more unusual weeping form, C. a. 'Gaulca Pendula'.

The Japanese Cedar Cryptomeria japonica 'Elegans', is a total different tree. One of its attractions lies in its autumn colour something rare in conifers, the majority of which are evergreen. Th dense and feathery foliage turns a deep rosy-red or purplish colo at the onset of winter.

Another fascinating conifer with an interesting story, and not the least conifer-like in appearance, is the Maidenhair Tree (Ginkg biloba). It was once known only from fossil records, but it wa discovered growing in northern China. Its leaves are two-lobe

-shaped and soft green, resembling a Maidenhair Fern. They turn
low before falling in autumn. It is an attractive tree, but needs
otection from cold winds.

Junipers are among the most suitable conifers for chalky soils,
d there are a great many of them, large and small. One nursery
ers over forty varieties of dwarf kinds alone, and there are just as
any larger kinds with foliage ranging from green and glaucous-
ue to golden-bronze. The aromatic foliage is poisonous to cattle,
avoid planting it where this could be a problem.

The Irish Juniper (*Juniperus communis* 'Hibernica') forms a dense
very-blue pillar, though it may be necessary to hold the branches
gether with bands. (Illustrated on page 152.)

Larch (larix) is a deciduous conifer, and most attractive in spring
nen the pale green foliage expands. Again, it is not for a small
rden, but in the right setting can be an impressive tree.

More suited in scale for most gardens are the Yews, among
hich there is a fastigiate (upright) form useful for limited space,
d the Westfelton Yew (*Taxus baccata* 'Dovastonii'), which has a
orizontal habit with wide-spreading branches, sometimes forming
leaderless bush. There is a golden form. Like Junipers, the foliage
Yews is poisonous to cattle, so the same precautions need to be
ken. (*Taxus baccata* is illustrated on page 187.)

Thujas are suitable for most kinds of soil provided it is well-
ained. This pyramidal tree or large shrub, the American Arbor-
tae, has aromatic foliage, rather like Cedar. The leaves usually
onze in winter.

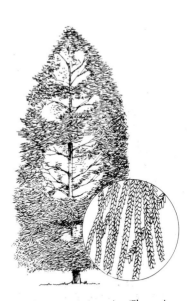

Cryptomeria japonica 'Elegans'
Japanese Cedar (4.5m+/15ft+)
(see page 188)

Dwarf conifers

ttractive though the large trees are, it is undoubtedly among the
warf and slow-growing kinds that the most useful plants can be
und. There are some subjects which are suitable for ground
over, the rock or Heather garden, or as small specimens.

Dwarf conifers are not easy to identify and name, and for many
ears the nomenclature has been extremely confused. At one time
ven specimens in our botanic gardens could not always be relied
pon to have the most accurate or up-to-date name. Things have
nproved, however, and the popular kinds most widely available
an be ordered from your nurseryman with confidence.

The key to wise planting is to keep a sense of scale. Always plant
an open part of the garden, or among low-growing plants, and
ot near large plant masses. They look magnificent when planted
mong low plants such as alpines or Heathers, but can fade into
nsignificance if set amid taller plants.

Rather than dotting dwarf conifers here and there, much better
mpact and effect is produced if they are grouped together, although
the Heather garden a few isolated specimens look best.

It must not be assumed that all dwarf or low-growing conifers are
uitable for rock garden planting, as some of the prostrate kinds can
pread horizontally for a considerable distance and would smother
urrounding plants in all but the largest rockery. These plants are,
owever, ideal for planting as a specimen, for ground cover, and to
ide manholes and similar objects.

Pinus pinaster
Maritime Pine (7.5m+/25ft+)
(see page 189)

181

Dwarf conifers are not particularly fussy about soil, thou[gh] chalky soil indicates the choice should be between varieties [of] *Juniperus* and *Taxus*. This may sound restricting, but these t[wo] genera contain so many good plants of varied habit and colour, th[at] it is not a serious restraint.

Peat is not required, and indeed can make firm planting diffic[ult] – an important point with these plants. If the roots are contained [in] a ball of soil, some of the surface of the root-ball should be brok[en] and a few roots spread out, to ensure a good bond betwe[en] root-ball and surrounding soil. Planting is best done between ea[rly] autumn and late spring, but if possible avoid December, Janua[ry] and early February.

Aspect is not critical as all conifers thrive in sun, but they w[ill] also tolerate a reasonable amount of shade. Most are also extreme[ly] hardy, although dwarf forms of chamaecyparis, cupressus a[nd] podocarpus may suffer some damage in an extreme winter. Whit[e]-tipped and golden forms seem particularly susceptible, so it is wor[th] giving these a sheltered spot, away from cold winds and draught[s].

Deciding which plants to grow is never easy – it would [be] possible to grow only Junipers and have a fascinating collectio[n,] but there are other equally interesting genera. The following plan[ts] and those discussed on page 185 are only a representative selecti[on] of the plants available.

Junipers are particularly useful as they are tolerant of a wi[de] range of conditions and will grow well on alkaline soil. They ran[ge] from ground-hugging types such as *J. sabina* 'Tamariscifolia'·a[nd] *J. horizontalis*, to the erect, slim pencil shapes of *J. scopuloru[m]* 'Skyrocket', which will reach 1·8–2·4m (6–8ft). (*Juniperus sabi[na]* 'Tamariscifolia' is illustrated on page 186.)

Below, right: The Balsam Fir, *Abies balsamea* 'Hudsonia', is ideal for rock gardens. It is slow-growing, and very hardy. (See pages 184 and 185.)
Below: The Irish Juniper, *Juniperus communis* 'Hibernica', is a popular conifer with a columnar habit. (See pages 181 and 188.)

Another Juniper with plenty of height, but still small by tree standards, is *J. scopulorum* 'Blue Heaven', which grows to 2·4m (8ft), and is a good choice for a sunny position, where its pyramid of bright silver-blue foliage looks most attractive. Of very different habit is *J.* x *media* 'Mint Julep', a semi-prostrate kind with arching branches and a fresh green colour. Another, yet totally different, variety of *J.* x *media* is *J. m.* 'Pfitzeriana' (also known as the Knap Hill Savin or Pfizer Juniper). It is a wide-spreading shrub with branches at an angle of about 45 degrees to the ground and branchlets that droop at the tip. It will grow to 1·8m (6ft) high and 2·4m (8ft) across, even larger in time, so it is best planted as a single specimen in isolation. It is a fine plant for disguising a manhole cover in a lawn — it will cover quickly, yet the branches can be lifted for access to the drains.

For the rock garden something like *J. communis* 'Compressa' is a better choice. This makes a compact, column-shaped plant of about 30–45cm (1–1½ft).

Just as *Chamaecyparis* offers a wide choice of tall-growing conifers, so it is among the dwarfs. A useful variety for the rock

Left: *Chamaecyparis lawsoniana* 'Minima Aurea' forms dense growth of golden-green foliage, and is ideal for the small garden or rock garden. (See pages 184 and 185.)

garden is C. *obtusa* 'Pygmaea', which has flat fan-shaped sprays of bright green foliage, which in winter take on a slight bronze tinge. It is always broader than it is high.

One of the strangest of this genus is C. *pisifera* 'Filifera Aurea', which produces a mop-head of golden thread-like foliage. It will grow too large for most rock gardens, but it contrasts well among Heathers.

Another attractive golden conifer, this time like a flat-topped cone in outline, is C. *lawsoniana* 'Minima Aurea'. Its growth is dense and the colour bright. (Illustrated on page 183.)

One of the more recent introductions is C. *l.* 'Boulevard', which makes a feathery bush of blue-grey foliage, although the colour tends to be less bright on limy soil.

One of the most popular and widely-planted dwarf chamaecyparis is C. *l.* 'Ellwoodii'. Not for the small rock garden, but excellent as a specimen or accent plant in a small garden – growing to 1·8m (6ft) or more, but no more than 30cm (1ft) across, being somewhat oval in outline. 'Ellwood's Gold' is gold-tinged in summer, and there is now a miniature green form, ideal for the rock garden, only growing to 1·2m (4ft) and known as C.*l.* 'Ellwood's Pillar'.

Suitable for rock gardens of any size is the Balsam Fir, (*Abies balsamea* 'Hudsonia'), which makes a slow-growing flat-topped bush of rich glossy green foliage, arranged regularly either side of the mid-rib. (Illustrated on the title page and page 182.)

For a dwarf Scots Pine, *Pinus sylvestris* 'Beauvronensis' is worth trying. This rather beautiful plant is dense and broadly branched, the foliage being grey-green. It looks a typical pine, but grows to about 1·2m (4ft), with a somewhat greater spread.

A delightful fastigiate or upright-growing dwarf conifer can be found in *Taxus baccata* 'Standishii', a slow-growing Yew of considerable merit and charm. It is golden-yellow in colour and will grow as a narrow column to 1·5m (5ft).

One of the popular golden dwarf conifers is *Thuja occidentalis* 'Rheingold', a broad plant that will grow to about 1·5m (5ft) and produce a dense mound of gold to glow brightly in the winter sunshine.

Ground-cover plants are always in demand, and there is no reason why suitable varieties of conifers should not be used for this purpose. Once established they are efficient in their task and most attractive in appearance. Certainly prostrate conifers will require little maintenance.

The Junipers offer several possible candidates. *Juniperus sabina* 'Tamariscifolia' and *J. horizontalis* have already been mentioned. There are several varieties of the latter, with various shades of foliage. *J. squamata* 'Blue Carpet' is a more recent introduction, which although completely prostrate soon forms a sheet of silvery-blue foliage.

One of the Yews, *Taxus baccata* 'Repandens' has a dense, spreading habit that makes it suitable for ground cover.

It is often beneficial to prune back the leading tips of shoots of these prostrate conifers once they have reached a reasonable size, to contain growth and encourage a more bushy framework of branches.

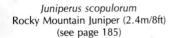

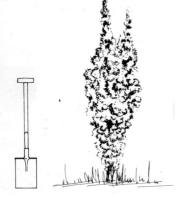

Juniperus scopulorum
Rocky Mountain Juniper (2.4m/8ft)
(see page 185)

Taxus baccata 'Standishii'
(1.5m/5ft)
(see page 185)

DWARF AND PROSTRATE CONIFERS

Species and Varieties	Height*	Ever-green	Ground cover	Hardiness	Description
Abies balsamea 'Hudsonia' Balsam Fir	60cm (2ft)	●		★★★★	A pygmy form, growing only very slowly. Makes a dark green bush, with prominent winter buds.
Chamaecyparis lawsoniana 'Ellwoodii'	1.8m (6ft)	●		★★★★	A useful and widely grown plant, upright-oval in outline. A gold form is also available.
C. l. 'Minima Aurea'	90cm (3ft)	●		★★★★	An attractive golden conifer, a flat-topped cone in outline. Bright yellow the year round.
C. obtusa 'Pygmaea'	75cm (2½ft)	●		★★	Flatish, fan-shaped branchlets held horizontally. Semi-prostrate habit; bright green foliage, bronzing in winter.
C. pisifera 'Boulevard'	1.2m (4ft)	●		★★★★	Beautiful silvery blue-grey foliage, although on limy soil it tends to be browner. Attractive bush shape. An outstanding plant.
C. p. 'Filifera Aurea'	1.5m (5ft)	●		★★★	Golden thread-like foliage. Looks nice planted among heathers, where its colour and mop-headed shape contrasts well.
Cryptomeria japonica 'Elegans Compacta'	90cm (3ft)			★★★★	The long, thin leaves and branches are often gracefully curved. Turns an attractive bronze-red during winter.
Juniperus x media 'Mint Julep'	90cm (3ft)	●		★★★★	Semi-prostrate branches give a feathery appearance to the plant. The rich green foliage looks nice with heathers.
J. sabina 'Tamariscifolia' Savin	90cm (3ft)	●	☁	★★★★	A low, spread shrub with prostrate branches of considerable 'architectural' value.
J. scopulorum 'Blue Heaven' Rocky Mountain Juniper	2.4m (8ft)	●		★★★★	Bright silver-blue foliage that is quite striking in the sun. Strong growth and pyramidal habit.
J. squamata 'Blue Carpet'	30cm (1ft)	●	☁	★★★★	A low-growing, almost prostrate conifer, silvery-blue foliage. A very distinctive plant.
Pinus sylvestris 'Beauvronensis'	1.2m (4ft)	●		★★★★	A dwarf Scots Pine with grey-green foliage. Forms a densely branched little bush.
Taxus baccata 'Standishii'	1.5m (5ft)	●		★★★★	This slow-growing Yew is a most desirable little plant, with dense upright habit and bright golden-yellow foliage.

Juniperus x media 'Mint Julep'
(90cm/3ft)
(see this page)

Juniperus squamata 'Blue Carpet'
(30cm/1ft)
(see this page)

Chamaecyparis pisifera 'Filifera Aurea'
(1.5m/5ft)
(see this page)

DWARF AND PROSTRATE CONIFERS Continued

Species and Varieties	Height*	Ever-green	Ground cover	Hardiness	Description
T. b. 'Repandans'	45cm (1½ft)	●	☁	★★★★	A strong-growing, spreading variety — up to 2.5m across with a large specimen. Shining deep green leaves.
Thuja occidentalis 'Rheingold'	1.5m (5ft)	●		★★★★	A wonderful conifer to bring a touch of gold to a small garden. The colour is especially attractive in winter.
T. plicata 'Rogersii'	1m (3½ft)	●		★★★★	This plant forms a dense, rounded bush. Leaves inside the bush are green, but those exposed have copper-bronze tips.

*: Likely ultimate height. Many are slow-growing and may take years to reach this height. Do not be deterred by the small size of the plants when purchasing the true pygmies, as these grow very slowly — perhaps less than 2.5cm (1 in a year.

Below: *Juniperus sabina* 'Tamariscifolia', commonly known as Savin, is an attractive prostrate conifer, which blends well with Heathers. (See pages 182 and 185.)

TALL CONIFERS

Species and Varieties	Height*	Evergreen	Suitable specimen tree	Hardiness	Description
Araucaria araucana Monkey Puzzle	6m+ (20ft+)	◆	◆	★★★	A tree of unique appearance, with branches standing out from the trunk rigidly and dark, glossy leaves in an overlapping spiral.
Cedrus atlantica 'Glauca' Blue Cedar	7.5m+ (25ft+)	◆	◆	★★★★	One of the most beautiful conifers. Arching, semi-pendulant branches. Glaucus-blue foliage. Becomes a large, flat-topped tree.
C. a. 'Glauca Pendula'	7.5m+ (25ft+)	◆	◆	★★★★	An unusual weeping form of *C. atlantica*.
C. deodara Himalayan Deodar	6m+ (20ft+)	◆	◆	★★★★	Most graceful of the Cedars, with drooping branches of soft green foliage. It will tolerate pruning to form a screen.

Below: The familiar Yew, *Taxus baccata*, forms a wide-spreading tree with dense growth and attractive red fruits. Although often used for hedges, single specimens can be most impressive. (See page 189.)

TALL CONIFERS Continued

Species and Varieties	Height*	Ever-green	Suitable specimen tree	Hardiness	Description
Chamaecyparis lawsoniana 'Allumii' Lawson Cypress	6m+ (20ft+)	●		★★★★	Pyramidal in habit, with glaucus blue foliage. Seen at its best up to about 3m (10ft), but can be beheaded to form a screen.
C. l. 'Columnaris'	6m+ (20ft+)	●	●	★★★★	A fine specimen tree, making a dense, narrow column. Glaucus blue foliage.
C. l. 'Fletcheri'	4.5m (15ft)	●		★★★★	Feathery blue-grey foliage, and neat, upright habit. A handsome medium-sized tree.
C. l. 'Green Hedger'	4.5m+ (15ft+)	●	●	★★★★	Dense, pyramidal habit and bright green foliage. Useful as a specimen or a hedging plant.
C. l. 'Pendula'	4.5m+ (15ft+)	●	●	★★★★	A useful form where variety is needed. The branches droop, providing a change of outline.
C. nootkatensis 'Pendula' Nastka Cypress	7.5m+ (25ft+)	●	●	★★★★	Similar to the Lawson Cypress, but with long pendulous branchlets of dark green leaves.
Cryptomeria japonica 'Elegans'' Japanese Cedar	4.5m+ (15ft+)	●	●	★★★	Needs shelter from strong winds to grow really well. The leaves have a purplish tinge from autumn to spring. Tall, bushy habit.
X *Cupressocyparis leylandii*	12m+ (40ft+)	●	●	★★★★	A fast-growing hybrid of columnar habit. Grey-green foliage. Excellent for forming a rapid screen.
Cupressus macrocarpa Cypress	12m+ (40ft+)	●	●	★★★★	Another conifer useful for hedges and screens. Bright green foliage sets off the brown cones. Rapid growth.
Ginkgo biloba Maidenhair Tree	7.5m+ (25ft+)		●	★★★	An interesting and beautiful conifer with leaves resembling the Maidenhair Fern. The leaves turn yellow in autumn.
G. b. 'Pendula'	7.5m+ (25ft+)		●	★★★	A form with spreading, more or less weeping habit.
Juniperus communis 'Hibernica' Irish Juniper	4.5m+ (15ft+)	●		★★★★	Pillar-like growth and glaucous foliage. Looks nice in a formal garden.
Larix leptolepis 'Pendula' Japanese Larch	6m+ (20ft+)		●	★★★	A vigorous tree with bright green foliage. Reddish twigs look nice in winter sunshine. Pendulous branches.
Metasequoia glyptostroboides Dawn Redwood	12m+ (40ft+)			★★★	Fresh green feathery foliage, which turns salmon in autumn. Vigorous, upright habit.

Chamaecyparis lawsoniana 'Columnaris'
Lawson Cypress (6m+/20ft+)
(see this page)

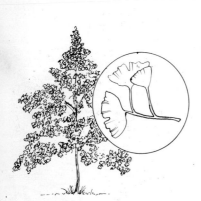

Ginkgo biloba
Maidenhead Tree (7.5m+/25ft+)
(see this page)

TALL CONIFERS Continued

Species and Varieties	Height*	Ever-green	Suitable specimen tree	Hardiness	Description
Picea abies Norway Spruce	7.5m+ (25ft+)	●		★★★★	More popularly known as the Christmas Tree, and therefore needs little description.
P. pungens 'Glauca' Colorado Spruce	4.5m+ (15ft+)	●		★★★★	Dense whorls of branches, with closely packed glaucous blue foliage. A broad pyramid in outline.
P. sitchensis Sitka Spruce	9m+ (30ft+)	●		★★★★	Narrowly conical in outline, this fast-growing tree has arching branches and bluish-green foliage.
Pinus nigra 'Austriaca' Austrian Pine	9m+ (30ft+)	●		★★★★	A broad-headed, densely branched tree with dark green needles about 13cm (5in) long. Very useful for screening.
P. pinaster Maritime Pine	7.5m+ (25ft+)	●		★★★★	A tall tree forming a dark, rugged trunk, old specimens being bare for two thirds of their height. Useful coastal tree.
P. radiata Monterey Pine	9m+ (30ft+)	●		★★	Grassy green needles about 13cm (5in) long are formed in bundles of three. Useful for coastal planting, but avoid lime.
P. sylvestris Scots Pine	7.5m+ (25ft+)	●		★★★★	A useful tree as a screen, vigorous and pyramidal when young. Old specimens become mushroom-topped, but the red of the trunk and branches are attractive in winter.
Taxodium distichum Swamp Cypress	10.5m+ (35ft+)			★★★★	A beautiful tree with bright green feathery foliage, which turns red in the autumn. Purplish cones.
Taxus baccata English Yew	3m+ (10ft+)	●		★★★★	A familar sight in old churchyards. Short-trunked and wide-spreading, the Yew is fine as a specimen or hedge.
T. b. 'Dovastonii' Westfelton Yew	3m+ (10ft+)	●		★★★★	A tree with spreading branches and long, drooping branchlets. There is a form with golden foliage.
Thuja occidentalis American Arbor-vitae	6m+ (20ft+)	●	●	★★★★	A pyramidal tree or large shrub, leaves usually bronze in winter. There are numerous forms of the tree. Aromatic foliage.

Pinus sylvestris
Scot's Pine (7.5m+/25ft+)
(see this page)

Metasequoia glyptostroboides
Dawn Redwood (12m+/40ft+)
(see page 188)

*: Probable height after 20 years.
A + sign indicates the species will continue to grow beyond this, and ultimate height may be considerably more.

Plants For Patios

...ios have become increasingly important in recent years as
...ople have realized how effective they can be, even in a small
...den. Regardless of scale, there is every reason to consider a patio
...whether a summer sitting-out area within a large garden, or a
...ally paved small, town garden. If the garden is particularly small,
...s is one of the most effective ways of using the space; any attempt
...proper beds and lawn would only emphasize the problem,
...ereas a patio looks designed and offers endless scope to create
...ever-changing scene, and an opportunity to grow a surprising
...ge of plants.

...One advantage of a patio from a gardener's point of view is its
...edom from many of the sometimes tiresome aspects of garden-
..., such as cutting lawns and hedges. It also provides an opportun-
...to 'rearrange', the garden frequently by moving the containers;
...almost continuous display of plants can be enjoyed by replanting
...flowers fade (something impractical on a larger scale). A
...advantage is that although a wide range of plants can be grown
...ccessfully in containers, choice is inevitably restricted in com-
...rison with the open garden. Watering is also far more critical than
...s in conventional flower beds, and large amounts of water will be
...eded *every* day during the summer. The use of a hosepipe makes
...s job easier.

...Plants often benefit from being grown in a container, because it
...easier to provide them with good soil of a type to suit their needs,
...d generally plants in containers tend to receive more attention
...an those in the open garden. As already mentioned, the main
...fficulty lies with the risk of dryness at the roots. Sometimes, wind
...also a problem – particularly with raised containers and hanging-
...skets.

...It is a mistake to think of patio plants and container gardening in
...e restricted sense of a paved area on the ground. Balconies and
...t roofs offer almost as much scope, although here wind is more of
...problem, and there are structural considerations. The roof must be
...ong enough to take the weight (although the use of peat composts
...elps in this respect), and window-boxes and hanging baskets must
...e well secured.

Hebe 'Autumn Glory'
Veronica
(see page 204)

...ypes of containers

...hether the container garden is to be confined to a window-box or
...full range of troughs and tubs on a paved area, the containers can
...e almost as important as the plants in them.

Far left: Grouping plants on patios often
enhances their appearance. Here, the
Century Plant, *Agave americana*, with its
dull green leaves edged yellow, nestles
close to echeverias and *Senecio laxifolius*.

Impatiens
Busy Lizzie
(see page 202)

Pendulous begonia
(see page 216)

Old tins can be used, with holes pierced in the bottom – th
sometimes are in garden centres – but they are hardly things
beauty. The need is for something functional, having a good dep
to it, yet attractive in its own right. No matter how attractive t
container is, do not be tempted to buy it unless there is suffici
depth to take 20cm (8in) of soil. By the time there are about 5
(2in) of rubble and coarse material at the bottom for drainage, th
only leaves 15cm (6in) for compost. This depth is required not on
for the mass of roots produced by some of the subjects, but
reduce the likelihood of the compost drying out too quickly.

Dish-shaped, asbestos-cement containers can have plenty
depth in the centre, but if the design is low and wide, the edges c
dry out very quickly and only plants that will tolerate this should
planted round the edge.

With the proviso about depth, there is almost no limit to t
containers that can be used, from old wheelbarrows and even c
baths, to very expensive specially-made clay or pottery urns. A
good garden centre will have a wide range, and usually cost is t
only restraint. Some of the containers will cost much more than t
plants you put in them, but if you have the finance available, t
more attractive kinds will enhance your garden for many years.

The materials used in these containers can be important. Th
plastics do not afford much protection in severe winter weath
and in the summer the soil can heat up excessively. They also te
to lack stability. Some of the heavier plastics, however, overcon
these problems. Although the thin plastics are cheap, they oft
have a fairly short life in the garden as they are easily damaged
broken by impact, and as they age they become more brittle.

Wood is a natural product that blends in well in the garden, a
although it is likely to rot in time, if treated with a suitable wo
preservative (not creosote, which may damage the plants) a
raised off the ground on a few bricks, the life compares favourab
with many other materials.

Old barrels make very good containers if cut in half and provid
with drainage holes, but as fewer wooden barrels are being ma
they are very scarce.

Wood has the advantage that it does not heat up rapidly li

terra-cotta, and therefore may be the best choice for a sun-baked position. Another advantage of wood is that you can make a trough or tub to fill a particular space.

Asbestos-cement looks rather whitish to start with, but it soon weathers, and stands up well to general wear and tear. Some attractive modern shapes are available, but be sure they are practical from the growing aspect.

Clay or terra-cotta pots perhaps give the most pleasing courtyard look, and normally they have a good depth of soil. They can heat up in the summer, and if unglazed dry out very quickly. There is also the danger of severe frosts causing damage, particularly if there are cracks into which water can seep and freeze.

Concrete is a robust material, and looks acceptable in the right setting, but both this and the asbestos-cement type look unpleasing if mixed with wooden or terra-cotta containers.

Keep the image either modern (concrete and similar materials) or traditional (wood and terra-cotta), but try to avoid mixing the two, otherwise the scene will not look well planned.

Avoid too many tubs and urns — if the area becomes cluttered it will look a mess. Choose a few large containers rather than too many small ones.

Positioning is part of the art of good container gardening. Don't overlook the possibility of a tub beside a door, or either side of a flight of steps (but not where someone might fall over them in the dark). Above all, avoid too much symmetry, unless you are deliberately setting out to make a formal design, perhaps with raised beds and a sunken pool.

Pelargonium
Geranium
(see page 200)

The other trap easily fallen into is a lack of contrast in height. Containers are, by nature, going to raise plants off the ground, yet it is important to have some colour and greenery at foot level. This can be provided by having an area devoted to small beds within the paving, especially round the edges, and by using trailing plants to take the colour down from the container as well as upwards.

Even on roof gardens and balconies it is possible to have 'ground level' plantings. By making low, raised beds, perhaps two bricks high, or using low troughs, plants can cascade from these and trailers tumble over the ground.

Height is provided by hanging baskets, climbers, and trees. Obviously, the range and height of the trees is severely restricted by practical considerations, but there are several suitable kinds and some of these are listed on pages 204 and 205. *Eucalyptus gunnii*, for instance, is so easily grown from seed, and is such a quick grower, that it is even worth sowing a few seeds each year, growing the plants on for a few seasons until they become too large for the containers or the site, and then discarding them.

Vinca minor
Periwinkle
(see page 109)

Climbers are dealt with later, but these should never be neglected at the planning stage. Climbers should be high on the priority list of plants for the patio. Wall space should never be wasted, and climbers will help to take any sense of bleakness away from walls. Trained over an arched entrance, a climber can create an impression of entering a secret and wonderful world beyond — which is what a well-planned patio should be.

The plants discussed here are representative of the many fine examples that can be used for container and patio gardening. But remember to group suitable plants together – not only in visual terms, but in soil and light requirement too. It would also be foolish to plant a rampant grower in the same container as a more restrained kind, as the weaker plant would soon be smothered.

Shrubs and trees

Shrubs and small trees form the backbone of a well-planned patio, around which other plants are incorporated within the design. They are likely to command the largest containers, and because of their perennial and woody nature will be the most permanent fixtures (herbaceous plants will come up each year but they are not so evident during winter). For all those reasons, planning and planting should start with these plants.

One of the tallest subjects to try is the Gum (eucalyptus), which has already been mentioned. *E. gunnii* is the hardiest species, and most attractive with its round, aromatic, blue-grey juvenile foliage, which becomes oval in outline as the tree matures. The tree can be contained by pruning it back hard each spring. It will survive most winters in the South, but may succumb in cold districts.

Acers are available in many forms – the vast majority of them totally unsuitable for the patio. However, the Japanese Maple (*A. palmatum*) is different. It makes a beautiful patio plant if given a sheltered position out of draughts and biting winds, in sun or partial shade. There are many good forms, all with divided leaves varying in shade from green to purple. A good example is *A. p.* 'Dissectum Atropurpureum', a slow-growing tree of graceful habit – the normally purple leaves turn vivid scarlet before they fall. Others have leaves so finely divided that they look feathery. (*Acer palmatum* 'Dissectum' is illustrated on page 91.)

Right: Fuchsias, with their exotic and colourful flowers, give summer colour to the patio, although all types except the winter-hardy ones will need greenhouse protection in winter. (See pages 197 and 205.)

The symmetry of conifers makes them useful tub plants, although they should not be used too freely otherwise the patio is likely to look like a chess set. Select just one or two of the taller-growing kinds to give emphasis to a focal point, although the very dwarf and prostrate kinds can be used more freely.

Sure to add interest is the pencil outline of *Juniperus scopulorum* 'Skyrocket', a slim conifer with grey-blue foliage. Although it will grow tall, its narrow, columnar effect makes the proportions perfectly acceptable for this form of gardening.

Chamaecyparis lawsoniana 'Ellwoodii' is conical in shape, with dense, glaucous blue-green foliage which will reach about 90cm (3ft) about five years from planting, and not increase much beyond this height in a container. There is a golden form, *C. l.* 'Ellwood's Gold'. There are even conifers suitable for a window-box, though if they are not to be left as a permanent feature they need to be grown in pots and plunged in the window-box compost. *Juniperus communis* 'Compressa' is a choice plant, forming a dense, bluish-grey pillar, and growing only very slowly, and even then only rarely does it exceed 60cm (2ft). *Picea abies* 'Nidiformis' is another slow-grower, making a miniature shrub with fan-like branches.

There are many other dwarf and prostrate conifers well worth growing on the patio or balcony, such as the charming *Chamaecyparis pisifera* 'Filifera Aurea', with its golden thread-like foliage and lovely arching habit. This and others are described on page 184.

One of the classic tub plants is *Laurus nobilis* (Bay), frequently seen in tubs flanking the entrance to restaurants. This evergreen stands up to atmospheric pollution well, does not object to confined roots, but good drainage is essential.

Evergreen foliage plants are always valuable, and besides the Bay and conifers already mentioned, there are shrubs such as the Gold-dust Tree (*Aucuba japonica* 'Variegata'), The Wood Olive

Below, left: Nasturtiums, with their bright flowers, are ideal rambling annuals for scrambling over the edges of containers. (See pages 23, 200 and 203.)

Below: *Ipomoea rubro-coerulea* is one of the loveliest annual climbers for growing in pots or for a sunny position outdoors. (See pages 23 and 27.)

Cassiope
(see page 204)

Fatsia japonica
Fig-leaved Palm
(see page 205)

Hosta
Plantain Lily
(see page 201)

(*Elaeagnus pungens* 'Maculata') and the Fig-leaf Palm (*Fatsia japonica*), all of which will hold interest during winter as well as form a focal point around which summer plants can be arranged.

Aucuba is a tough plant, and ideal for a shady position, and quite at home in towns and cities, where it will tolerate atmospheric pollution. The large, glossy-green leaves are splashed with gold, and it makes a neat shrub of compact habit. Small plants can be grown in a window-box, but tubs are needed for larger specimens. They are sometimes used as houseplants, but are perfectly hardy.

The Wood Olive also has green foliage splashed with gold, but the leaves are smaller than aucuba, and unlike that plant will not enjoy heavy shade. Use this one in a sunny or semi-shaded position. It is especially useful for a windy site.

Fatsia japonica, the Fig-leaf Palm, is a shrub of great merit, having a striking architectural value, but unlike the previous two is not dependably hardy except in mild areas. It has large, evergreen leaves about 30cm (1ft) across, the shape of a fig-leaf, and an established plant will carry globular heads of milky-white flowers during autumn and early winter.

Camellias are superb flowering evergreens. These plants, with large, rose-like flowers borne at the end of winter and beginning of spring need an acid compost, and the buds require protection from early sun following a severe frost, but if given this will reward with a spectacular display. In northern districts, a sunny position may be needed to ripen the wood, but generally they prefer shade. They need a large tub. (Illustrated on page 87.)

The evergreen (Japanese) azaleas also produce a spectacular display in April and May in a sheltered and shady position. Their gay and colourful flowers, mainly in shades of pink, mauve and yellow, cover the plants, but out of flower are not as attractive as camellias.

The deciduous azaleas are similar to the evergreen one in their requirements, liking an acid peaty soil, but the flowers are larger.

Other plants requiring an acid compost include the Heathers (callunas) and cassiope. Cassiopes are grown for their white, bell-shaped flowers on dwarf plants in April and May, but Heathers are grown for flowers and foliage. Pink, mauve, purple and white are the main shades for flower, and some have golden foliage, though 'Multicolor' is an example of one with vivid red, orange-yellow and green foliage nearly all year. (See pages 127 to 137.)

If you like Heathers but can't provide lime-free soil, try some of the Ericas described on pages 133, 134, 136 and 137.

Another popular shrub sensitive to compost is the hydrangea. Acid soil produces blue flowers, limy soil pink to red flowers. Magnificent though these shrubs are, they are not always easy to grow in containers — their roots must never become dry, and they may need protection in winter. See page 95 for 'blueing' hydrangeas.

Hebes and fuchsias are other examples of superb patio plants that will need winter protection in all but the most favoured areas. They are best taken indoors for winter. Hebes are useful evergreens with neat glossy leaves attractively arranged, and most species have attractive flowers too.

Fuchsias are magnificent plants for patios and balconies. They are adaptable to a range of uses – some will cascade from a hanging basket, others will grow upright in tubs, and they can even be trained into standards. These have a clean stem for about 1·2m (4ft) and then a bushy head of large pendant flowers. Half-standards have a 60cm (2ft) stem.

The Tree Hollyhock (*Hibiscus syriacus*) is an excellent tub shrub with spectacular large flowers rather like those of a Hollyhock. But it needs a sunny position protected from cold winds. It does not like root disturbance and may take a season to settle down, but will then flower prolifically from August to October, although individual blooms are short-lived. The plant is not hardy except in favourable districts and should be taken in the house or greenhouse for the winter.

For a sunny or semi-shaded wall, the Flowering Quince (*Chaenomeles speciosa*) is a valuable plant. It is not a climber, but can be trained against a wall, where its branches will bear red, pink or white flowers during spring. Usually, these are followed by attractive, edible, quince fruits. For further details, see page 118. (Illustrated on page 107.)

Some other shrubs suitable for container gardening are listed on pages 204 and 205. Generally, shrubs in containers will not grow as rapidly, nor to the same ultimate height, as those in the open soil.

Phyllitis scolopendrium
Hart's-tongue Fern
(see page 201)

Climbers and trailers

After the shrubs, climbers must be considered the next priority. The contribution they make in hiding and disguising unwanted brick-work or other features cannot be over-estimated. They also add much charm and atmosphere. Some, such as clematis, are brilliant in flower.

If there is not already an archway or framework for climbers to clamber up and clothe, it is worth making one. Even straight pillars, wooden or brick, can be a magnificent sight clothed with a pillar rose (see page 145).

Annual climbers have a part to play, and several are listed on page 22, it is the shrubby kind that must be planned as part of the permanent planting. Such climbers usually like a cool root run, even if their heads are in the sun, and wherever possible it is best to plant straight into the soil, even if it means lifting a paving stone.

Among the flowering climbers, pride of place must go to clematis. They are very floriferous, and there are many shapes and colours to choose from among the species and large-flowered hybrids. These desirable plants are dealt with more fully on pages 116 and 121.

Polystichum setiferum
Soft-shield Fern
(see page 201)

Among the foliage climbers, the Ivies must be the most useful, although for a spectacular display of autumn colour there is little to beat *Vitis coignetiae* when its 25cm (10in) leaves turn shades of brilliant orange and crimson. The Ivies, however, are more versa-tile. They can be used to trail from window-boxes or tubs, or to clothe a whole wall. There are varieties of the common Ivy (*Hedera helix*) with an amazing range of leaf shapes and colours, and they have the merit of being self-clinging. Some varieties are described on page 115. Another striking species is *H. colchica* 'Dentata Variegata', the Persian Ivy, which has dark green leaves with yellow variegation. (Illustrated on pages 114 and 122.)

Trailing plants should not be overlooked, and many those worth trying are pendulous begonias, trailing lobelia, *Lysimachia nummularia*, Ivy-leafed Geraniums (pelargoniums), *Saxifraga stolonifera*, and vincas.

Herbaceous and rock plants

There is no merit in trying to create a miniature herbaceous border, nor in trying to build a full-blown rock garden on a patio or balcony. These plants are best used in tubs and troughs with other plants. They are best planted around shrubs and small trees in containers, where they can remain undisturbed. A few, however, such as the African Lily (agapanthus), are best in a tub on their own.

Agapanthus are among the few herbaceous perennials that usually grow better in a container than in the open border. The cramped root conditions seem to suit them and make them flower more prolifically. They have thick fleshy roots which send up long, deep green strap-shaped leaves, which are topped during July and August with heads of blue flowers. They are not hardy plants, though Headbourne Hybrids are among the hardiest. Full sun and plenty of water is necessary for these impressive plants.

A particularly useful plant, because it flowers from March to

Right: Lobelia is a favourite annual for edging borders close to patios, where the bold colours look decisive.

May, is *Bergenia cordifolia*, sometimes known as Elephant's Ears. Both the pink flowers and large rounded leaves are attractive.

Hostas are even more useful as foliage plants, ideal for a shady spot. Among the types to choose from are *H. albomarginata*, lance-shaped leaves edged creamy-white; *H. crispa*, crinkly creamy-white edge; *H. fortunei*, glaucous leaves; *H. f.* 'Albopicta', buff or gold variegation in spring and early summer; *H. sieboldiana*, bluish grey-green; *H. undulata* 'Medio-variegata', smallish leaves with wavy-edges; and *H. ventricosa* 'Aureo-variegata', prominent yellow variegation contrasting with deep green leaves. Besides desirable leaves the flower spikes have an attraction of their own in July and August.

For a damp, shady spot some of the hardy ferns can look most attractive, though they are best planted straight into the ground rather than in containers. Two dependable types are the Hart's Tongue Fern (*Phyllitis scolopedrium*) and the Soft-shield Fern (*Polystichum setiferum*). The first has strap-shaped leaves, the second pinnate foliage. Both require copious watering if they are not in a naturally damp position. More ideas for herbaceous and rock plants to grow in containers appear on page 201.

Bulbs for patios

The use of bulbs opens even brighter possibilities. Most of them will grow well in containers. A few will need to be left undisturbed as a

Below, left: A variety of the Common Ivy, *Hedera helix* 'Glacier', with its distinctive leaves and attractive colour, is well worth using for year-round attractiveness. (See pages 115, 197 and 218.)

Below: Hanging baskets burgeoning with bright pelargoniums (commonly but incorrectly called geraniums) really state that summer has arrived. Do ensure that the supporting bracket is well secured to the wall. (See hanging baskets on page 193.)

permanent feature, but most of them can be planted afresh each year and used as a form of seasonal bedding – but in this case, fresh bulbs will be required each year (the old ones can be put out in the main garden). You cannot expect bulbs to continue to flower at their peak if lifted and replanted each season, with no opportunity to build up into a good flowering-sized bulb. This may not matter so much in the open garden, but in containers every bulb should be at its best if the display is not to look second-rate.

For a spring display, include *Anemone blanda*, 'De Caen' or 'St. Brigid' anemones, crocuses, hyacinths, muscari, and dwarf varieties of tulip.

Summer-flowering bulbs for the patio include cannas (not hardy), *Fritillaria meleagris*, *Galtonia candicans*, bulbous iris, ranunculus, and *Lilium regale* if a deep container can be provided.

Autumn flower can be provided by *Colchium autumnale*, *Crocus speciosus*, and *Nerine bowdenii* (best at the foot of a warm wall).

Bulbs to flower at the end of winter are chionodoxa, *Crocus chrysanthus*, *Eranthis hyemalis*, snowdrops, *Iris reticulata* and *I. danfordiae*, and *Scilla sibirica*.

Descriptions and planting advice appear on pages 63 to 81.

Bedding plants

Bedding plants are widely used in window-boxes, but they are just as valuable for all kinds of containers. Some require the depth of a tub rather than a trough or window-box, and the chart on pages 202 and 203 indicates which these are.

The treatment of bedding plants is described on page 15, and although there is the possibility of sowing some annuals in the autumn (page 16) unless the back-up garden space is available you will be limited to the availability of plants in the shops and garden centres.

Half-hardy perennial subjects such as pelargoniums (Geraniums), and begonias will have to be taken indoors for the winter. In the case of tuberous-rooted begonias the tubers are dried off and stored, but the fibrous-rooted *B. semperflorens* can be potted up carefully and taken indoors to continue flowering for a further period as a houseplant. Impatiens can be treated in the same way.

Window-box plants

If you make your window-boxes large enough, and sufficiently deep, you should be able to sustain interest throughout the year and avoid the bleak times between the summer bedding being cleared and the spring bulbs flowering.

Plant some permanent subjects, such as Ivies and vinca, to trail down at the front, and dwarf conifers, little Box plants, or small aucubas to add interest the year round with their evergreen foliage. Then plant the seasonal colour around these.

Don't overlook trailers such as *Lysimachia nummularia* (Creeping Jenny), and Nasturtiums. Be careful to select plants of roughly equal vigour to go together though – Nasturtiums, for instance, are lovely plants and make a bright show, but they can swamp weaker plants. (Illustrated on page 15.)

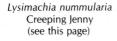

Lysimachia nummularia
Creeping Jenny
(see this page)

Dianthus
Pinks
(see page 201)

HERBACEOUS AND ROCK PLANTS
FOR THE PATIO

Species and Varieties	Height	Flowering period	Aspect	Container	Hardifss	Description
Agapanthus 'Headbourne Hybrids' African Lily	60cm (2ft)	7-8	○	pot	★★	Strap-shaped leaves, heads of blue lily-like flowers. Impressive subjects for pots or tubs.
Alchemilla mollis Lady's Mantle	45cm (1½ft)	6-7	◉	pot	★★★★	Soft, downy rounded foliage, surmounted by sprays of greeny-yellow flowers.
Alyssum saxatile Gold Dust	30cm (1ft)	4-6	○	trough	★★★★	An easily grown plant, a mass of bright yellow flowers.
Arabis albida 'Plena' Snow in Summer	15cm (6in)	3-5	◑	trough	★★★★	Grey-green leaves and masses of small white flowers.
Armeria maritima Thrift	15cm (6in)	6-7	○	pot	★★★★	Grass-like foliage and round heads of pink flowers.
Aubrieta	15cm (6in)	3-5	○	trough	★★★★	Lovely plants that form a mass of colour — usually in shades of blue or purple.
Bergenia cordifolia Elephant's Ears	30cm (1ft)	3-5	◑	pot	★★★★	Large, round, glossy green leaves. Deep pink flowers.
Dianthus Carnations and Pinks	15-45cm (6-18in)	6-8	○	pot	★★★★	Well-known plants with grey, elongated leaves and colourful, often fragrant, flowers.
Dicentra spectabilis Bleeding Heart	60cm (2ft)	4-6	◉	pot	★★★★	A very pretty plant, with feathery foliage and dangling sprays of rose and white flowers.
Festuca glauca	12-23cm (6-9in)		◉	pot	★★★★	A pretty grass with tufted habit and slender glaucous leaves. Useful as an edging for tubs.
Helleborus niger Christmas Rose	30cm (1ft)	12-3	●	pot	★★★	A most welcome sight early in the year. Purple or white flowers.
H. orientalis Lenten Rose	30-45cm (1-1½ft)	2-3	●	pot	★★★	Similar to Christmas Rose. Flowers vary from white to purple.
Hosta Plantain Lily	30-60cm (1-2ft)	7-8	●	pot	★★★★	Although the sprays of mauve trumpet-shaped flowers are pleasant, it is for the foliage that hostas are grown. There are various species, with various shades of green and variegations.
Iberis sempervirens Perennial Candytuft	23cm (9in)	5-6	○	pot	★★★★	White flowers are carried above a mat of evergreen leaves.
Nepeta mussinii Catmint	30cm (1ft)	5-9	○	pot	★★★★	Pleasant plant with aromatic grey-green foliage and blue spiky flowers.
Phlox subulata Dwarf Phlox	15cm (6in)	4-5	○	trough	★★★★	An attractive rock plant, suitable for containers. Plants become a mound of lavender, pink or red flowers.
Phyllitis scolopendrium Hart's-tongue Fern	30cm (1ft)		●	pot	★★★★	Strap-shaped fern leaves. Requires a damp situation or copious watering.
Polygonum vacciniifolium Alpine Knotweed	15cm (6in)	8-10	◉	pot	★★★★	Deep pink flowers. Vigorous creeping growth.
Polystichum setiferum Soft-shield Fern	30cm (1ft)		●	pot	★★★★	A fern with pinnate leaves, useful for a damp, shady corner.
Saxifraga umbrosa London Pride	30cm (12in)	5-7	◑	pot	★★★★	Minute star-shaped flowers on heads rising from a rosette of leaves.
Sedum spectabile Ice Plant	45cm (1½ft)	9-10	○	pot	★★★★	Among the finest herbaceous plants, and especially valuable late in the season. Succulent leaves, and dazzling heads of pink or red flowers.

BEDDING PLANTS FOR THE PATIO

Species and Varieties	Height	Flowering period	Aspect	Container	Treatment	Description
Ageratum	15-45cm (6-18in)	7-8	○	▽	HHA	Heads of small, blue powder-puff flowers. Most varieties, less than 25cm (10in) are best for window-boxes.
Alyssum	10cm (4in)	5-8	○	▽	HA	Useful edging plant, most varieties being white, but some are violet.
Antirrhinum (dwarf varieties) Snapdragon	30cm (12in)	7	○	▽	HHA	The tall varieties are not suitable for containers, but dwarf, bushy kinds are very useful.
Begonia (tuberous-rooted, large-flowered)	30cm (1ft)	6-10		▽	HHP	Spectacular flowers, rather like full roses. Needs a sheltered position for good results.
Begonia semperflorens	20cm (8in)	7-10	○	▽	HHP	Very gay, floriferous flowers — mainly in shades of red and pink, with white varieties too. Not hardy.
Bellis perennis Double Daisy	15cm (6in)	3-5	⊙	▽	HB	Large, double flowers on small plants — useful for edging. Red, pink, white.
Calendula officinalis Pot Marigold	30-60cm (1-2ft)	7-9	⊙	▽	HA	Plants that will grow with the minimum of attention. Bright and gay, in shades of orange and yellow.
Cheiranthus Wallflower	15-30cm (6-12in)	3-5	○	▽	HB	Popular fragrant spring flowers. Grow only the dwarf, compact varieties for container planting.
Clarkia	60cm (2ft)	7	⊙	▽	HA	Graceful and easily grown annuals, best planted in a small group.
Delphinium (annual) Larkspur	45cm (1½ft)	7-8	○	▽	HA	A small-spiked version of the delphinium, in blue, red, and white. Grow only dwarf varieties — the taller kinds reach 1.2m (4ft).
Impatiens Busy Lizzie	30cm (12in)	7-9	⊙	▽	HHP	Well-known as a houseplant, but can also be planted out during the summer.
I. balsamina Balsam	30-45cm (1-1½ft)	7-8	○	▽	HHA	Showy plants with flowers resembling small camellias.
Kochia scoparia Burning Bush	60cm (2ft)	—	○	▽	HHA	Neat oval bushes, light green in summer turning to brilliant scarlet and bronze in autumn.
Linum grandiflorum Flax	45cm (1½ft)	6-7	○	▽	HA	Crimson flowers freely produced. Grow in a group for impact.
Lobelia	15cm (6in)	7-8	⊙	◓	HA	Popular blue bedding plant, widely used as an edging. A trailing form is available for hanging baskets and window-boxes.
Matthiola bicornis Night-scented Stock	30cm (1ft)	7-8	○	▽	HA	Flowers are not spectacular, but it is a plant for fragrance.
M. incana Stock	45cm (1½ft)	7-8	○	▽	HHA	Stocks come in many shades and sizes, and it is possible to be fairly certain of double flowers.
Myosotis Forget-me-not	15-30cm (6-12in)	3-6	◑	▽	HB	Popular spring flowers, the masses of small blue flowers being most effective when massed.
Nemesia strumosa	23-30cm (9-12in)	6-7	◑	▽	HHA	Small flowers cover these delightful summer bedding plants. Good compact habit and wide range of colours.
Nicotiana alata Tobacco Plant	45-75cm (1½-2½ft)	7-8	⊙	▽	HHA	Pleasant tubular flowers in several colours, but the principal attraction if the delightful fragrance.
Nigella damascena Love-in-a-mist	30-60cm (1-2ft)	7-8	○	▽	HA	Blue flowers set in a sea of feathery green foliage.

Plants
For The Home

Plants in pots are fortunate regarding soil, for it isn't difficult to provide them with a suitable growing medium – whether one of the traditional composts such as John Innes is used, or a newer loamless type. These will suit the vast majority of plants, but for the small number that need something special there are the traditional formulae that can be mixed for the occasion. Houseplants also have the further advantage of a frostproof, usually warm environment in which to grow.

These advantages are countered by very poor lighting conditions in comparison with outdoors, an artificially dry atmosphere, and difficulties with watering.

Compost, watering and humidity problems can be dispensed with by resort to hydroponics (growing the plants in nutrient solutions, without soil), but even then, and assuming the light requirement is fulfilled, there is no guarantee of success. The room may be too cold, too warm, or too draughty.

The protected surroundings of the home is no perfect growing environment, and as with outdoor plants it is vital to choose and site plants carefully.

There are many difficult sites in the home – kitchens with cooking fumes and often sudden rises of temperature; bathrooms that alternate between a hot, steamy 'jungle' atmosphere and a riveting coldness; dull hallways, cold stairways, to mention a few – but there are plants that will thrive in all of them. The tables on pages 216 to 219, and the following advice should enable the right plant to be chosen for each place.

Bathrooms and kitchens

These two rooms are often steamy – but the similarity ends there. A kitchen often has much more light than a bathroom, and generally a more consistently high temperature. On the other hand, kitchens are sometimes bursting with cooking fumes, including those of hot fat and gas if that is the method of cooking; there can also be a considerable temperature gradient towards the upper half of the room, which can affect plants placed in a high position.

How good the bathroom is for plants depends largely on the lifestyle of the occupants of the house. If the room is kept at a constant 18°C (65°F), it will be an ideal position for many plants, and especially useful as a place in which to introduce new plants to the home for the first couple of weeks.

Dracaena
Dragon Plant
(see page 217)

Far left: The Madagascar Jasmine, *Stephanotis floribunda*, displays fragrant, waxy, white flowers surrounded by glossy green leaves. (See page 219.)

Coleus
Flame Nettle
(see page 217)

Fatshedera
(see page 217)

Peperomia
(see page 218)

PLANTS FOR ROOMS WITHOUT DIRECT SUN
Aglaeonema
Aspidistra
Aucuba
Begonia (decorative leaved kinds)
Chlorophytum
Cissus
Cyperus
Dieffenbachia
Dracaena
X Fatshedera
Fatsia
Ficus pumila
Hedera
Helxine
Impatiens
Maranta
Monstera
Peperomia
Philodendron
Pilea cadierei
Rhoeo discolor
Rhoicissus
Saintpaulia
Sansevieria
Saxifraga stolonifera
Schefflera
Scindapsus
Spathiphyllum
Syngonium
Tolmiea
Tradescantia
Zebrina

PLANTS FOR BOTTLE GARDENS
Adiantum
Chlorophytum
Dracaena godseffiana
Ficus pumila
Fittonia
Hedera (small-leaved varieties)
Helxine soleirolii
Maranta
Pellionia pulchra
Peperomia
Pilea
Pteris cretica
Saintpaulia
Saxifraga stolonifera
Tradescantia

PLANTS FOR SHADE
Araucaria
Aspidistra
Cyperus
Dizygotheca
X Fatshedera
Fatsia
ferns
Ficus elastica 'Decora'
Ficus pumila
Fittonia
Hedera
Helxine
Maranta
Philodendron scandens
Rhoicissus
Saxifraga stolonifera
Syngonium podophyllum

PLANTS FOR A DRY ATMOSPHERE
Aechmea
Ananas
Aspidistra
Billbergia
cacti
Grevillea
Guzmania
Howea
Hoya
Pelargonium
Sansevieria
Saxifraga stolonifera
succulents

CLIMBING HOUSEPLANTS
Cissus
Cobaea
Dipladenia
Hedera
Hoya
Ipomoea
Jasminum
Philodendron scandens
Rhoicissus
Scindapsus
Stephanotis
Thunbergia

TRAILING OR HANGING HOUSEPLANTS
Achimenes
Asparagus densiflorus (A. sprengeri)
Begonia (pendulous)
Campanula isophylla
Ceropegia
Chlorophytum
Columnea
Ficus pumila
Hedera
Saxifraga stolonifera
Setcreasea
Thunbergia
Tradescantia
Zebrina

PLANTS FOR ROOMS WITH FUMES
(cooking, gas, tobacco)
Aechmea
Aspidistra
Aucuba
Billbergia
Dieffenbachia
Dracaena
Fatshedera
Fatsia
Ficus
Grevillea
Guzmania
Hippeastrum
Hoya
Impatiens
Monstera
Philodendron
Rhoicissus rhomboidea
Sansevieria
Schefflera
Scindapsus
Sedum sieboldii
Tolmiea
Tradescantia

PLANTS FOR UNHEATED AREAS SUCH AS HALLS AND STAIRWAYS	PLANTS FOR SUNNY WINDOWS
Araucaria	Beloperone
Aspidistra	cacti
Billbergia	Campanula
Chlorophytum	Capsicum
Cissus	Ceropegia
Cyperus	Citrus
X Fatshedera	Cobaea
Fatsia	Coleus
Grevillea	Guzmania
Hedera	Hippeastrum
Helxine	Impatiens
Jasminum polyanthum	Pelargonium
Philodendron scandens	Sansevieria
Saxifraga stolonifera	Solanum
Schefflera	succulents

Hoya carnosa
Wax Flower
(see page 218)

However, if the heating is only on a couple of times a day for a few hours, or when a bath is being taken, such fluctuating temperatures can be harmful.

The other major drawback to bathrooms is the increasing use of aerosol sprays. Besides a regular dusting of talcum powder, the chances are the plants will also have to share a variety of chemicals in the form of deodorants and hair sprays. Some of these can cause damage to the leaves of many plants. The leaves will, in any case, need regular wiping with a damp cloth, or a mist spray of water to prevent them becoming clogged with powder.

Philodendrons are some of the most useful houseplants, and although *Philodendron scandens* (Sweetheart Plant) is a prime candidate for the bathroom, it is suitable for other aspects too. The common name probably comes from the heart-shaped leaves, green and shiny, and attractively arranged on climbing stems. If there is nothing for the plant to clamber up, it will be happy to trail.

Two other good plants for a warm bathroom are spathiphyllum (Peace Lily) and anthurium (Flamingo Flower), both grown for their spathes. *Spathiphyllum wallisii* has rich, dark green leaves rather like those of an aspidistra, and long-lasting white arum-like bracts to frame a small and less significant flower spike. Wipe the leaves regularly and keep the plants out of direct sunlight in mid-summer.

Anthurium scherzerianum also has bright green leaves, but the spathe or bract is bright red and downward curving. The edges of the leaves may turn yellow if the temperature drops below 10°C (50°F). Use rainwater or soft tap water, and feed with a dilute fertilizer once a fortnight.

Almost any other glossy-leaved foliage plant is suitable for the bathroom, and the tables on pages 216 to 219 will indicate the temperature range for each plant.

Kitchens are usually light places, especially in modern homes. The window space is larger than in the bathroom, and is not usually curtained with heavy material, as in a living-room. This has the potential to make it one of the best 'growing rooms' in the home — but the presence of so many fumes restricts the ideal choice to those listed on page 208.

The list includes some dependable and popular foliage plants, including the very accommodating philodendron, already men-

Spathiphyllum
Peace Lily
(see page 219)

Anthurium
Flamingo Flower
(see page 216)

Ficus pumila
(see page 218)

tioned for bathrooms, the Swiss Cheese Plant (*Monstera deliciosa*) with its very large, deeply cut and slashed leaves, Rubber Plant (ficus) and the Umbrella Tree (schefflera), with its glossy green leaflets radiating out from the stem like an umbrella. The once almost-despised aspidistra should not be overlooked, because of its good nature.

For something a little more colourful the various dracaenas are well suited. There are various types, some with narrow ribbon shaped leaves, others broader and strap-shaped, and usually with variegated stripes down the centre of the leaves or along the edges.

A plant with a truly exotic look is Queen's Tears (*Billbergia nutans*). The long grass-like leaves, growing in a funnel-shaped cluster, are pleasant but unspectacular; in spring, however, sprays of weird, hanging flowers appear. Tassels of long flowers emerge from a bright red sheath — each yellowish-green bloom having a navy-blue edge to the petals and a pink-flushed calyx. They are not difficult if given a peaty compost and not exposed to too much direct light, which tends to turn the leaves rather yellow.

Nowhere near as beautiful, but interesting in a different way, is the Pick-a-back Plant (*Tolmiea menziesii*). The attraction of this hardy plant lies in the heart-shaped hairy leaves, which produce young plants on the surface. These will root if they come into contact with soil. Plenty of water and a little shade are the only requirements of this fun plant.

Right: The Boat Lily, *Rhoeo discolor* 'Variegata', is an undemanding yet very attractive plant, ideal for a shady area. The strap-like leaves have purplish undersides. (See page 213.)

Although climbers may not seem practical plants for a kitchen, they can be particularly useful if there is a dining area set aside from the main cooking part, where they can climb a light plastic trellis to form a pleasant screen. For sheer screening power, the Grape Ivy (*Rhoicissus rhomboidea*) is difficult to better. Shiny, deep green, diamond-shaped leaves are produced in threes along the stems, and tendrils are used to cling to the support. It grows quickly, but needs shade to thrive.

For a climber with flowers, the Wax Flower (hoya) is very beautiful, bearing waxy-white star-shaped flowers. One of the variegated forms of *Hoya carnosa* should be chosen, for the thick evergreen cream and green leaves are an attraction in their own right.

Plants for shade

Light of the quality required by plants is one of the conditions over which we have least control in the home. Humidity can be provided in a variety of ways, and warmth can be controlled, but short of using special growing lights the plants have to manage with the amount of natural light that penetrates the room. The illumination on a windowsill is usually adequate to grow most plants, but many of us like to see plants within the room too. Suitable plants are available, but the choice has to be made carefully unless you have a greenhouse and are prepared to rotate the plants between greenhouse and home on a regular basis.

Inner walls away from the window usually receive the least light, and here only plants happy in complete shade should be grown.

Two of the climbers already mentioned are suitable – *Philodendron scandens* and *Rhoicissus rhomboidea* – along with trailing *Ficus pumila* and the Rubber Plant (*F. elastica*).

Ivies are extremely obliging plants and will grow almost anywhere, but for best results the variegated kinds require reasonable light, which restricts the choice for dark areas to the green-leaved kinds. This is no hardship, as there are some excellent green ivies

Below, left: *Tradescantia fluminensis* 'Quicksilver' is one of the popular house plants. It is one of the easiest plants for the home. (See page 219.)

Below: The Norfolk Island Pine, *Araucaria excelsa*, is a stately and distinctive houseplant, with whorls of flat, pine-like branches. During the summer it can be placed outside on a patio. (See page 215.)

Scindapsus aureus
Devil's Ivy
(see page 219)

Cyperus alternifolius
Umbrella Grass
(see this page)

Chlorophytum
Spider Plant
(see page 217)

with attractive leaves – *Hedera helix* 'Sagittaefolia' has deeply lobed spiky-looking leaves with an elongated central lobe 'Chicago' is a small-lobed kind, sometimes blotched with purple and *H. h.* 'Cristata' has wavy, crimpled edges to the leaves. (Ivie are illustrated on pages 114 and 119.)

A delightful small plant for a mantlepiece (but not if the fire i alight) is *Fittonia argyroneura*, a gem with creeping habit and smal oval leaves made delightfully attractive by the white net-lik patterning of the veins. They need plenty of water.

Baby's Tears (*Helxine soleirolii*) forms a low creeping mound o tiny, green or yellowish-green leaves borne on thin, fragile stems. I is one of the few plants that will tolerate constantly damp roots, and the pot is best stood in a saucer of water, as dryness is certain deatl to this plant.

Another houseplant with a similar liking for constant moisture i the very different Umbrella Grass (*Cyperus alternifolius*) a grass-lik plant with stems up to 30–60cm (1–2ft) at the top of whicl blade-like leaves radiate umbrella-fashion. The pot should stand i a saucer of water all the time.

Ferns are also shade and moisture lovers, but as high humidity i vital round the leaves they do not grow well in centrally-heated rooms. Among the ferns worth trying are the Japanese Holly Fern (*Cyrtomium falcatum*) or the various pteris, some of which are variegated.

Other plants suitable for shady positions are listed on page 208 but the range of plants that can be grown in lighter positions, bu without direct sun, is much wider. There are many positions where the light is comparatively good, although direct rays of the sun do not fall for more than a short part of the day, if at all. Many of those mentioned as being suitable for shade will grow well here too – including aspidistra, cyperus, *Ficus pumila*, hedera, helxine, phi lodendron and rhoicissus.

A climber much resembling rhoicissus, and which does well in a cool, slightly shaded position, is the Kangaroo Vine (*Cissus antarc tica*).

Two other plants of climbing or semi-climbing habit worth growing are Devil's Ivy (scindapsus) and the Goosefoot Plan (syngonium). The Devil's Ivy looks like a philodendron and i attractive grown up a mossed stake or supported on cork bark There are variegated kinds, such as *S. aureus* (streaked with pale yellow). The Goosefoot plant will form a short-jointed plant i deprived of support, but will climb a sphagnum moss or cork bark pole by using its aerial roots. The heart-shaped leaves are green in the normal species (*Syngonium podophyllum*), but there are varieties with light and dark green variegation, such as *S. p.* 'Emerald Gem'.

Two more variegated foliage plants are aglaonema and aucuba. Several good aglaonemas are available, all with large green leaves variegated in some way, usually spotted or blotched with cream. They are not easy plants, however, and require draught-free warmth and humidity, and they are sensitive to gas or paraffin fumes. Much tougher, and quite able to tolerate most fumes, is *Aucuba japonica*. This is a hardy plant, but the variety 'Crotonifolia makes an attractive houseplant because its leaves have a yellow mottling. Wash the leaves occasionally if they become dusty, and plant outdoors when the plant eventually becomes too large.

For really attractive colourings, however, the ornamental-leaved begonias are excellent. There are many from which to choose, and all are well suited to a light area out of the direct sun's rays. A humid atmosphere is important for these superb plants.

Variegation of a striking kind is also presented by the marantas. The oval leaves are carried on stems that rise from the base of the plant, and are blotched or veined in lighter or darker shades, sometimes with red veins, according to species and variety. They make neat, compact plants of great attraction, but are not particularly easy to grow successfully. Ideally, it needs the kind of warmth and moist atmosphere of a bottle garden.

Undoubtedly, one of the most widely grown houseplants is the Spider Plant (chlorophytum). The reason for its popularity lies partly in its extreme ease of cultivation, often managing to survive conditions that are far from ideal. If kept in a light but not directly sunlit room, and given a large enough pot and plenty of water throughout the summer, this accommodating plant will be seen at its best — with long, narrow leaves striped cream and green, and masses of arching sprays of tiny white flowers and small plantlets eager to root wherever they can touch soil.

Rhoeo discolor is an undemanding yet impressive plant — with broadly strap-shaped leaves, green with yellowish variegation on top and rich purple beneath.

African Violets (saintpaulias) have been improved tremendously during recent years as a result of skilful breeding, and most of them carry large yet compact heads of flowers well clear of the hairy foliage. They flower profusely over a long period. There are also double-flowered forms. The key to success, apart from adequate but indirect light, is a peat-based compost and careful watering from beneath to keep the compost evenly moist during flowering.

The Dumb Cane (dieffenbachia) has the reputation for making the tongue swell up if the sap gets anywhere near the mouth. It is, therefore, prudent to wash your hands after taking cuttings or removing a leaf. Nevertheless the Dumb Cane is a most attractive foliage plant, with large green leaves attractively marked with yellow or cream.

Plants for sunny windows

Cacti and succulents are the most obvious candidates to cope with the hot, scorching rays of summer sun through glass. And for many gardeners these plants hold a special fascination. A good collection can be contained in a small space, and there are few worries about watering when it comes to holiday time.

Cacti and succulents can give brilliant displays of flowers when they are mature, but for more dependable flowering on a sunny window the Shrimp Plant (*Beloperone guttata*) can hardly fail to please. The overlapping dull shrimp-pink bracts of the flowers look effective against the dark green leaves. The bracts remain colourful for a long period, and if the plant becomes straggly and bare at the

Saintpaulia
African Violet
(see page 219)

Grevillea
Silk Oak
(see page 218)

Dieffenbachia
Dumb Cane
(see page 217)

Aspidistra
Cast Iron Plant
(see page 216)

base new growth can be encouraged by pruning the shoots b·
about half in spring.

Pelargoniums, or Geraniums as they are frequently called, are
often regarded as plants more suited to outdoor summer bedding
than as houseplants. The Zonal Pelargoniums (*P. zonale*) and
Ivy-leafed Geranium (*P. peltatum*) are splendid to brighten the
outdoor garden in summer, but they are also fine indoor plant
(although the Ivy-leafed kind will need to be planted in a hanging
basket or provided with a cane for support). The Regal Pelargonium
(*P. x domesticum*) is an especially beautiful pot plant and continues
to produce some flowers long after its main flush in May and June.

A beautiful sight when trailing over a pot in full flower is the blue
Campanula isophylla, and its white variety 'Alba'.

If coleus were difficult to grow they would probably have a
bigger following. The range of rich colour on the leaves, and the
seemingly endless variations and permutations to the markings
make these truly remarkable foliage plants.

Busy Lizzies (impatiens) are among the best-known houseplants
but sadly many inferior varieties are grown, and often in poor light
which causes them to become leggy. They flower almost continuously but need to be pinched back to keep the plant compact.

Another popular, but very different, plant for a sunny position is
Mother-in-law's Tongue (*Sansevieria trifasciata* 'Laurentii').

Oranges on the windowsill are an enchanting thought, and quite
feasible if you are content with miniatures. The Calamondin
Orange (*Citrus mitis*) grows to about 45cm (1½ft) and the fragrant
white flowers open in spring, continuing at intervals throughout
summer. Spray the flowers with water occasionally and keep the air
humid, then the reward should be a crop of tiny oranges about 4cm

Right: The Prayer Plant, *Maranta
leuconeura*, is so-called because its leaves
fold up at night, resembling hands folding
in prayer. (See page 218.)

214

1½in) across. The fruit is edible but rather sharp in taste.

Fruit of a different kind can be provided by the Peppers (Capsicum annuum). The fruits are conical or round, and although red is the common colour, they can be yellow, purple or black.

Plants for a hot, dry atmosphere

Central heating may seem an asset – the even, warm temperature should present no problem to overwintering and tender plants – but few like the dryness it creates. To grow the plants that require high humidity it is necessary to create a localized climate by packing peat between the plant-pot and an outer container, which is kept moist. The alternative is to grow those plants able to tolerate low humidity.

Among the plants already mentioned, the following are suitable for centrally-heated rooms: aspidistra, billbergia, hoya, pelargonium, sansevieria, cacti and succulents. To that list can be added some exotic plants such as pineapples, aechmeas, and a palm.

One of the longest-lasting of all houseplants is the Urn Plant (aechmea), so-called because of the urn-shaped vase formed by the rosette of leaves, which holds water.

Pineapples (ananas) sound exciting to grow, and they do make splendid houseplants where the temperature is high enough. But the best kinds are those grown for their foliage, not the fruit. Several kinds are available, with long narrow leaves radiating from a central vase. These are saw-toothed and usually variegated, and edged with white or yellow.

Silk Oak (Grevillea robusta) is an Australian tree. In our homes it makes a pleasant pot plant with feathery fern-like foliage. The plant can be raised from seed. A little summer shade is required, and a cool winter temperature of not more than 10°C (50°F) is best.

One of the palms popular with the Victorians and steadily regaining popularity is the Kentia Palm (Howea forsteriana).

Saxifraga stolonifera (Mother of Thousands) will cascade its runners bearing miniature plants from a hanging basket or from a pot holder.

Plants for cool halls and stairways

In homes without central heating, halls and stairways are sometimes cold, and are frequently poorly lit by natural light. Such conditions are not good for any plant for a long period, and even the plants recommended here will benefit from a period in a better position.

The Norfolk Island Pine (Araucaria excelsa) is a really easy houseplant. (Illustrated on page 211.)

Fatsia japonica is an almost hardy evergreen with large hand-shaped leaves, green in the type, but with creamy-white variegation in the variety 'Variegata'.

A cross between Fatsia and Hedera (Ivy) resulted in a new bigeneric hybrid – X Fatshedera lizei. The habit is upright, and the leaves resemble a large but deeply lobed Ivy. Other plants able to withstand a period in these conditions are listed on page 209.

Sansevieria
Mother-in-law's Tongue
(see page 219)

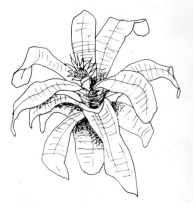

Aechmea
Urn Plant
(see page 216)

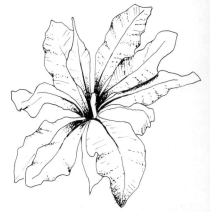

Asplenium nidus
Bird's-nest Fern
(see page 216)

PLANTS FOR THE HOME

Species and Varieties	Size	Minimum temperature	Flowering period	Flower or foliage	Ease of cultivation	Description
Achimenes Hot Water Plant	S	13°C (55°F)	6-10	✿	★★	An upright or trailing plant with purple, blue, violet or rose-pink flowers. Ideal for pots, troughs or hanging baskets.
Adiantum Maidenhair Fern	M	7°C (45°F)	—	🍃	★★	Popular ferns. They dislike draughts and prefer a humid atmosphere.
Aechmea Urn Plant	M	15°C (59°F)	6-10	✿🍃	★	A rosette of grey-green leaves. They need a lime-free compost, and prefer a light position even though they will survive in shade.
Aglaonema	S	16°C (61°F)	4-5	🍃	★★	Attractive leaves, usually about 20cm (8in) long, and variegated.
Ananas Pineapple	M	15°C (59°F)	—	🍃	★	Long, strap-shaped leaves with saw-tooth edge, often variegated. Require a higher temperature to bear fruit.
Anthurium Flamingo Flower	M	13°C (55°F)	1-4	✿	★★★	Beautiful plants with a brilliant red or pink (sometimes white) spathe, set off against attractive green leaves.
Aphelandra Zebra Plant	M	10°C (50°F)	9-11	✿🍃	★★	Rich dark green leaves striped white. There is also a bonus of yellow flowers.
Araucaria Norfolk Island Pine	M	7°C (45°F)	—	🍃	★	An attractive conifer, making a distinctive house plant with its whorls of flat, pine-like branches.
Asparagus densiflorus Asparagus Fern	M	7°C (45°F)	—	🍃	★	This plant is perhaps better known as *A. sprengeri,* the popular trailing form of Asparagus Fern.
A. setaceus Asparagus Fern	M	7°C (45°F)	—	🍃	★	Widely known as *A. plumosus,* this attractive plant has feathery foliage and more upright growth than *A. densiflorus.*
Aspidistra Cast Iron Plant	M	7°C (45°F)	—	🍃	★	This well-known plant of the Victorian era is enjoying a revival. A resilient plant for all homes.
Asplenium nidus Bird's-nest Fern	M	13°C (55°F)	—	🍃	★★	A fern with the distinction of having undivided fronds,, growing in rosette fashion.
Aucuba	M	Hardy	—	🍃	★	A popular evergreen shrub which makes a hardy foliage plant for a cool room.
Azalea	M	10°C (50°F)	11-4	✿	★★	These floriferous winter-flowering plants are available in a wide range of colours, from white to crimson. Do not allow the compost to dry out.
Begonia (decorative leaved kinds)	M	10°C (50°F)	—	🍃	★★	These plants are grown for their decorative leaves, providing year-round interest. Two good species are *Begonia rex* and *B masoniana.*
Begonia (pendulous)	Tr	10°C (50°F)	7-9	🍃	★	Pendulous begonias provide colour during the summer and into the autumn, and are excellent for window-boxes and hanging baskets.
Beloperone guttata Shrimp Plant	M	7°C (45°F)	4-10	✿	★	The shrimp-like flowers, formed of green and yellow bracts.
Billbergia nutans Queen's Tears	M	15°C (59°F)	5-6	✿	★	Most distinctive plants with drooping yellowish-green, blue and red flowers. They can be flowered in winter if the temperature is high enough.
Calceolaria Slipper Flower	M	10°C (50°F)	3-5	✿	★	Pouch-shaped flowers in a wide range of colours, often prettily mottled.

Species and Varieties	Size	Minimum temperature	Flowering period	Flower or foliage	Ease of cultivation	Description
Campanula isophylla Italian Bellflower	Tr	1°C (34°F)	7-9	✿	★	An attractive plant for trailing over pots, with its blue bell-shaped flowers. There is also a white form, *C. i.* 'Alba'. Good for hanging baskets.
Capsicum Christmas Pepper	M	10°C (50°F)	—	❦	★★	A plant grown for its decorative bright red fruits, which make it popular for winter decoration.
Ceropegia Hearts Entangled	Tr	10°C (50°F)	9-10	⬭	★	The flowers are fairly insignificant, the plant's main attraction being the heart-shaped mottled grey-green leaves.
Chlorophytum Spider Plant	M	7°C (45°F)	—	⬭	★	A very popular plant with narrow, variegated leaves and small plantlets borne at the ends of arching stems.
Chrysanthemum	M	Hardy	1-12	✿	★	Too well known to need detailed description. They were once regarded as autumn-flowering plants, but modern treatments enable them to flower at any season.
Cineraria	M	8°C (46°F)	11-5	✿	★	Spectacular plants with colourful heads of daisy-like flowers, in a range of colours.
Cissus antarctica Kangaroo Vine	Cl	10°C (50°F)	—	⬭	★	A climbing plant grown for its glossy green leaves, which form a pleasing screen.
Citrus mitis Calamondin Orange	M	15°C (59°F)	7-9	❦	★★	Heavily scented white flowers are followed by green fruits which mature into perfect miniature oranges.
Cobaea scandens Cathedral Bells	Cl	7°C (45°F)	7-10	✿	★	Vigorous climber best treated as an annual. Large purple bell-shaped flowers.
Codiaeum Croton	M	18°C (64°F)	—	⬭	★★★	A striking foliage plant with leaves patterned in shades of orange, red, yellow, white, cream, purple and black.
Coleus Flame Nettle	M	13°C (55°F)	—	⬭	★★	A spectacular foliage plant, usually grown as an annual. Infinite variations of colour and markings.
Columnea x banksii	Tr	15°C (59°F)	11-4	✿	★	Spectacular trailing plant with a blaze of orange-brown hooded flowers. Ideal in a hanging pot or basket.
Cyclamen persicum	S	10°C (50°F)	10-4	✿	★★	Eye-catching flowering plants for Christmas decoration. Available in a wide range of colours. Leaves often attractively marbled.
Dieffenbachia Dumb Cane	M	15°C (59°F)	—	⬭	★★	Attractive foliage plants with large green leaves mottled yellow or white.
Dipladenia rosea	Cl	13°C (55°F)	6-9	✿	★★★	A beautiful evergreen climber with bright pink trumpet-shaped flowers.
Dizygotheca False Aralia	M	15°C (59°F)	—	⬭	★★★	Handsome, deep-copper leaves that change to dark green as they age.
Dracaena deremensis 'Bansei' Dragon Plant	M	15°C (59°F)	—	⬭	★★	Narrow, rigid leaves with light coloured stripes along the edges, and a white central stripe. Other species have different colours and variegation.
Euphorbia pulcherrima Poinsettia	M	15°C (59°F)	11-1	✿	★★	The well-known Christmas-flowering Poinsettia, with showy red flower bracts.
Exacum affine Persian Violet	S	13°C (55°F)	4-10	✿	★	A mass of flattish violet-blue yellow-centred flowers. Neat, compact habit.
X Fatshedera	L	7°C (45°F)	—	⬭	★	Five-lobed large green leaves on erect stems.

Species and Varieties	Size	Minimum temperature	Flowering period	Flower or foliage	Ease of cultivation	Description
Fatsia japonica False Castor Oil Plant	L	Hardy	—	foliage	★	Rich, shiny green leaves make this a useful houseplant for cool rooms.
Ficus elastica Rubber Plant	L	7°C (45°F)	—	foliage	★	A justifiably popular houseplant, with large, glossy green leaves. A very obliging plant.
F. pumila	S	7°C (45°F)	—	foliage	★	Small leaves, ideal for trailing over the sides of pots or hanging baskets.
Fittonia argyroneura Snakeskin Plant	S	16°C (61°F)	—	foliage	★★★	White-veined leaves and trailing habit. A pretty plant, ideal for bottle gardens.
Gloxinia	M	13°C (55°F)	8-10	flower	★★	Trumpet-shaped single or double flowers in shades of red, purple, pink or white, often nicely shaded or mottled.
Grevillea Silk Oak	M	7°C (45°F)	—		★	Feathery light green, almost fern-like foliage.
Guzmania	S	15°C (60°F)	5-12	flower & foliage	★★	Forms a rosette of strap-shaped leaves, sometimes variegated, and a brilliant red flower formed in the centre of the cluster of leaves.
Hedera (small-leaved varieties)	M	Hardy	—	foliage	★	Too well known to need description. There are many very attractively variegated small-leaved forms suitable for indoor cultivation.
Helxine soleirolii Mind Your Own Business	S	1°C (34°F)	—	foliage	★	A plant which forms mounds of minute green leaves. There is also a golden form, H. s. 'Aurea'.
Hippeastrum Amaryllis	M	10°C (50°F)	12-4	flower	★★	Striking, large trumpet-shaped flowers carried on top of strong stems. Colours are usually pink, white or red.
Howea Kentia Palm	L	10°C (50°F)	—	foliage	★★	A graceful palm suitable for growing in the home. Use soft water otherwise the tips of leaves may turn brown.
Hoya Wax Flower	Cl	10°C (50°F)	7-9	flower	★★	A climbing evergreen plant with fragrant waxy white flowers.
Impatiens Busy Lizzie	M	7°C (45°F)	3-10	flower	★	A very popular houseplant, easily propagated and a rampant grower.
Ipomoea tricolor Morning Glory	Cl	7°C (45°F)	7-9	flower	★	Large trumpet-shaped flowers in various colours — blue and white striped; blue with a white centre; crimson.
Jasminum polyanthum Jasmine	Cl	10°C (50°F)	1-3	flower	★	A climber with highly scented pink flowers carried amid attractive foliage.
Kalanchoe	M	5°C (41°F)	1-12	flower	★	Kalanchoes flower naturally in the spring, but commercially are flowered the year round. Eye-catching colours, from red to pink, white and cream.
Maranta Prayer Plant	S	15°C (59°F)	—	foliage	★★★	Attractive leaves with variously coloured blotches and patterns, according to species. Leaves close up at night.
Monstera deliciosa Swiss Cheese Plant	L	10°C (50°F)	—	foliage	★	Large leaves with holes and gashes make this an impressive foliage plant for the home.
Pelargonium Geranium	M	7°C (45°F)	5-8	flower	★	Traditional plants for the home and garden. The Zonal type can also be used for bedding, but Regal pelargoniums are primarily houseplants.
Peperomia	S	13°C (55°F)	—	foliage	★★	This is a large family and there are many species suitable for the home.

Species and Varieties	Size	Minimum temperature	Flowering period	Flower or foliage	Ease of cultivation	Description
Philodendron scandens	Cl	15°C (59°F)	—	🍂	★	Heart-shaped, glossy green leaves on trailing stems. Can be trained up a frame.
Pilea cadierei Aluminium Plant	S	10°C (50°F)	—	🍂	★★	Metallic silvery markings on oval green leaves. A distinctive plant on its own or set among a grouping of other plants.
Primula malacoides	M	10°C (50°F)	12-4	✿	★	A dainty primula, with spikes of delicate flowers on neat plants during winter and spring.
P. obconica	M	10°C (50°F)	12-4	✿	★	A valuable winter and spring flowering plant, having heads of orange, purple, blue, red, pink, or white shades.
Pteris cretica Ribbon Fern	M	10°C (50°F)	—	🍂	★	A good easy fern for the home, having crested edges to the leaves. Provides winter interest.
Rhoeo discolor Boat Lily	M	10°C (50°F)	5-6	🍂	★★	Boat-shaped flowers produced between the lance-shaped metallic-green and purple leaves.
Rhoicissus rhomboidea Grape Ivy	M	10°C (50°F)	—	🍂	★	An attractive foliage plant, climbing by tendrils. The ivy-shaped leaves are glossy and green.
Saintpaulia African Violet	S	13°C (55°F)	4-10	✿	★★	One of the most attractive flowering houseplants, a good specimen being covered with heads of small lilac, purple, red or white flowers.
Sansevieria Mother-in-law's Tongue	M	10°C (50°F)	—	🍂	★	Tough and distinctive long, upright leaves, often edged in yellow. A particularly useful houseplant.
Saxifraga stolonifera Mother of Thousands	S	7°C (45°F)	6-8	🍂	★	Kidney-shaped leaves, dark green with white or purplish variegation. Small runners bear small plantlets at the tips.
Schefflera actinophylla Umbrella Plant	L	10°C (50°F)	—	🍂	★★	Handsome green leaves, joined to the stem three to seven at a time, sometimes more.
Scindapsus aureus Devil's Ivy	Cl	10°C (50°F)	—	🍂	★★	A climbing plant grown for its attractive leaves. Aerial roots are produced, which help it to climb.
Setcreasea	Tr	13°C (55°F)	—	🍂	★	Distinctive deep purple lance-shaped leaves. A useful trailer where the light is good.
Solanum capsicastrum Christmas Cherry	M	10°C (50°F)	—	❀	★★	A cheerful plant with red marble-shaped fruits, popular for winter decoration.
Spathiphyllum Peace Lily	M	13°C (55°F)	4-5	✿	★★	Shiny oval-shaped green leaves and large white flowers. A very ornamental plant.
Stephanotis floribunda Madagascar Jasmine	Cl	10°C (50°)	4-8	✿	★★	Fragrant, waxy white flowers, popular in wedding bouquets.
Syngonium Goosefoot Plant	Cl	15°C (59°F)	—	🍂	★★	The common name comes from the shape of the attractive leaves, though young foliage is not so divided. Is slow to climb.
Tolmiea Pick-a-back Plant	S	Hardy	—	🍂	★	A curious plant, mature leaves bearing small plantlets on the upper surface.
Tradescantia Wandering Jew	Tr	10°C (50°F)	—	🍂	★	Popular and easy plants, with trailing stems of silver, pink, white and purple leaves.
Zebrina	Tr	10°C (50°F)	—	🍂	★	Similar to tradescantia, but with rather larger leaves with a pronounced purple hue.

S: Small   M: Medium   L: Large   Cl: Climbing   Tr: Trailing   * Easy   ** Some care needed   *** Difficult

Symbols used in the Tables	
☉	sun + shade
○	sun
◑	partial shade
●	shade
·	tender
··	hardy in mild climate
···	protect from frost
····	hardy
▽	tub
▼	large tub
▬	window box
◓	hanging basket
✿	grown for flowers
✿	cut flower
⌀	grown for foliage
❦	grown for foliage and flowers
✿	fragrant flowers
⌀	fragrant foliage
✱	berries
▮	requires protection
♦	evergreen
♦	suitable for small garden
♦	specimen tree
▬	ground cover
▲	rock garden

Acknowledgements
Edited by Caroline Sheldrick, Tony Whittle, and David Hoy Limited
Designed by Bridgewater and Grain.
Line illustrations by V.C. Cook.
Colour photographs by Michael Warren, and David Hoy Limited.
Jacket design by Ebury Press Ltd.